SO-AHV-594

THE WRITER'S WORKPLACE
Essays

PE
1413
.S36
1997

THE WRITER'S WORKPLACE
Essays

Building College Writing Skills

SANDRA SCARRY
*Recently with the
Office of Academic Affairs,
City University of New York*

JOHN SCARRY
*Hostos Community College,
City University of New York*

Harcourt Brace College Publishers

Fort Worth   Philadelphia   San Diego   New York   Orlando   Austin   San Antonio
Toronto   Montreal   London   Sydney   Tokyo

KVCC KALAMAZOO VALLEY
COMMUNITY COLLEGE
LIBRARY

JAN 2 0 2003

Publisher	Christopher P. Klein
Senior Acquisitions Editor	Carol Wada
Developmental Editor	Tia Black
Project Management	Publications Development Company
Senior Production Manager	Kathleen Ferguson
Project Editor	John Haakenson
Manager of Art & Design	Pat Bracken
Photo/Literary Rights	Shirley Webster
Cover Illustration	Phil Boatwright

Copyright © 1997 by Harcourt Brace & Company

All rights reserved. No part of this publication may be reproduced or transmitted in any form or by any means, electronic or mechanical, including photocopy, recording or any information storage and retrieval system, without permission in writing from the publisher.

Requests for permission to make copies of any part of the work should be mailed to: Copyrights and Permissions Department, Harcourt Brace College Publishers, 6277 Sea Harbor Drive, Orlando, Florida 32887.

Address for editorial correspondence: Harcourt Brace College Publishers, 301 Commerce Street, Suite 3700, Fort Worth, Texas 76102

Address for orders: Harcourt Brace College Publishers, 6277 Sea Harbor Drive, Orlando, Florida 32887. 1-800-782-4479, or 1-800-433-0001 (in Florida)

Harcourt Brace College Publishers may provide complimentary instructional aids and supplements or supplement packages to those adopters qualified under our adoption policy. Please contact your sales representative for more information. If as an adopter or potential user you receive supplements you do not need, please return them to your sales representative or send them to:

Attn: Returns Department
Troy Warehouse
465 South Lincoln Drive
Troy, MO 63379

ISBN: 0-15-503833-8

Library of Congress Catalog Card Number: 96-76517

Printed in the United States of America

6789012345 053 987654321

For
Elsa Nuñez
Office of Academic Affairs, CUNY
Vice Chancellor for Student Affairs and
University Dean for Academic Affairs

with gratitude for her generous support in all the work
of students and their teachers

The Writer's Workplace Three-Book Series

The Writer's Workplace: Sentences
The Writer's Workplace: Paragraphs
The Writer's Workplace: Essays

The Writer's Workplace three-book series is a fully integrated grammar and writing program that challenges students while helping them master and retain basic college writing skills. These books provide students with all the skills needed to write well-constructed sentences, paragraphs, and essays. *The Writer's Workplace: Essays* is one part of a unique and extensive series of books and supplementary materials designed as a sequence and intended to be used from semester to semester by students who need to demonstrate an increasing level of writing competence. Each of the three books in this series contains a significant section devoted to the study of sentence level skills which are so necessary for beginning writers to master. As the books increase in difficulty, the number of sentence-level practice exercises decreases. Each book in the series provides a set of model readings that are especially suited to the writing projects in which students will be engaged. Students are encouraged throughout the series to work together in groups, to keep writing portfolios, and to sharpen their computer skills as well. In all three books, the main focus is on the student's ability to write coherently and clearly.

PREFACE

The Writer's Workplace: Essays guides the developing writer in the construction of the traditional five-paragraph college essay. Students who use this book will have the advantage of studying the work of several outstanding prose writers, and will learn how to use the work of those writers as models for their own writing. Reading selections and writing topics are closely related to students' own experiences and also reflect many of the current concerns of our multicultural society.

The starting point: Writing is a process that can be learned

The Writer's Workplace: Essays begins with an inviting overview of the basic steps in the writing process. With the presentation of each step, an activity gives the student an immediate opportunity to practice what is being discussed. Composing the thesis statement, brainstorming, organizing, drafting, editing, and proofreading will familiarize students with the writing process at the outset and give them a good sense of how essays evolve.

A flexible tool for students

The Writer's Workplace: Essays focuses on the step-by-step development of student essays, from first draft to final copy. Students have plentiful opportunities to practice writing thesis statements, and to study model paragraphs for ideas how to write introductory and concluding paragraphs, and how to incorporate supporting details into their essays. In addition, detailed chapters teach students how to write an essay with a specific method of development. These methods are needed in virtually every college English course, not to mention in the work of most other areas of college study.

The comprehensive essay section of *The Writer's Workplace: Essays* is supported by an extensive section that teaches sentence skills in the second half of the book. Students request this section because they know they need these sentence skills in order to revise and edit their own work. Here in this section, students can practice whatever areas of skill that need strengthening. Plentiful exercises are provided to offer adequate reinforcement. Instructors may assign chapters from this section to accompany the students' work on developing their essays.

Important features in the book

- An inviting first chapter is designed to help the student experience an overview of the entire writing process. This chapter helps the student identify the skills needed for success in a writing course at this level.

- An early chapter shows, step-by-step, the progress of a student essay from first draft to final version.

- A complete chapter discusses the importance of using example, illustration, and anecdotes for support in all essays, regardless of the main method of development.

- Five chapters give detailed guidance on how to write essays using specific methods of development: illustration, narration, process, comparison or contrast, and persuasion. These methods of development are used in nearly every college composition course.

- A detailed section on grammar provides a guide for students as they revise and edit their own writing. These topics include many practice exercises to reinforce such sentence level skills as making subjects and verbs agree, correcting fragments and run-ons, understanding coordination and subordination, and making sentence parts agree.

- Working Together is a collaborative writing feature that ends each chapter in the essay section of the book. This feature actively encourages class members to work in groups as they plan, develop, and revise their essays. This approach to writing demonstrates the benefits of working as a writing community.

- An appendix has been added as a further reference tool. The appendix contains an alphabetical listing of irregular verbs in addition to a concise description of the parts of speech.

- Fourteen contemporary multicultural reading selections have been included, each one chosen for its appeal, its accessibility, and its effective illustration of one or more of the rhetorical modes.

Supplements

The Writer's Workplace three-book series comes with one of the most unique and extensive supplementary packages ever. An Instructor's Manual, written by J'lain Robnolt at Camden County College, contains a wealth of information for both the novice and experienced instructor. In addition to sample syllabi, plentiful writing process activities, other types of activities, and writing prompts, the Instructor's Manual will help you integrate journal writing, reading activities, and good study skills into your curriculum. There are also essays from experts on working with learning disabled students; implementing a portfolio grading method; managing a class that is doing collaborative and group work; using the Internet; and training adjuncts and part-timers effectively.

An Answer Key to the grammar exercises in *The Writer's Workplace: Essays* is available. Written by Jessica Carroll at Miami Dade Community College, this answer key provides answers with complete questions from the book.

An Exercise Book is also available for students and teachers. This Exercise Book, written by Lloyd Larson of Madison Area Technical College, contains diagnostic tests, additional grammar exercise sheets, grammar mastery tests, and cumulative mastery tests. Answers are provided in the exercise book, so this material can be used independently by the student or for more practice or in a lab or classroom setting.

Finally, Harcourt Brace is proud to introduce its new series of developmental writing software created by Joe Reese and the staff at Cedar Valley College: Culture and Grammar Software Series. This software teaches your students grammar in a fun way through the context of a story from a different culture. Also included in the software is information about a culture's music, art, and literature.

Other versions of *The Writer's Workplace*

For courses with different needs or semester schedules, another series is available. This additional series presents material especially suited to a course which runs for two semesters.

> *The Writer's Workplace: Sentences to Paragraphs*
> *The Writer's Workplace: Paragraphs to Essays*

The original textbook upon which this series is based is also available in its complete form for those instructors who prefer to have all the material in one source.

> *The Writer's Workplace, 4th edition*
> *The Writer's Workplace with Readings, 2nd edition*

Contact your local Harcourt Brace sales representative to get copies or more information about any of these supplements.

We are deeply grateful to those individuals who have contributed material to our present editions. First, our very special gratitude goes to Vermell Blanding, whose experience and skill added so much to the work of these books. For Siobhán Scarry, our older daughter, we take pride in her many contributions to this edition. We also thank Moira Malone, John Medalis, Sterling Warner, and Jennifer Koponen-Hsu for their help.

Our work could not have been successful without the kindness and support of our colleagues at City University, specifically President Isaura Santiago Santiago of Hostos Community College, Cynthia Jones of the Hostos English Department, Vice Chancellor Elsa Nuñez and Deborah Douglass at the Office of Academic Affairs, CUNY.

We would also like to thank the following reviewers for their helpful critiques and recommendations:

Jan Barshis, City College of Chicago; Lisa Berman, Miami Dade Community College; Paul Berman, McLennon Community College; Joann Brown, Miami Dade Community College; Georgia Carmichael, North Harris Community College; Jessica Carroll, Miami Dade Community College; Bill Dodd, Augusta College; Donald Edge, Camden County College; Joan Feague, Baker College; Valerie

Flournoy, Manatee Community College; Eddye Gallagher, Tarrant County Junior College; Stella Gildemeister, Palo Alto Community College; Bonnie Hilton, Broward Community College; Cynthia Krausk, Wilbur Wright College; Douglas Kreinke, Sam Houston University; Bill McKeever, Sinclair Community College; Mary Ann Merz, Oklahoma City Community College; Kathleen Olds, Erie Community College; Michael Orlando, Bergen Community College; Abraham Oseroff, Miami Dade Community College; Linda Patterson, State Technical Institute; Sharon Reedy, Pellissippi State Community College; Sarah Lee Sanderson, Miami Dade Community College; and David White, Walters State Community College.

Finally, we want to express our thanks to the staff at Harcourt Brace College Publishers, most especially to our always attentive acquisitions editor, Carol Wada, and to our always encouraging developmental editor, Tia Black. We are grateful to Shirley Webster, who researched the photos and literary permissions for the books. We also wish to express our appreciation to Nancy Marcus Land and her staff at Publications Development Company for all their careful handling of our work.

All of these efforts have come together with gratifying results in the latest edition of *The Writer's Workplace,* the second edition of *The Writer's Workplace with Readings,* and in the new two-book series and three-book series of *The Writer's Workplace* (each volume containing readings). Each version in *The Writer's Workplace* series offers an unusually extensive set of ancillary materials, making the series a fully integrated grammar and writing program that will support the ongoing work of both teachers and students.

BRIEF CONTENTS

CONTENTS

Rhetorical List of Further Readings

Rhetorical List

Example/Illustration/Anecdote

Narration

Process

Comparison and Contrast

Definition and Analysis

Classification

Cause and Effect

Argumentation/Persuasion

Index   **389**

Step 1

LOOKING AT THE WHOLE

CONTENTS

THE WHOLE

The Writing Process for the College Essay

Sometimes we think that people are born painters or dancers, and that their talent comes from an almost magical inspiration. It is true that a few lucky people are gifted in this way, but these people are the exceptions. Most artists, including writers, have to work long and hard to develop their skills. It might seem that an opera star like Luciano Pavarotti just opens his mouth and music pours out, but his singing is based upon years of rigorous preparation beginning with simple musical scales. When Stephen King comes out with a new novel that promises to scare us to death, the success of his story comes out of years of careful observation and writing. Like all creative individuals, these artists have learned that success is a result of hard work—daily.

Just as no two chefs or no two singers have exactly the same approach to their work, no two writers work in exactly the same way. In spite of this individuality, each writer, no matter how experienced or inexperienced, follows a remarkably similar sequence of steps to move from the blank page to the finished product.

Many students believe they can write an essay in one step—writing the essay from start to finish in one sitting. Actually, this approach often leads to a very high level of anxiety, and can even cause writer's block. These students are often the ones who complain, "I don't have anything to say."

The step-by-step approach is much more likely to ensure successful writing. It not only leads to more thoughtful and better organized work, but the writer's anxiety level is reduced. Careful preparation before writing and careful revisions afterwards lead to major improvements in what a writer can produce. You will probably be surprised as you watch your initial ideas change. Knowing there is a process that enables your ideas to take shape and blossom will help you feel more in control of your task. No longer will you feel overwhelmed by a writing assignment.

The box on page 4 lists the steps in the writing process. In the chapters that follow, you will use this basic sequence to guide you through the creation of several essays. Writing an essay is a craft like any other and can be learned through daily practice.

Whatever your level of skill right now, by the time you have practiced writing several essays in the guided assignments that follow, you will be able to observe improvements in your writing.

STEPS IN THE WRITING PROCESS

1. Find a topic and controlling idea for the thesis statement.

2. Gather the information using brainstorming techniques or research.

3. Select and organize material.

4. Write the rough draft.

5. Revise the rough draft for greater clarity of ideas. (Many writers work on several drafts before a satisfactory final version is reached.)

6. Edit the revised draft for correctness. (Correct errors such as misspellings or faulty grammar.)

7. Prepare the final typed copy, print it out, and proofread.

Find the topic and controlling idea for the thesis statement

Usually when you sit down to write, you know the general topic. For a report in a history class, you may have been assigned an essay on the two-party system in the United States; for a psychology take-home exam, you might have to write on the methods of coping with stress. Perhaps you are angry about a toxic waste site near your home, and you decide to write a letter to the local newspaper to convince your community to do something about the situation. Perhaps your employer has asked you to write a report to describe the ways in which productivity could be increased in your department. In all these cases, the topic is set before you and the purpose is clear. You do not have to say to yourself, "Now what in the world shall I write about?" In school, most students prefer an assigned topic or a number of topics from which to choose. Therefore, in the assignments that follow, suggestions are given to help you find a suitable topic. However, keep this fact in mind as you prepare to write any essay: You cannot hope to hold your reader if the material does not first interest you! The writer who is involved in the material puts forth more effort, and this always shows in the finished product.

Even though you may be assigned a particular topic, you will need to spend some time thinking of a possible approach that can make use of your experience or knowledge. In writing, this approach is called the ***controlling idea.*** One of our students, for example, loved to play chess. Toward the end of his final year, he described to us how he had used his interest in and knowledge of chess to help him complete several of his college writing assignments. When his psychology teacher asked for a paper entitled "Stereotypes—Are They True?" he wrote about the characteristics of people who play chess. For a political science class, this same student discussed the importance of international games, including chess, of course. For a paper in his literature course, he wrote about four writers who used games in their writing. You can see from these examples how this student used his own special interests and knowledge to make his writing interesting for himself and undoubtedly interesting to the teachers who read his papers. Don't ever think that you have nothing to write about. The secret is in finding your own angle.

Once you have decided what your topic will be and what your controlling idea could be, you have what is needed to write your thesis statement. The thesis statement is a sentence that usually occurs somewhere in the first paragraph. It announces the topic and controlling idea of the essay. The thesis statement may also indicate what method of development will be used (such as explaining, comparing, defining, or persuading).

ACTIVITY 1   Composing the Thesis Statement

Below are three general topics. (1) Narrow each one down to a more specific topic, something you would be interested in writing about. (2) Give a controlling idea for the topic you select. (3) Combine the topic and controlling idea into a sentence that could become the thesis statement for an essay. An example is given.

General topic: Pets
Narrowed topic: Dogs
Controlling idea: Disadvantages of owning

Thesis statement: You should be aware of the many disadvantages of owning a dog.

or (a more creative approach)

If you think you would like to own a dog, think again!

1. General Topic: Pets

   Narrowed topic: _____

   Controlling idea: _____

   Thesis statement: _____

   _____

2. General Topic: Discussion of a social problem

   Narrowed topic: _____

   Controlling idea: _____

   (Suggestion: You could discuss causes or effects.)

   Thesis statement: _____

   _____

3. General Topic: Relationships

   Narrowed topic: _____

   Controlling idea: _____

   (Suggestion: You could compare your view of the topic with your parent's or grandparent's opinion on the same topic.)

   Thesis statement: _____

   _____

Gather the information using brainstorming techniques

Once you have your topic and controlling idea in mind, a short time spent gathering ideas and details about the topic will prove helpful. If the assignment calls for your own opinions or experiences, outside research—working in the library or conducting interviews—will be unnecessary. In this case, you can begin with the technique known as *brainstorming.* Writers use brainstorming to discover what they already know and feel about a given topic.

> When you *brainstorm,* you allow your mind to roam freely around the topic, letting one idea lead to another, even if the ideas seem unrelated or irrelevant. You jot down every word and phrase that comes into your mind.

Since your brainstorming list is for your personal use, you can jot down single words, phrases, or entire sentences—whatever makes sense to you. Don't concern yourself with listing your ideas in any order. What matters is that you get all your thoughts down on paper as quickly as they come to mind. Brainstorming often stimulates your thinking, and you do not want to be sidetracked during this time. Organizing comes later.

Depending on the assignment, it can be very useful to brainstorm with another person or a group of people. With a group effort, each person's idea may bring an idea to another person's mind. In this way, you can stimulate each other's thinking and produce a wealth of material for each other's writing projects.

Finally, the details you produce during brainstorming will often get you more involved and excited about your topic. You will feel more confident as you move to the next stage of your writing.

ACTIVITY 2   Brainstorming a Topic

Choose one of the topics selected in the first activity and spend at least ten minutes jotting down every word, phrase, or thought that comes to mind as you focus on the topic. Don't judge any thought as relevant or irrelevant; just jot everything down. Let your mind follow its own path.

_____

_____

_____

_____

_____

_____

_____

_____

_____

_____

_____

_____

_____

Select and organize material

When you brainstorm, ideas come to your mind in no particular order, and you jot them down as they come. Your next step in the writing process is to look over your list and consider ways to organize the material. At this point, try to find a logical sequence for your ideas. This need not be the final order, but this sequence will help you plan the organization of the first draft.

As you study the details on your list, do not hesitate to cross out items you know you will not use. Fill in any additional details that come to mind and continue to entertain new ideas for main points you want to make. Finally, group all the details under the three or four headings that seem to be your major points. You will want to develop each of these major points with at least one good example, a story, a description, or an explanation. Do you have the material to develop each point? If you need to, develop an outline to use for writing the draft.

ACTIVITY 3

Look at the brainstorming list in the second activity. How could you group the items on your list? Do you still want to have the same controlling idea that you selected in the first activity, or does your material seem to point you in a new direction? Group the material you wish to use into at least three different parts. (Each part would eventually become a separate paragraph in your essay.) List your three parts or main points:

1. _____

2. _____

3. _____

Write the rough draft

After you have gone through the brainstorming process, and you have organized the material into some kind of order, the time has come to write a rough draft. Some students write their drafts in the traditional way, using pen and paper. Many others, however, find it easier to compose directly on a word processor, changing or rearranging words, sentences, and even entire paragraphs as they go along.

A rough draft is just what its name implies: your first attempt to write your essay. The first attempt will undoubtedly undergo many changes before it is finished: parts may be missing, paragraphs may lack sufficient detail, or certain words may seem to be repetitive or inappropriate. Some sentences will sound awkward.

They will need to be rewritten later. The experienced writer expects this. All that you should try to accomplish in the rough draft is to get down on paper as many of your initial ideas as possible. These first ideas will provide the seeds that can be developed later on.

Armed with a first draft, you will now have something with which to work. No longer is a blank paper before you; this is a great relief to most writers.

ACTIVITY 4   Developing an idea in a paragraph

In the third activity, you grouped your material into three parts. Refer back to your three parts and select one of those parts to develop into a paragraph. Using any material from your brainstorming list that would help to develop your point, write a paragraph (at least seven or eight sentences) to develop that idea. Keep in mind that this paragraph could become part of an essay that you will want to complete later on.

_____

_____

_____

_____

_____

_____

_____

_____

_____

_____

_____

_____

_____

_____

Revise the rough draft for unity and coherence

Put aside your rough draft for a day or two. Then, when you reread it, you will look at it with a fresh mind. In this important revision stage, you should be concerned with how you have organized your ideas into paragraphs and if the ideas are clear. Do not worry about grammar, spelling, and punctuation at this stage.

Ask yourself the following questions:

1. Is the essay unified? Do you stick to the topic you have announced and have you focused on the controlling idea established in the first paragraph? Go through the essay and take out irrelevant material.

2. Do you repeat yourself? Look back over your essay to determine whether or not you have said the same thing more than once. Unless you are summarizing your points at the conclusion, you should not repeat ideas. Take out any repetitious material.

3. Is the essay coherent; that is, does it make sense? Can a reader follow your logic or train of thought? You may want to give the rough draft to someone else to read at this point, to get an answer to this question. If the essay is confusing to the reader, you must decide how to fix it. Sometimes when you read your writing out loud, you will hear a sentence that seems to come suddenly out of nowhere or a paragraph that doesn't seem to follow from what came before. All that may be needed is the careful use of a transitional expression or a sentence of explanation. Reading it out loud may bring the words to mind that are needed to make one idea flow to the next.

4. Are the paragraphs roughly the same length? If you see one paragraph that has only one sentence, you know something is wrong. Each paragraph usually needs at least five sentences to develop a point. Check through your essay. Do you need to change the paragraphing? You may need to develop one point more fully, or a one-sentence "paragraph" may really belong with the paragraph that comes before or with the paragraph that follows.

5. Do you have all the types of paragraphs essential to an essay? These include the introductory paragraph with its topic sentence, at least three well-developed body paragraphs with transitional words or phrases to connect ideas, and a concluding paragraph.

6. Can you add more specific details? Most writing teachers agree that nearly every paper they read could be improved by more specific details, more descriptive verbs, and more sensory images to make the writing come alive.

7. Can you add dialogue or a quote from someone?

8. Could you make the introduction, conclusion, or title more creative?

ACTIVITY 5   Revising a Student Paragraph

The following paragraph is from the main body of a student's rough draft on the disadvantages of owning a dog. This paragraph explains what the writer thinks is the third disadvantage. At this stage in the writing process, the student must consider making revisions.

Consider how you would revise this paragraph. Without thinking about spelling, grammar, and other such corrections, concentrate on the ideas in the paragraph. Is the paragraph *unified* (all sentences help to develop a single idea)? Is the paragraph *coherent* (one idea flows into the next)? To improve the paragraph, consider adding more details, rearranging sentences, crossing out sentences that do not belong, and rewriting parts of sentences.

Another issue to consider if you think you want a dog is whether or not you are prepared for the extra expenses. Every week or so you will have to buy dog food. A family's food budget is already too high. The cost of fish, for instance, is practically out of sight. Dog food could cost you over $10.00 a week. Then there are the vitamins, medicines, or food for dogs with special diets (especially as they grow older). If the pet should become ill, you must take it to a veterinarian and now your talking big bucks. If you take any pet to an animal doctor, their professional fees are always too high. And then what about when you want to go away? You will have to pay somebody to take care of the dog. Finally, what about guilt? Most pet owners feel guilty if they don't have time every day to spend with the dog.

_____

_____

_____

_____

_____

_____

_____

_____

_____

_____

_____

_____

_____

_____

_____

_____

_____

_____

_____

_____

_____

_____

_____

_____

_____

Edit the second draft for correctness (look for mistakes in spelling, grammar, punctuation, and diction)

Now that you have made all the major revisions in the content of your essay, the time has come to check your paper for any mistakes in spelling, grammar, or punctuation. Most writers make mistakes as they compose. You should also expect this and be sure to leave enough time for this stage of the writing process. Use a dictionary or the spell-check feature on the computer. Read out loud to have a clear sense of the actual sound of your writing. By doing this, you will often hear a word that has been overused, or you will think of a better word choice or a smoother way to express an idea. If you can find someone else to read your essay, that person may catch errors you may not have noticed.

Sometimes an instructor will read a rough draft and mark a number of the sentence level errors. If your instructor does this, consult the editing marks reproduced on the back cover of this book. These marks are the abbreviations instructors often use to correct student papers. Most importantly, you should concentrate on developing an awareness of your weaknesses. If you know you have a problem with spelling, plan to pay special attention to that skill area.

Many students find it helpful to keep a record of their errors. Such a record is useful because it keeps you aware of what to look for when you edit. The following is an illustration of how a student could keep a record of errors.

Sentence in student essay:

Your going to have to walk that dog in the pouring rain and more then once you'll have to leave a great party and come home to feed it.

Entries in Student Record Book:

Error	Correct to	Type of Error
1. your going	you're going . . .	confusion of *your* (a possessive pronoun) and *you're* (the contraction for *you are*)
2. more then once	more than once	confusion of *then* and *than*

While you grow as a writer, mistakes such as these will become easier to spot. You will become more analytical about your writing and thus better able to recognize your typical mistakes. Once you become aware of these errors, you will begin to avoid some of them as you write and be able to correct many others as you revise.

ACTIVITY 6   Editing a Student Paragraph

In the fifth activity, you revised a paragraph to improve the content. In the following paragraph, correct other errors such as mistakes in spelling, grammar, or punctuation.

What will you do if your pet turn out to have a terrible disposition? For example a dog may bark all night or not be good with children. In fact some dogs have been known to become very jealus of a new baby and has actually attacked infants or toddlers. If you find yourself in this situation, what will you do? Some people have gone so far as to hire special trainers or animal psycologists, these approaches do not always work. Others live for years being miserable with a dog who is never quiet housebroken. Or with a dog who may snap at it's family members and guests. The worst situation is when a pet owner decides the pet must go. This is a terribly painful and often traumatic experience for everyone in the family.

Prepare the final copy, print, and proofread it

The typing of the final version should follow the traditional rules for an acceptable submission.

CHECKLIST FOR THE FINAL COPY

Use only 8½-by-11 inch paper (never paper torn out of a spiral bound notebook).

Type on one side of the paper only.

Double space.

Leave approximately 1½-inch margins on each side of the paper.

Center the title at the top of the page. Do not put quotation marks around the title and do not underline it.

Do not hyphenate a word at the end of a line unless you are willing to consult a dictionary to check on the acceptable division of the word into syllables.

You may put your name, the date, and the title of your paper on a separate title page. Ask your instructor for specific advice on what information to include.

Indent each paragraph five spaces.

Leave two spaces after each period.

If your paper is more than one page, number the pages and staple them together so they will not get lost.

Do not forget to make a copy before you submit the paper.

Note: In most cases, college teachers will not accept handwritten work. However, if you are submitting handwritten work, you must be sure to write on every other line and have good legible handwriting. Begin today to learn to type on the computer. You will be at a disadvantage if you cannot use the current technology.

Once you have typed your final version and printed it out, an important step still remains. This step can often mean the difference of an entire letter grade. You must *proofread* your paper. Even if you have used a spellcheck feature available on your word processing program, there still could be errors in your paper.

The spellcheck feature only finds groupings of letters that are not words. For example, if you typed the word *van* when you meant to type *han,* the spellcheck would not catch this error.

The secret of good proofreading is to look at each word and sentence construction by itself without thinking about the paper's contents.

CHECKLIST FOR PROOFREADING

Study each sentence: One way to proofread is to read backwards, starting with the last sentence and examining every sentence, one at a time. First, check that the sentence is really complete and not a fragment or a run-on. Then check the punctuation. Go on to the next sentence and do the same. In this way, you will develop a critical eye for spotting any problems with sentence level errors.

Study each word: Read the paper again, this time studying each word in every sentence. Look at the letters of the words. Have you transposed any letters or have you left off an ending such as the *-ed* or the *-s?* If there are any words you are not sure how to spell, do not forget to check for the correct spelling. Is there any word you have omitted?

ACTIVITY 7   Proofread a Student Paragraph

The sentences in this activity are taken from the rough draft of a student essay. Using the guidelines for proofreading, see if you can find at least ten errors.

We are all familiar with the benefits of having a dog. Dogs offer companionchip without any complaints. You can come home everynight to a loving dog who wags his tail at the sight of you. Many expert claim that peopel who have dogs are healthier and happier than those who alone. Of course the best of all situations is if you can enjoy your dog but pass along all the work to someone else in your family. An older sister or a spouse if you are marry. Let someone else vacum the dog hair all day, take the pet out four or five times during a blizzard, go to the store in the middle of the night because you ran out of dog food, and basically stay home home all the time to be sure the dog is happy and the neighbors are happy. (Dogs have been known to drive neighbors crazy.) Can you manage this arrangement. If so by all means get a dog.

Working Together

Sometimes a writer can gather material for an essay by conducting an interview or taking a survey of a particular group of people who have something in common. For this exercise, make a survey of the students in your class to discover their attitudes and experiences with writing. Feel free to add additional questions or change the questions provided. This information could become the basis for a later essay.

Each student should answer the questionnaire below so the answers can be discussed in class and compiled to see what the range of answers are.

1. Where do you do your best writing? In the library, at home, or someplace else? What makes some places better than others?

   _____

   _____

   _____

   _____

   _____

   _____

2. Is a certain time of day better for you than other times? When do you concentrate the best?

   _____

3. How long can you write with concentration before you have to take a break?

   _____

4. What fears do you have when you write?

   _____

5. What do you believe is your major weakness as a writer?

   _____

6. Are you comfortable using a computer to compose?

   _____

7. In high school, how many of your classes included writing opportunities? How often did you write?

   _____

8. Keeping in mind that most people today use a telephone to keep in touch, how often do you find yourself writing a letter?

   _____

9. Which of the following best describes your feeling about writing up until this point in your school career?

   _____ I enjoy writing most of the time.

   _____ I occasionally like to write.

   _____ I usually do not like to write.

   _____ I don't have any opinion about writing at all.

   How could the responses in this survey be used as the basis for an essay? What could be the purpose of such an essay?

Step 2

STRUCTURING THE COLLEGE ESSAY

CONTENTS

THE ESSAY

Chapter 2

Watching a Student Essay Take Form

It's an exciting experience for most writers to see a beginning thought or inspiration evolve into a fully developed essay. In this chapter, you will follow a student writer as she works through the sequence of steps, from the initial assignment to the final proofreading of her essay.

The sequence of steps in the writing process are given here so you can review them before you study the student's development of her essay.

STEPS IN THE WRITING PROCESS

1. Find a topic and controlling idea for the thesis statement.

2. Gather the information using brainstorming techniques or research.

3. Select and organize material.

4. Write the rough draft.

5. Revise the rough draft for greater clarity of ideas. (Many writers work on several drafts before a satisfactory final version is reached.)

6. Edit the revised draft for correctness. (Correct errors such as misspellings or faulty grammar.)

7. Prepare the final typed copy, print it out, and proofread.

As you follow the student's progress through this chapter, you should maintain a critical attitude. That is, you should be prepared to analyze how well the student succeeds in producing a finished essay. Ask yourself what you might have done with the same topic. You may eventually want to write your own essay on the same topic, but with a very different controlling idea.

Choose a topic and a controlling idea for the thesis statement

The student's first task is to think over what topic would be appropriate and what approach should be taken. This leads the writer in the direction of developing a tentative thesis—the sentence that states the main idea—for the entire essay. Although not all essays come right out and state the thesis directly, the writer must always have a main idea if the writing is to be focused. A reader should never have to wonder what your main idea is.

In this case, the student has been asked to write an essay about a social issue using cause or effect as the method of development. Having this assignment from the beginning is helpful because it gives the student a good sense of direction. With the help of several members of the class, she begins by making a list of possible topics on social issues that come to mind.

The causes of children failing in school

The causes of children succeeding in school

The effects of dishonesty in business

The causes of couples choosing to have small families

The effects of growing up in a large city

The effects of consumerism on the environment

The effects on the family when both parents work

The effects of being an only child

The topic she chooses is important because her success will depend on selecting a topic that is of interest to her. Writing on a topic that you don't care about will not produce a very creative result.

The student reviews the list, talks over the ideas with others and finds herself responding most directly to the topic of families with two wage earners. Although she doesn't work at present and her mother never worked outside the home, she intends to find a job as soon as she finishes her education. She has been thinking about the changes that going to work might mean for her family, particularly her husband. Not only is the topic of real interest to her, but she suspects most people in her class, many of whom are young mothers, will also have a strong interest in the topic.

Once a student knows the subject for the essay, there still is the question about what the point should be for this essay. Many students may find it difficult to figure this out before they actually do some brainstorming and see what material they have to develop. In this case, the instructor has already asked the students in the class to develop their essay by discussing the causes or the effects. This limits how our student can handle the material. Her main form of development will not be to tell a story about a friend who works (narration). She will not contrast a woman who works outside the home to a woman who stays at home (comparison and contrast); she will not give advice on how a woman can manage a job and a family at the same time (process). Although writing often can combine methods of development, she will focus on the *effects* on the family when both parents work.

Gathering information using brainstorming techniques

Here is what the student listed when she thought about her topic, *Working Parents:*

no time to cook

more microwavable dinners

more fast food

no hot meals for children

nobody at home for deliveries

hard to get to bank and to medical appointments

grocery shopping on weekends

no time to entertain

dads have to do more household chores—more than just take out the garbage

dads may be resentful

some marriages could fail

moms have to clean house at night

mom not home for children's emergencies

Some writers like to cluster their ideas when they brainstorm. ***Clustering*** is a visual map of your ideas rather than a list. Had the student clustered her ideas, they might have looked like this:

You might want to try both ways of generating ideas to see which approach works best for you.

Selecting and organizing the material

When the student has listed as many ideas as she can think of and has also asked her classmates for their ideas, she then looks over the list to see how she might group the words, phrases, or ideas into sections. Perhaps some ideas should be crossed out and not used at all. Maybe other ideas could be further developed. The student must also remember that once she starts to write, some creative flow may also direct her writing away from the exact outline she has developed by this point. That is fine. The outline is useful if it keeps the focus of the essay in mind.

Many instructors require the student to write a tentative thesis statement and an outline at this point so the instructor can verify that the student is on the right track.

Here is the outline the student wrote:

Topic: Parents who work outside the home

Method of Development: Discuss the effects on the family

Tentative Thesis: When economic needs force both parents to work, the effects on the family are noticeable.

   I. Introductory paragraph: Economy makes it necessary for both parents to work

 II. Support paragraphs: Effects on the family

     A. Effects on children

       1. No hot meals

       2. No sympathetic ear

     B. Effects on local businesses and services

       1. Medical appointments

       2. Banking and other businesses

       3. Grocery shopping

     C. Effects on dads

       1. More household chores

       2. More child care

       3. More meal preparation

     D. Effects on family eating habits

       1. More convenience foods

       2. More microwaveable foods

III. Concluding paragraph: Effects on marriage

     A. Dads could feel threatened

     B. Dads could feel resentful

Writing the rough draft

This student went to the computer lab where she knew she could work without interruption. With her outline and brainstorming list in front of her, she wrote the first draft of her essay. At this point, she was not concerned about a polished piece of work. The writer's goal was to get all her thoughts written down as a first draft. When she finished this rough draft, she not only saved it on a diskette of her own, she also printed out her draft so she could take the hard copy (actual printed pages) with her for later review. At that time, she would be ready to consider making revisions.

Read the student's rough draft and discuss your first impressions of it with your classmates. What are the strengths and weaknesses of this draft?

When Both Parents Work

1 The economy today has made it necessary for both parents to work. Rising prices have made two-income families the norm. What has been the effect?

2 The most noticeable change for most families is that Mom is no longer home during the day. She is not there to fix hot lunches or to soothe scraped knees and bruised egos.

3 Another effect of Mom's absence from the home is that businesses are discovering that she is no longer available to let meter readers in, accept furniture deliveries, take children to the doctor and dentist, or take care of banking needs. Just as many supermarkets have changed to a twenty-four-hour selling day, retail stores and service industries are begining to realize that they must also adapt if they want to keep the working woman's business.

4 Even when Mom comes home in the evening, life is still not normal. Housecleaning is becoming a shared activity, when it gets done at all. Dad's duties are no longer confined to mowing the lawn and taking out the garbage, he is now expected to do lots of other things.

5 It's always a pleasure to see fathers taking their children out on weekends. Sometimes they are trying to give their wives a break, so they take the children out for a few hours or even for an entire day. This is a positive experience for the children, for they will remember these as happy hours spent with the exclusive attention of one parent.

6 So now we have Dad helping with the household chores and with the children. What about meals? Again, Dad may be asked to help out. But many men (and women) still feel the kitchen is the woman's domain. The idea that women belong in the kitchen is a popular one. Enter time-saving appliances, such as the microwave oven and convenience foods such as boil-in-the-bag frozen entrees. Mom simply doesn't have the time or the energy to prepare traditional meals. Instant meals are no longer considered a luxury and the food industry is cashing in on the demand. Even old standby items on the grocery shelves now proclaim that they are microwavable. A fact that is not hurting their sales one bit.

7 How does the family feel about Mom as a late bloomer? Dad may feel somewhat threatened, especially if he was raised to believe that a womans place is in the home. He may resent her working even more when the financial need is severe. Because he feels it announces to the world that he cannot provide for his family. In

marriages that are not solid to begin with, this perceived loss of dominance by the husband may lead to divorce.

Revising the rough draft for greater clarity of ideas

When the student has left the rough draft for a day or more and then returns to make revisions, she must consider what needs to be changed. Some of the questions that follow should help in the revision process. Go through these questions with your classmates and discuss what revisions need to be made. Remember that at this stage the writer should be concerned about the ideas and the organization of the ideas, not how a word is spelled or where a comma belongs.

1. Is the essay unified? Does the writer stick to the topic? Does any material need to be cut?

2. Does she repeat herself anywhere? If so, what needs to be cut?

3. Does the essay make sense? Can you follow her logic? If any spot is confusing, how could she make her idea clear? Sometimes the use of transitional expressions such as *another effect, the most important effect,* or *the second effect* will help show the writer is moving to the next point.

4. Are the paragraphs roughly the same length? If you see one sentence presented as a paragraph, you know something is wrong.

5. Does the essay follow essay form? Is there an introductory paragraph with the thesis statement? Are there at least three supporting paragraphs in the body of the essay? Is there a concluding paragraph?

6. Are there places where more specific details could be added to develop an idea further or to add more interest?

7. Could the introduction, conclusion, or title be more creative?

Now let's look at what the student's writing instructor suggested. Here is the rough draft again with the instructor's comments written in the margins. Notice that no corrections of punctuation, spelling, or grammar have yet been considered. See if you agree with the instructor's comments. Think about what other comments you would have added if you had been the instructor.

You might be able to think of a more catchy title.

When Both Parents Work

Introductory paragraph needs more development. You might tell us more about the economy.

1 The economy today has made it necessary for most women to work. What has been the effect?

2 The most noticeable change for most families is that Mom is no longer home during the day. She is not there to fix hot lunches or to soothe scraped knees and bruised egos.

Is anyone available for this? More development please!

3 Another effect of Mom's absence from the home is that businesses are discovering that she is no longer available to let meter readers in, accept furniture deliveries, take children to the doctor

and dentist, or take care of banking needs. Just as many super-markets have changed to a twenty-four-hour selling day, retail stores and service industries are begining to realize that they must also adapt if they want to keep the working woman's business.

good specific details

4   Even when Mom comes home in the evening, life is still not normal. Housecleaning is becoming a shared activity, when it gets done at all. Dad's duties are no longer confined to mowing the lawn and taking out the garbage, he is now expected to do lots of other things.

What exactly does Dad do now? Be more specific. Give examples.

This ¶ is not relevant to this essay, is it? Omit it in your next draft or revise it.

5   It's always a pleasure to see fathers taking their children out on weekends. Sometimes they are trying to give their wives a break, so they take the children out for a few hours or even for an entire day. This is a positive experience for the children, for they will remember these as happy hours spent with the exclusive attention of one parent.

6   So now we have Dad helping with the household chores and with the children. What about meals? Again, Dad may be asked to help out. But many men (and women) still feel the kitchen is the woman's domain. The idea that women belong in the kitchen is a popular one. Enter time-saving appliances, such as the microwave oven and convenience foods such as boil-in-the-bag frozen entrees. Mom simply doesn't have the time or the energy to prepare traditional meals. Instant meals are no longer considered a luxury and the food industry is cashing in on the demand. Even old standby items on the grocery shelves now proclaim that they are microwavable. A fact that is not hurting their sales one bit.

Don't these two sentences say the same thing?

In your concluding ¶, you might look to the future for more positive solutions or summarize all your points.

7   How does the family feel about Mom as a late bloomer? Dad may feel somewhat threatened, especially if he was raised to believe that a womans place is in the home. He may resent her working even more when the financial need is severe. Because he feels it announces to the world that he cannot provide for his family. In marriages that are not solid to begin with, this perceived loss of dominance by the husband may lead to divorce.

This ¶ presents another effect. It is not a conclusion.

Editing the revised draft for correctness

Until now, the student has been concerned with the content and organization of the essay. After the student is satisfied with these revisions, it is time to look at the sentences themselves for errors such as faulty grammar, misspelling, incorrect punctuation, and inappropriate diction.

Now she should take each sentence by itself, perhaps starting with the last sentence and working backwards. (This will help her focus on the correctness of the sentences and words themselves rather than on the ideas.) She should concentrate on any weaknesses that usually cause problems for her. Many of the errors we make are unconscious and therefore hard for us to spot. Some attention from another student may be helpful and may lead to finding some of her particular errors.

When you edit your draft, look for problems such as those suggested in the following list:

1. Sentence level errors: run-ons and fragments, often corrected by use of the proper punctuation.

2. Misspellings.

3. Lack of understanding about when to use the comma.

4. Possessives: *dog's* collar, but *its* collar.

5. Diction: wordiness, use of slang, informal language or abbreviated forms, wrong word.

6. Grammar errors: subject-verb agreement, parallel structure, pronoun consistency.

Here is the fourth paragraph from the student's revised draft. The student has responded to the instructor's comments and has added more specific details, along with examples. Edit the paragraph for correctness, finding at least one mistake from each of the problem areas just listed.

Even when Mom comes home in the evening, life is still not normal. Housecleaning is becoming a shared activity, when it gets one at all. Dads duties are no longer confined to mowing the lawn and taking out the garbage, he is now expected to vacuum wash dishes bathe children fold laundry—chores that no self-respecting man of a generation ago would have done. Has Dad's ego suffered? Maybe. But possibly, just possibly, his sense of being part of a family unit, not just the bread winner and disciplinarian, have increased. Because he is now forced to deal with his kids on a less exalted level, he may find that he is closer to them and they to him. Certainly, both parent and kid will be effected by this more active fathering.

Preparing the final copy

Read the student's final version which she has typed, printed, and proofread. Compare it to the rough draft. Did the student make the changes suggested by the instructor? In what ways has the essay improved? What criticisms do you still have?

Goodbye, Mom's Apple Pie

1 Inflation. Stagflation. Recession. No matter what you call the current state of our economy, virtually all of us have been touched by its effects. Rising prices and the shrinking dollar have made two-income families, once a rarity, now almost the norm. Besides fattening the family pocketbook (if only to buy necessities), how else has this phenomenon changed our lives?

2   The most noticeable change for most families is that Mom is no longer home during the day. She is not there to fix hot lunches or to soothe scraped knees and bruised egos. So who does? The answer, unfortunately, often is "No one." Countless numbers of children have become "latchkey children," left to fend for themselves after school because there aren't enough dependable, affordable babysitters or after-school programs for them. Some children are able to handle this early independence quite well and may even become more resourceful adults because of it, but many are

not. Vandalism, petty thievery, alcohol and drug abuse may all be products of this unsupervised life, problems that society in general must deal with eventually. Some companies (although too few) have adapted to this changing lifestyle by instituting on-site childcare facilities and/or "flextime" schedules for working mothers and fathers. Schools have begun to provide low-cost after-school activities during the schoolyear, and summer day camps are filling the need during those months.

3   Another effect of Mom's absence from the home is that businesses are discovering that she is no longer available to let meter readers in, accept furniture deliveries, take children to the doctor and dentist, or take care of banking needs. Just as many supermarkets have changed to a twenty-four-hour selling day, retail stores and service industries are beginning to realize that they must also adapt if they want to keep the working woman's business.

4   Even when Mom comes home in the evening, life is still not normal. House-cleaning is becoming a shared activity, when it gets done at all. Dad's duties are no longer confined to mowing the lawn and taking out the garbage. He is now expected to vacuum, wash dishes, bathe children, fold laundry—chores that no self-respecting man of a generation ago would have done. Has Dad's ego suffered? Maybe. But possibly, just possibly, his sense of being part of a family unit, not just the breadwinner and disciplinarian, has increased. Because he is now forced to deal with his children on a less exalted level, he may find that he is closer to them and they to him. Certainly, both parent and child will be affected by this more active fathering.

5   So now we have Dad helping with the household chores and with the children. What about meals? Again, Dad may be asked to help out, but many men (and women) still feel the kitchen is the woman's domain. Enter time-saving appliances, such as the microwave oven and convenience foods such as boil-in-the-bag frozen entrees. Mom simply doesn't have the time or the energy to prepare traditional meals, including apple pie and home-baked bread. Instant meals are no longer considered a luxury and the food industry is cashing in on the demand. Even old standby items on the grocery shelves now proclaim that they are microwavable, a fact that is not hurting their sales one bit. However, even with quickie meals Mom is sometimes just too tired to cook. At those times fast-food restaurants enjoy the family's business. They offer no fuss, no muss, and someone to clean up after the meal. And "clean up" the restaurants have. At a time when food prices were rising almost daily and supermarket sales were dropping, fast-food restaurants were enjoying even higher sales. Maybe part of the reason was that women were beginning to realize that their time was valuable too, and if food prices were high anyway, they reasoned, they might as well eat out and not have to spend their few precious hours at home in the kitchen.

6   How does the family feel about Mom as a late bloomer? Dad may feel somewhat threatened, especially if he was raised to believe that woman's place is in the home. He may resent her working even more when the financial need is severe because he feels it announces to the world that he cannot provide for his family. Sometimes in marriages that are not solid to begin with, this perceived loss of dominance by the husband may even lead to divorce.

7   Yes, the two-income family has played havoc with our lifestyles but it hasn't been all bad. There are problems that must be solved, changes that are difficult to accept, priorities that must be rearranged. However, with increased pressure from the growing number of two-income families, these problems will be addressed. Hopefully, society in general and individual families in particular will find even better ways to deal with these changes regarding how we raise our children, how we care for our homes, and how we view our marriages and ourselves.

Working Together

1. Imagine yourself in the following situation: you and your classmates are guidance counselors in a high school. You have been asked to produce a brochure that will be entitled, "When a Young Person Quits School." This brochure is intended for students who are thinking of dropping out of school. You and the other counselors meet to brainstorm on the topic. Divide into groups. Each group will choose a method of brainstorming: clustering, mapping, or listing. Work for 15 minutes or so, and then come together again as a class. Discuss what brainstorming method you chose and then on the board make a final grouping of the ideas for this topic.

2. In groups or as a class, construct an outline for the essay on "When a Young Person Quits School" using the information gathered in the brainstorming activity above. Organize the information into main points and supporting details under those main points.

THE ESSAY

Chapter 3

Understanding Essay Form

When you studied paragraphs and their development, you realized that each paragraph you wrote had to have a topic sentence, supporting details, and an organization that was unified and coherent. Similarly, the fully developed essay must have a thesis and a unified and coherent organization with supporting details and examples. The resulting essay, however, develops a topic in greater depth than a single paragraph. Making these parts work together in a longer composition is a real challenge for every student writer.

The length of an essay is usually five or more paragraphs. This longer piece of writing can also be called a composition, a theme, or a college paper. Your development of this longer piece of writing is the central work of the course you are now in, and it will be an important part of nearly every other college course you will take.

In the preceding chapter, you examined a student essay in progress. You observed a writer revising paragraphs while also paying close attention to grammar and the mechanics of writing. Each expanded and improved version of the essay you studied in that chapter was a separate stage in the development of the final version.

In this chapter, you will become familiar with what is needed for each of the three kinds of paragraphs in the essay:

- Recognizing and developing the thesis statement
- The effective introductory paragraph
- The use of transitions in the body of the essay
- The effective concluding paragraph
- Creating the title

What kinds of paragraphs are in an essay?

In addition to support paragraphs, the essay has two additional kinds of paragraphs:

1. The **introductory paragraph** is the first paragraph of the essay. Its purpose is to be so inviting that the reader will not want to stop reading. In most essays, this introduction contains a **thesis statement.**

2. **Support paragraphs** (also called **body paragraphs**) provide the evidence that shows your thesis is valid. An essay must have at least three well-developed

support paragraphs. One paragraph must flow logically into the next. This is accomplished by the careful use of **transitional expressions.**

3. The **concluding paragraph** is the last paragraph of the essay. Its purpose is to give the reader a sense of coming to a satisfying conclusion. The reader should have the feeling that everything has been said that needed to be said.

Before you begin to write your own college essays, study this chapter to become familiar with these special essay features:

- Thesis statement
- Introductory paragraph
- Transitional expressions
- Concluding paragraphs

What is a thesis?

> A *thesis* is a statement of the main idea of an essay.

The thesis of an essay states what you are going to explain, defend, or prove about your topic. It is usually placed at the end of the introductory paragraph.

How to recognize the thesis statement

The thesis statement is a complete sentence.

Thesis: The government should provide financial and training support for athletes who want to represent this country in Olympic events.

Do not confuse a thesis with a title. Remember that titles are usually phrases rather than complete sentences.

Title: Government support of Olympic athletes

The thesis statement presents a viewpoint about the topic that can be defended or explained in your essay. Notice that the sample thesis argues that governments should support Olympic athletes.

Thesis: The government should provide financial and training support for athletes who want to represent this country in Olympic events.

Do not confuse a thesis with a statement of fact which can be proven and is not a topic for debate. (Facts can, of course, be used to support a thesis.)

Fact: The government presently provides no direct support for athletes who want to be in the Olympics.

• PRACTICE

Read each of the following statements. If you think the statement is a thesis, write Th on the blank line. If you think the example is a title, mark T. If you think the statement is a fact, mark F.

_____ 1. Jesse Owens won the 100-meter run in the 1936 Olympic Games held in Berlin.

_____ 2. The procedure for getting tickets to an Olympic event

_____ 3. The summer Olympics will be held in Atlanta, Georgia in 1996.

_____ 4. Several other countries support their Olympic hopefuls with training, direct money allowances, and other specific forms of help.

_____ 5. Citizens of this country should write to their congressional representatives asking for direct government support for our Olympic athletes.

EXERCISE 1   Recognizing the Thesis Statement

Identify each of the following as a *title* (T), a *thesis* (Th), or a *fact* (F) that could be used to support a thesis.

_____ 1. The United Nations' growing burden of debt

_____ 2. Several celebrities, among them the singer Harry Belafonte and the actress Audrey Hepburn, have served as good-will ambassadors for the United Nations.

_____ 3. The first fifty years of the United Nations

_____ 4. In 1980, the United Nations' World Health Organization announced complete victory over smallpox.

_____ 5. Despite its failures in some areas, the United Nations should be supported by every nation.

_____ 6. The skyrocketing number of United Nations' peacekeeping operations

_____ 7. The annual United Nations' budget of nearly 5 billion dollars is excessive and must be reduced.

_____ 8. The most frequently asked question of United Nations' tour guides is, "Where did Khrushchev bang his shoe?"

_____ 9. One nation, Israel, was founded under United Nations' sponsorship in 1948.

_____ 10. The United Nations has six official languages and 526 translators.

EXERCISE 2   Recognizing the Thesis Statement

Identify each of the following as a *title (T)*, a *thesis (Th)*, or a *fact (F)* that could be used to support a thesis.

———   1. Electronic money should solve the problem of the expense of storing, moving, and protecting paper money.

———   2. Everything from shells to cattle has been used as legal tender.

———   3. People should welcome the coming convenience of electronic money.

———   4. Already, Swindon, a town in England, allows 8,000 of its citizens to do all transactions using only cybermoney.

———   5. Planning for the transformation into a cashless society

———   6. The delicate balance of public money and individual privacy

———   7. The 30 billion checks written every year cost as much as one dollar each by the time they are processed.

———   8. The costliness of processing checks

———   9. In January of 1996, the Mark Twain Bank of St. Louis became the first institution to allow customers to download account balances into their home computers.

———   10. In this new cashless world, governments and banks must protect everyone against counterfeiting and other abuses likely to take place.

Writing the effective thesis statement

An effective thesis statement has the following parts:

1. **A topic that is not too broad:** Topics that are too broad usually cause trouble for the writer. Essays with broad topics end up with very general or vague ideas. Broad topics should be narrowed in scope. You can do this by *limiting the topic* (changing the term to cover a smaller part of the topic), or *qualifying the topic* (adding phrases or words to the general term).

   Broad topic: Running for office

   Limited topic: The campaign funding of presidential candidates in the 1996 election

   Qualified topic: Running for office in the California primaries

   A topic can be narrowed in many ways. Choose what will fit into the proper essay length and what will fit your own experience and knowledge.

2. **A controlling idea that you can defend:** The controlling idea is what you want to show or prove about your topic; it is your attitude about that topic. Often the word is an adjective.

The present campaign funding practices are *controversial.*

Proposed reforms of campaign funding would be *beneficial* to every part of the election process.

3. **An indication of what strategy of development is to be used:** Often you can use words such as *description, steps, stages, comparison, contrast, causes, effects, reasons, advantages, disadvantages, definition, analysis, persuasion.*

Although not all writers include the strategy in the thesis statement, they must always have in mind what major strategy they plan to use to prove their thesis. Professional writers often use more than one strategy within the same essay. However, in this book, you are asked to develop your essays by using one major strategy at a time. By working in this way, you can concentrate on understanding and developing the skills needed for each specific strategy. What strategy of development does the writer plan to use in the following thesis?

In order to prevent the use of the internet for pornographic purposes, several steps must be taken to regulate the industry.

Now look back and check the parts of this thesis statement.

General topic:	pornography
Qualified topic:	pornography on the internet
Controlling idea:	need for regulation
Strategy of development:	steps that need to be taken to prevent improper use of the internet

EXERCISE 1   Writing the Thesis Statement

Below are five topics. For each one, develop a thesis sentence by (1) limiting or qualifying the general topic, (2) choosing a controlling idea (what you want to explain or prove about the topic), and (3) selecting a strategy that you could use to develop that topic. An example is done for you.

General topic: Senior citizens
   a. *Limit or qualify the subject:*
      Community services available to the senior citizens in my town
   b. *Controlling idea:*
      To show the great variety of programs
   c. *Strategy for development* (narration, process, cause and effect, definition and analysis, comparison or contrast, classification, argument):
      Classify the services into major groups

Thesis statement:
The senior citizens of Ann Arbor, Michigan, are fortunate to have three major programs available that help them deal with health, housing, and leisure time.

1. Winter sports

   a. Limit or qualify the subject:

   _____

   b. Controlling idea:

   _____

   c. Strategy for development (narration, process, cause and effect, definition and analysis, comparison or contrast, classification, or argument):

   _____

   Thesis statement:

   _____

   _____

2. Grocery stores

   a. Limit or qualify the subject:

   _____

   b. Controlling idea:

   _____

   c. Strategy for development (narration, process, cause and effect, definition and analysis, comparison or contrast, classification, or argument):

   _____

   Thesis statement:

   _____

   _____

3. Public schools

   a. Limit or qualify the subject:

   _____

   b. Controlling idea:

   _____

   c. Strategy for development (narration, process, cause and effect, definition and analysis, comparison or contrast, classification, or argument):

   _____

   Thesis statement:

   _____

   _____

4. Gambling

   a. Limit or qualify the subject:

   _____

   b. Controlling idea:

   _____

   c. Strategy for development (narration, process, cause and effect, definition and analysis, comparison or contrast, classification, or argument):

   _____

   Thesis statement:

   _____

   _____

5. Taxes

   a. Limit or qualify the subject:

   _____

   b. Controlling idea:

   _____

   c. Strategy for development (narration, process, cause and effect, definition and analysis, comparison or contrast, classification, or argument):

   _____

   Thesis statement:

   _____

   _____

EXERCISE 2   Writing the Thesis Statement

Below are five topics. For each one, develop a thesis sentence by (1) limiting or qualifying the general topic, (2) choosing a controlling idea (what you want to explain or prove about the topic), and (3) selecting a strategy that you could use to develop that topic. Review the example in Exercise 1 (page 33).

1. News commentators

   a. Limit or qualify the subject:

   _____

   b. Controlling idea:

   _____

c. Strategy for development (narration, process, example, cause and effect, definition and analysis, comparison or contrast, classification, or argument):

_____

Thesis statement:

_____

_____

_____

_____

2. Amusement parks

 a. Limit or qualify the subject:

_____

 b. Controlling idea:

_____

 c. Strategy for development (narration, process, example, cause and effect, definition and analysis, comparison or contrast, classification, or argument):

_____

Thesis statement:

_____

_____

_____

_____

3. Psychology (or another field of study)

 a. Limit or qualify the subject:

_____

 b. Controlling idea:

_____

 c. Strategy for development (narration, process, example, cause and effect, definition and analysis, comparison or contrast, classification, or argument):

_____

Thesis statement:

_____

_____

_____

_____

4. Politicians

   a. Limit or qualify the subject:

   _____

   b. Controlling idea:

   _____

   c. Strategy for development (narration, process, example, cause and effect, definition and analysis, comparison or contrast, classification, or argument):

   _____

   Thesis statement:

   _____

   _____

   _____

   _____

5. Part-time jobs

   a. Limit or qualify the subject:

   _____

   b. Controlling idea:

   _____

   c. Strategy for development (narration, process, example, cause and effect, definition and analysis, comparison or contrast, classification, or argument):

   _____

   Thesis statement:

   _____

   _____

   _____

   _____

Ways to write an effective introductory paragraph

> An *introduction* has one main purpose: to "grab" your readers' interest so that they will keep reading.

There is no one way to write an introduction. However, since many good introductions follow the same common patterns, you will find it helpful to look at a few examples of the more typical patterns. When you are ready to create your own introductions, you can consider trying out some of these patterns.

1. *Begin with a general subject that can be narrowed down into the specific topic of your essay.* Here is an introduction to an essay about a family making cider on their farm:

> The number of children who eagerly help around a farm is rather small. Willing helpers do exist, but many more of them are five years old than fifteen. In fact, there seems to be a general law that says as long as a kid is too little to help effectively, he or she is dying to. Then, just as they reach the age when they really could drive a fence post or empty a sap bucket without spilling half of it, they lose interest. Now it's cars they want to drive, or else they want to stay in the house and listen for four straight hours to The Who. There is one exception to this rule. Almost no kid that I have ever met outgrows an interest in cidering.
>
> From Noel Perrin,
> "Falling for Apples"

2. *Begin with specifics (a brief anecdote, a specific example or fact) that will broaden into the more general topic of your essay.* Here is the introduction to an essay on the place of news programs in our lives:

> Let me begin with a confession. I am a news addict. Upon awakening I flip on the *Today* show to learn what events transpired during the night. On the commuter train which takes me to work, I scour *The New York Times,* and find myself absorbed in tales of earthquakes, diplomacy and economics. I read the newspaper as religiously as my grandparents read their prayerbooks. The sacramental character of the news extends into the evening. The length of my workday is determined precisely by my need to get home in time for Walter Cronkite. My children understand that my communion with Cronkite is something serious and cannot be interrupted for light and transient causes. What is news, and why does it occupy a place of special significance for so many people?
>
> From Stanley Milgram,
> "Confessions of a News Addict"

3. *Give a definition of the concept that will be discussed.* Here is the introduction to an essay about the public's common use of two addictive drugs, alcohol and cigarettes:

> Our attitude toward the word "drug" depends on whether we are talking about penicillin or heroin or something in-between. The unabridged three-volume Webster's says a drug is "a chemical substance administered to prevent or cure disease or enhance physical and mental welfare" or "a substance affecting the structure or function of the body." Webster's should have added "mind," but they probably thought that was part of the body. Some substances that aren't drugs, like placebos, affect "the structure or function of the body," but they work because we *think* they're drugs.
>
> From Adam Smith,
> "Some American Drugs Familiar to Everybody"

4. *Make a startling statement:*

    Man will never conquer space. Such a statement may sound ludicrous, now that our rockets are already 100 million miles beyond the moon and the first human travelers are preparing to leave the atmosphere. Yet it expresses a truth which our forefathers knew, one we have forgotten—and our descendants must learn again, in heartbreak and loneliness.

From Arthur C. Clarke,
"We'll Never Conquer Space"

5. *Start with an idea or statement that is a widely held point of view. Then surprise the reader by stating that this idea is false or that you hold a different point of view:*

    Tom Wolfe has christened today's young adults as the "me" generation, and the 1970s—obsessed with things like consciousness expansion and self-awareness—have been described as the decade of the new narcissism. The cult of "I," in fact, has taken hold with the strength and impetus of a new religion. But the joker in the pack is that it is all based on a false idea.

From Margaret Halsey,
"What's Wrong with 'Me, Me, Me'?"

6. *Start with a familiar quotation or a quotation by a famous person:*

    "The very hairs of your head," says Matthew 10:30, *"are all numbered."* There is little reason to doubt it. Increasingly, everything tends to get numbered one way or another, everything that can be counted, measured, averaged, estimated or quantified. Intelligence is gauged by a quotient, the humidity by a ratio, pollen by its count, and the trends of birth, death, marriage and divorce by rates. In this epoch of runaway demographics, society is as often described and analyzed with statistics as with words. Politics seems more and more a game played with percentages turned up by pollsters, and economics a learned babble of ciphers and indexes that few people can translate and apparently nobody can control. Modern civilization, in sum, has begun to resemble an interminable arithmetic class in which, as Carl Sandburg put it, "numbers fly like pigeons in and out of your head."

From Frank Trippett,
"Getting Dizzy by the Numbers"

7. *Give a number of descriptive images that will lead to the thesis of your essay.* Here is the opening of a lengthy essay about the importance of sports in our lives:

    I cannot remember when I was not surrounded by sports, when talk of sports was not in the air, when I did not care passionately about sports. As a boy in Chicago in the late Forties, I lived in the same building as the sister and brother-in-law of Barney Ross, the welterweight champion. Half a block away, down near the lake, the Sullivan High School football team worked out in the spring and autumn. Summers the same field was given over to baseball and men's softball on Sundays. A few blocks to the north was the Touhy Avenue Fieldhouse, where basketball was played, and lifeguards trained, and behind which, in a softball field frozen over in winter, crack-the-whip, hockey, and speed skating took over. To the west, a block or so up Morse Avenue, was the Morse Avenue "L" Recreations, a combined pool hall and bowling alley. Life, in short, was games.

From Joseph Epstein,
"Obsessed with Sport:
On the Interpretation of a Fan's Dreams"

8. *Ask a question that you intend to answer.* Many essays you will read in magazines and newspapers use a question in the introductory paragraph to make the reader curious about the author's viewpoint. Some writing instructors prefer that students do not use this method. Check with your instructor for his or her viewpoint. Here is an example of such an introduction:

Suppose there were no critics to tell us how to react to a picture, a play, or a new composition of music. Suppose we wandered innocent as the dawn into an art exhibition of unsigned paintings. By what standards, by what values would we decide whether they were good or bad, talented or untalented, successes or failures? How can we ever know that what we think is right?

From Marya Mannes,
"How Do You Know It's Good?"

9. *Use classification to indicate how your topic fits into the larger class to which it belongs, or how your topic can be divided into categories that you are going to discuss.* Here is how Aaron Copland began an essay on listening to music:

We all listen to music according to our separate capacities. But, for the sake of analysis, the whole listening process may become clearer if we break it up into its component parts, so to speak. In a certain sense we all listen to music on three separate planes. For lack of a better terminology, one might name these: the sensuous plane, the expressive plane, the sheerly musical plane. The only advantage to be gained from mechanically splitting up the listening process into these hypothetical planes is the clearer view to be had of the way in which we listen.

From Aaron Copland,
What to Listen For in Music

What *not* to say in your introduction

1. *Avoid telling your reader that you are beginning your essay:*

   In this essay I will discuss . . .

   I will talk about . . .

   I am going to prove . . .

2. *Don't apologize:*

   Although I am not an expert . . .

   In my humble opinion . . .

3. *Do not refer to later parts of your essay:*

> By the end of this essay you will agree . . .

> In the next paragraph you will see . . .

4. *Don't use trite expressions.* Since they have been so overused, they will lack interest. Using such expressions shows that you have not taken the time to use your own words to express your ideas. The following are some examples of trite expressions:

> busy as a bee

> you can't tell a book by its cover

> haste makes waste

Using transitions to move the reader from one idea to the next

Successful essays help the reader understand the logic of the writer's thinking by using transitional expressions when needed. Usually this occurs when the writer is moving from one point to the next. It can also occur whenever the idea is complicated. The writer may need to summarize the points so far; the writer may need to emphasize a point already made; or the writer may want to repeat an important point. The transition may be a word, a phrase, a sentence, or even a paragraph.

- Here are some of the transitional expressions that might be used to help the reader make the right connections:

1. To make your points stand out clearly:

the first reason	second, secondly	finally
first of all	another example	most important
in the first place	even more important	all in all
	also, next	in conclusion
	then	to summarize

2. To show an example of what has just been said:

> for example

> for instance

3. To show the consequence of what has just been said:

> therefore

> as a result

> then

4. To make a contrasting point clear:

> on the other hand

> but

> contrary to current thinking

> however

5. To admit a point:

> of course
>
> granted

6. To resume your argument after admitting a point:

> nevertheless
>
> even though
>
> nonetheless
>
> still

7. To call the reader's attention to your organization:

> Before attempting to answer these questions, let me . . .
>
> In our discussions so far, we have seen that . . .
>
> At this point, it is necessary to . . .
>
> It is beyond the scope of this paper to . . .

- A more subtle way to link one idea to another in an essay is to repeat a word or phrase from the preceding sentence. Sometimes instead of the actual word, a pronoun will take the place of the word.

8. To repeat a word or phrase from a preceding sentence:

> I have many memories of my childhood in Cuba. These *memories* include the aunts, uncles, grandparents, and friends I had to leave behind.

9. To use a pronoun to refer to a word or phrase from a preceding sentence:

> Like all immigrants, my family and I have had to build a new life from almost nothing. *It* was often difficult, but I believe the struggle made us strong.

EXERCISE 1   Finding Transitional Expressions

Below are the first three paragraphs of an essay on African art. Circle all the transitional expressions including repeated words that are used to link one sentence to another or one idea to the next.

> Like language and social organization, art is essential to human life. As embellishment and as creation of objects beyond the requirements of the most basic needs of living, art has accompanied man since prehistoric times. Because of its almost unfailing consistency as an element of many societies, art may be the response to some biological or psychological need. Indeed, it is one of the most constant forms of human behavior.
>
> However, use of the word *art* is not relevant when we describe African "art" because it is really a European term that at first grew out of Greek philosophy and was later reinforced by European culture. The use of other terms, such as *exotic art, primitive art, art sauvage,* and so

on, to delineate differences is just as misleading. Most such terms are pejorative—implying that African art is on a lower cultural level. Levels of culture are irrelevant here, since African and European attitudes toward the creative act are so different. Since there is no term in our language to distinguish between the essential differences in thinking, it is best then to describe standards of African art.

African art attracts because of its powerful emotional content and its beautiful abstract form. Abstract treatment of form describes most often—with bare essentials of line, shape, texture, and pattern—intense energy and sublime spirituality. Hundreds of distinct cultures and languages and many types of people have created over one thousand different styles that defy classification. Each art and craft form has its own history and its own aesthetic content. But there are some common denominators (always with exceptions).

Ways to write an effective concluding paragraph

A concluding paragraph has one main purpose: to give the reader the sense of reaching a satisfying ending to the topic discussed. Students often feel they have nothing to say at the end. A look at how professional writers frequently end their essays can ease your anxiety about writing an effective conclusion. You have more than one possibility. Here are some of the most frequently used patterns for ending an essay:

1. *Come full circle. That is, return to the material in your introduction.* Finish what you started there. Remind the reader of the thesis. Be sure to restate the main idea using a different wording. Here is the conclusion to an essay "Confessions of a News Addict." (The introductory paragraph appears on page 38.)

   Living in the modern world, I cannot help but be shaped by it, suckered by the influence and impact of our great institutions. *The New York Times, CBS,* and *Newsweek* have made me into a news addict. In daily life I have come to accept the supposition that if *The New York Times* places a story on the front page, it deserves my attention. I feel obligated to know what is going on. But sometimes, in quieter moments, another voice asks: If the news went away, would the world be any worse for it?

2. *Summarize by repeating the main points.* This example is the concluding paragraph to an essay on African art. (The first three paragraphs appear on pages 42–43.)

   In summary, African art explains the past, describes values and a way of life, helps man relate to supernatural forces, mediates his social relations, expresses emotions, and enhances man's present life as an embellishment denoting pride or status as well as providing entertainment such as with dance and music.

3. *Show the significance of your thesis by making predictions, giving a warning, giving advice, offering a solution, suggesting an alternative, or telling the results.*

This example is the concluding paragraph to "Falling for Apples."(The introductory paragraph appears on page 38.)

> This pleasure goes on and on. In an average year we start making cider the second week of September, and we continue until early November. We make all we can drink ourselves, and quite a lot to give away. We have supplied whole church suppers. One year the girls sold about ten gallons to the village store, which made them some pocket money they were prouder of than any they ever earned from baby-sitting. Best of all, there are two months each year when all of us are running the farm together, just like a pioneer family.

4. *End with an anecdote that illustrates your thesis.* This example is the concluding paragraph to the essay "Obsessed with Sport . . ." (The introductory paragraph appears on pages 39–40.)

> When I was a boy I had a neighbor, a man who, after retirement, had a number of strokes. An old man and a young boy, we had in common a love of sports, which, when we met on the street, was our only topic of conversation. He once inspected a new glove of mine, and instructed me to rub it down with neat's-foot-oil, place a ball firmly in the pocket, wrap string tightly around the glove, and leave it like that for the winter. I did, and it worked. After his last stroke but one, he seldom left his house. Afternoons he spent in a chair in his bedroom, a blanket over his lap, listening to Cub games over the radio. It was while listening to a ball game that he quietly died. I cannot imagine a better way.

What *not* to say in your conclusion

1. Do not introduce a new point.

2. Do not apologize.

3. Do not end up in the air, leaving the reader feeling unsatisfied. This sometimes happens if the very last sentence is not strong enough.

A note about titles

Be sure to follow the standard procedure for writing your title.

1. Capitalize all words except articles (*the, a, an*) and prepositions.

2. Do not underline the title or put quotation marks around it.

3. Try to think of a short and catchy phrase (three to six words). Often writers wait until they have written a draft before working on a title. There may be a phrase from the essay that will be perfect. If you still cannot think of a clever title after you have written a draft, choose some key words from your thesis statement.

4. Center the title at the top of the page, and remember to leave about an inch of space between the title and the beginning of the first paragraph.

Working Together

LIFE IN FRONT OF "THE TUBE"

For years before TV took hold in America, families gathered in the evening to listen to their favorite radio programs, so the switch to television would seem to be a natural evolution. But "the tube" was more seductive; it made you afraid that you would miss something if you didn't pay attention. It was no longer as easy to sew, play a game, or do homework while listening; you had to be able to watch too.

Most early televisions were substantial pieces of furniture connected to a roof-top antenna cable, and couldn't be taken from room to room. So that dinner could be prepared quickly and people could eat without missing their favorite show, Swanson's introduced its line of "TV Dinners" in 1954, starting with a turkey entrée in a tray that could be taken right in front of the television set.

By 1953, viewers could buy *TV Guide* to help them keep track of the increasing number of new programs. The premier issue hit the newsstands the week of April 3-9 that year with *I Love Lucy*'s "Little Ricky" on the cover.

More and more companies aimed their advertisements at what would come to be called the "television generation." Ads for the latest models of television sets proliferated. Some sets, like the one mentioned in the 1949 ad shown here, could cost more than $2,000; for many at the time, a year's salary.

Most sets, however, were more reasonably priced, and Americans were buying them—between 1949 and '55 the number of families with televisions in the U.S. increased more than 1,500 percent. In only a few years, television had become a source of information, a primary form of entertainment, a babysitter or companion, and an important sector of the national economy. ★

In this chapter, you have studied the essay form. The following essay appeared in *American History Magazine* in 1996 and reviews the earliest years of our television era, a time when our society was still getting used to this new source of entertainment. Have a member of the class read the essay out loud, and use a period of class discussion to answer the following questions.

1. What is the purpose of the essay?

2. Look at the introductory paragraph. Which sentence has the topic and controlling idea for the essay? What word would you pick for the controlling idea? Describe how the writer has used the introductory paragraph to introduce the topic.

3. How many paragraphs form the body of the essay? How does the writer develop the ideas?

4. What does the writer do in the conclusion?

5. This article was written for an audience interested in American history. How does this writer show his sensitivity to this fact?

You may want to make a copy of this essay to include in your portfolio. Writing about the significance of television in American life is an endlessly interesting subject and may be one you will want to write about. Many of the facts from this essay may be useful to you at that time.

Writing an Essay Using Examples, Illustrations, or Anecdotes

Exploring the topic: The fear of AIDS

One of our most serious medical situations today is the widespread menace of the AIDS virus, along with all the suffering the disease has caused. In this chapter, you will be working on an essay that emphasizes the use of *example*. As you answer the following questions, and as you read the selection in this chapter, you will be preparing to write an essay of your own, complete with examples that will illustrate and support the points you are making.

1. Based upon what you have read and what you have heard, do most people act reasonably or unreasonably when it comes to AIDS? Can you think of any other illnesses that carry this level of fear? Explain.

   _____

   _____

   _____

2. Based upon your discussions with others, do you believe most people know the proper precautions to take when it comes to protection against AIDS?

   _____

   _____

   _____

3. Some people in our society have different attitudes toward AIDS victims, depending on the circumstances under which those victims contracted the disease. How widespread are these attitudes? Are these attitudes fair or unfair?

   _____

   _____

   _____

4. Scientists are working continually to find a cure for AIDS. What evidence is there that they may eventually be successful? Some people are critical of the amount of money being spent to fight this illness when the same resources could be spent fighting other diseases. What is your opinion on this question?

_____

_____

_____

Reading a model essay to discover examples, illustrations, and anecdotes

The cure for AIDS remains to be found. The disease is an epidemic that has caused widespread misery and death. In the following essay, two prominent writers on medical subjects show us another aspect of the disease we know as AIDS: the pervasive fear that accompanies the very mention of its name and the immediate unthinking reaction some people have when they find themselves near someone who has been stricken by the virus.

AIDS: An Epidemic of Fear
MARGARET O. HYDE AND
ELIZABETH H. FORSYTH, M.D.

1 Some people are so frightened by AIDS that they shun all homosexuals. Many customers have changed hairdressers because they suspected that the ones they frequented were gay. They now insist on women doing their hair. Actresses have refused to be made up by men who might be homosexual. One couple visiting New Orleans was so concerned about the numerous gay waiters in the French Quarter restaurants that they stopped going out to eat. They bought food in supermarkets and ate it in their hotel room. A woman who was given a book purchased at a gay-lesbian book store called the store and asked if she could safely open the package without getting AIDS. Even people who do not think they know a homosexual person have expressed fear of the disease. All of these people were acting on unfounded fears.

2 The epidemic of fear has been evident in many places. Some television technicians refused to work on a program in which an AIDS patient was to be interviewed. Fourteen people asked to be excused from jury duty in the trial of a man who had AIDS and was accused of murder. The sheriff's deputies who had to walk with this murder suspect were so concerned about contracting the disease that they wore rubber gloves and other protective clothing when they escorted him into the courtroom.

3 There have been reports that funeral homes refused to handle the bodies of AIDS patients without using elaborate precautions. In one case, it was alleged that a funeral home charged a family an extra two hundred dollars for the gloves and

gowns used to handle an AIDS patient's body, and another funeral home tried to sell a family an expensive "germ-free" coffin. A Baltimore man, Don Miller, who is concerned about the rights of homosexuals, reported that he called ninety-nine funeral homes to see what response they gave when he told them he had AIDS and was making funeral arrangements in advance. Ten refused to deal with him, and about half of them said they would require special conditions such as no embalming and/or a sealed casket. Some groups have been working toward establishing guidelines for embalming and burying people who had AIDS.

4   Children with AIDS and those whose parents have AIDS have been the victims of the epidemic of fear that spread throughout the country. Prospective foster parents often shy away from children whose mothers died from infectious diseases because of AIDS, even though the children do not have the disease. For example, one little boy lived at Jackson Memorial Hospital in Miami, Florida, for two years after he was born because his mother had AIDS before she died. He showed no indication of having the virus.

5   While some babies die quickly after birth, others live well into school age. In a number of places, hospitals have begun day care programs for children with AIDS, and a California monastery has opened its doors to unwanted infants born with AIDS who might otherwise have to spend their lives in hospitals. For many children with AIDS, life outside the hospital is one in which they are shunned by friends, neighbors, and even relatives because of the fear that still surrounds the disease.

6   Controversies about whether or not children with AIDS should be permitted to attend school have reached far and wide. The case of Ryan White of Russiaville, Indiana, was well publicized. A hemophiliac, he contracted AIDS from a blood transfusion he received in December 1984. At one point, Ryan was forced to monitor classes at home by telephone because of a restraining order obtained by parents of the other children. In the fall of 1986, Ryan started school with his class for the first time in two years, after the parents who fought his return dropped their lawsuit because of legal costs. Ryan's school had been picketed in the past, but by 1986, some students just took the attitude that they did not mind his being in school as long as he did not sit near them. Ryan was assigned his own bathroom and was given disposable utensils in the cafeteria, even though scientists believe this precaution to be unnecessary. School staff members were instructed in handling any health emergencies that arose.

7   In New York City, when school opened in late August of 1985, the fear of AIDS created a great deal of excitement. Whether or not a child who had AIDS could attend public school in New York City was determined by a panel made up of health experts, an educator, and a parent. One child with AIDS had been attending school for three years and was identified only as a second grader. The child was said to have been born with AIDS but was in good health, the disease being in remission. She had received all the inoculations necessary for school admission, and had recovered from a case of chicken pox, managing to fight off this childhood illness uneventfully.

8   In Hollywood, many people were near hysteria after Rock Hudson's announcement that he was suffering from AIDS. Some actresses who had kissed people with AIDS were especially concerned, while others refused to work with anyone considered to be gay. After one actor became sick, make-up artists burned the brushes they had used on him. But Hollywood stars have been outstanding in their support

of care for persons with AIDS and research on AIDS. Shortly before he died, Rock Hudson sent a brief message to a benefit dinner, "I am not happy that I am sick. I am not happy that I have AIDS. But if that is helping others, I can, at least, know that my own misfortune has had some positive worth."

9   Only through education and further research can one strike a balance between fear of the disease, sensible precautions, and concern for people who suffer from AIDS. Fear makes people "block out" information. We need more campaigns which emphasize the lack of danger from casual contact since polls show that people are simply not listening.

Analyzing the writers' strategies

1. In the first paragraph of the essay, the writers choose a variety of examples to introduce their subject. Examine each sentence of the paragraph and underline each example. How do these different examples show the variety of the AIDS experience in our society?

2. One of the points the writers make throughout their essay is that AIDS is a nationwide problem. Review each paragraph and note the area of the country mentioned in the paragraph. How do the contents of the different paragraphs confirm the idea that AIDS is a widespread problem?

3. Throughout the essay, the writers use a number of short examples. They also use extended examples. Review the essay and find at least two paragraphs that contain several short examples. Then find at least two paragraphs that each contain one more fully developed example.

4. One method writers use to make their work more memorable is to be very specific when they use examples. Choose one paragraph in the essay and judge each example in that paragraph. How have the writers made a good example even better by being specific?

5. Can you find an anecdote in this essay? (An anecdote tells a brief story in order to illustrate a point.)

Writing an essay using examples, illustrations, or anecdotes

Of the many ways writers choose to support their ideas, none is more useful or appreciated than the *example.* All of us have ideas in our minds, but these ideas will not become real for our readers until we use examples to make our concepts clear, concrete, and convincing. Writers who use good examples will be able to hold the attention of their readers.

> *Example,* one of the methods for developing a writer's ideas, provides one or more instances of the idea, either briefly or in some detail, in order to clarify, make concrete, or convince readers of the more general idea or point.

The following terms are closely related:

example: a specific instance of something being discussed

extended example: an example which is developed at some length, often taking up one or more complete paragraphs

illustration: an example used to clarify or explain

anecdote: a brief story used to illustrate a point

Find a topic and controlling idea for the thesis statement

Suggested topics for writing

Here is a list of possible topics that could lead to an essay using example as the main method of development. The section that follows this list will help you work through the various stages of the writing process.

1. Doctors I Have Encountered
2. The Quality of Medical Care
3. Crises Children Face
4. What Makes a Class Exciting
5. Features to Look for When Buying a _____
6. The World's Worst Habits
7. The Lifestyles of College Students Today
8. The Increasing Problem of Homelessness
9. People I Have Admired
10. The Top Five Best Recording Artists

Using this list or ideas of your own, jot down two or three topics that appeal to you.

_____

_____

_____

From these topics, select the one you think would give you the best opportunity for writing. About which one do you feel strongest? About which one are you the most expert? Which one is most likely to interest your readers? Which one is best suited to being developed into a college essay containing examples?

Selected Topic: _____

Your next step is to decide what your controlling idea should be. What is the point you want to make about the topic you have chosen? For instance, if you choose to write about "Doctors I Have Encountered," your controlling idea may be "compassionate," or it may be "egotistical."

Controlling idea: _____

Now put your topic and controlling idea together into your thesis statement.

Thesis statement: _____

_____

Gather the information (use brainstorming techniques)

Take at least fifteen minutes to jot down every example you can think of that you could use in your essay. If your topic is not of a personal nature, you might form a group to help each other think of examples, anecdotes, and illustrations. Later, you may want to refer to material from magazines or newspapers if you feel your examples need to be improved. If you do use outside sources, be sure to take notes, checking the correct spelling of names and the accuracy of dates and facts.

_____

_____

_____

_____

_____

_____

_____

_____

_____

_____

_____

_____

_____

_____

Select and organize material

Review your list of examples, crossing out any ideas that are not useful. Do you have enough material to develop three body paragraphs? This might mean using three extended examples, some anecdotes, or several smaller examples that could be organized into three different groups. Decide the order in which you want to present your examples. Do you have any ideas for how you might want to write the introduction? On the lines that follow, show your plan for organizing your essay. You may want to make an outline that will show major points with supporting details under each major point.

_____

_____

_____

_____

_____

_____

_____

_____

_____

_____

_____

_____

_____

Write the rough draft

Now you are ready to write your rough draft. Approach the writing with the attitude that you are going to write down all your thoughts on the subject without worrying about mistakes of any kind. It is important that your mind is relaxed enough to allow your thoughts to flow freely, even if you do not follow your plan exactly. Just get your thoughts on paper. You are free to add ideas, drop others, or rearrange the order of your details at any point. Sometimes a period of freewriting leads to new ideas, ideas that could be better than the ones you had in your brainstorming session. Once a writer has something on paper, he or she usually feels a great sense of relief, even though it is obvious there are revisions ahead.

Coherence in the example essay

Keep in mind that in a paragraph with several examples, the order of these examples usually follows some logical progression. This could mean that you would start with the less serious and then move to the more serious, or you might start with the simpler one and move to the more complicated. If your examples consist of events, you might begin with examples from the more distant past and move forward to give examples from the present day. Whatever logical progression you choose, you will find it helpful to signal your examples by using some of transitional expressions that follow.

> ## TRANSITIONAL EXPRESSIONS IN ESSAYS USING EXAMPLES
>
> the following illustration
> to illustrate this
> as an illustration
> for example
> for instance
> specifically
> an example of this is
> such as
> one such case
> a typical case
> To prove my point, listen to what happened to
> Let me tell you a story.

Guidelines for revising the essay using examples

As you work on your rough draft, you may revise alone, with a group, with a peer tutor, or directly with your instructor. Here are some of the basic questions you should consider at this most important stage of your work:

1. Does the rough draft satisfy the conditions for the essay form? Is there an introductory paragraph? Are there at least three well-developed paragraphs in the body of the essay? Does each of these paragraphs have at least one example? Is there a concluding paragraph? Remember that one sentence is not usually considered an acceptable paragraph. (Many journalistic pieces do not follow this general rule because they often have a space limitation and are not expected to develop every idea.)

2. Have you used *example* as your major method of development? Could you make your examples even better by being more specific or by looking up statistics or facts that would lend more authority to your point of view? Could you quote an expert on the subject?

3. What is the basis for the ordering of your examples? Whenever appropriate, did you use transitions to signal the beginning of an example?

4. Is any important part missing? Are there any parts that seem irrelevant or out of place?

5. Are there expressions or words that need to be better chosen? Is there any place where you have been repetitious?

6. Find at least two verbs (usually some form of the verb "to be") that could be replaced with more descriptive verbs. Add at least two adjectives that will provide better sensory images for the reader.

7. Find at least one place in the draft where you can add a sentence or two that will make an example better.

8. Can you think of a more effective way to begin or end?

9. Show your draft to two other readers and ask each one to give you at least one suggestion for improvement.

Prepare the final copy, print, and proofread it

The typing of the final version should follow the traditional rules for an acceptable submission.

CHECKLIST FOR THE FINAL COPY

Use only 8½-by-11 inch paper (never paper torn out of a spiral bound notebook).

Type on one side of the paper only.

Double space.

Leave approximately 1½-inch margins on each side of the paper.

Center the title at the top of the page. Do not put quotation marks around the title and do not underline it.

Do not hyphenate a word at the end of a line unless you are willing to consult a dictionary to check on the acceptable division of the word into syllables.

You may put your name, the date, and the title of your paper on a separate title page. Ask your instructor for specific advice on what information to include.

Indent each paragraph five spaces.

Leave two spaces after each period.

If your paper is more than one page, number the pages and staple the pages together so they will not get lost.

Do not forget to make a copy before you submit the paper.

Note: In most cases, college teachers will not accept handwritten work. However, if you are submitting handwritten work, you must be sure to write on every other line and have good legible handwriting. Begin today to learn to type on the computer. You will be at a disadvantage if you cannot use the current technology.

Once you have typed your final version and printed it out, an important step still remains. This step can often mean the difference of an entire letter grade. You must *proofread* your paper. Even if you have used a spellcheck feature available on your word processing program, there still could be errors in your paper. The spellcheck feature only finds groupings of letters that are not words. For example, if you typed the word *van* when you meant to type *ban,* the spellcheck would not catch this error.

The secret of good proofreading is to look at each word and sentence construction by itself without thinking about the paper's contents.

CHECKLIST FOR PROOFREADING

Study each sentence: One way to proofread is to read backwards, starting with the last sentence and examining every sentence, one at a time. First, check that the sentence is really complete and not a fragment or a run-on. Then check the punctuation. Go on to the next sentence and do the same. In this way, you will develop a critical eye for spotting any problems with sentence level errors.

Study each word: Read the paper again, this time studying each word in every sentence. Look at the letters of the words. Have you transposed any letters or have you left off an ending such as the *-ed* or the *-s?* If there are any words you are not sure how to spell, do not forget to check for the correct spelling. Is there any word you have omitted?

Working Together

Brainstorming a topic as a group can create ideas and stimulate interest in the topic. A few fresh ideas will get everyone thinking and add to the list of possibilities. Students should work in groups to come up with a variety of anecdotes or illustrations that would be used in an essay on one of the following topics:

1. People who are fun to be around (or people who are annoying).

2. Courses most students like (or dislike).

3. Assignments that drive students crazy.

Twenty minutes of brainstorming may produce enough material to help everyone get started. Every person should then work on his or her own essay. Work for one hour to produce a first draft.

At the next class meeting, your instructor may want each group to discuss the drafts for possible revisions.

THE ESSAY

Chapter 5

Writing an Essay Using Narration

Exploring the topic: Confronting anxiety

At one time or another, we have all found ourselves in situations where we have been nervous or uncomfortable. Perhaps it was being overwhelmed by a large organization with its rules and regulations, or perhaps it was a new experience in an unfamiliar place. The essay you will write in this chapter will be a narrative essay, based on an experience that happened to you. As you answer the questions, and as you read the narrative selection in this chapter, you will be preparing to write your own personal experience essay.

1. From your own observation, what causes the most anxiety for a student on the first day in a new school?

   _____

   _____

   _____

2. When a person is about to go to a new school, or start a new job, or enter any other new situation, what is the best way to prepare?

   _____

   _____

   _____

3. How do you react when you are faced with an assignment such as making a report or presentation in front of a class?

   _____

   _____

   _____

4. How does it feel to be the only person in a situation where everyone else seems to know what's going on?

_____

_____

_____

Reading a model essay to discover narrative elements

First Day in Class
JAMAICA KINCAID

Jamaica Kincaid was born on the island of Antigua in the West Indies. Her work has appeared in *The Paris Review, Rolling Stone,* and *The New Yorker*. The following selection is taken from her 1985 novel *Annie John,* the story of a young girl's childhood and adolescence in Antigua.

1   On opening day, I walked to my new school alone. It was the first and last time that such a thing would happen. All around me were other people my age—twelve years—girls and boys, dressed in their school uniforms, marching off to school. They all seemed to know each other, and as they met they would burst into laughter, slapping each other on the shoulder and back, telling each other things that must have made for much happiness. I saw some girls wearing the same uniform as my own, and my heart just longed for them to say something to me, but the most they could do to include me was to smile and nod in my direction as they walked on arm in arm. I could hardly blame them for not paying more attention to me. Everything about me was so new: my uniform was new, my shoes were new, my hat was new, my shoulder ached from the weight of my new books in my new bag; even the road I walked on was new, and I must have put my feet down as if I weren't sure the ground was solid. At school, the yard was filled with more of these girls and their most sure-of-themselves gaits. When I looked at them, they made up a sea. They were walking in and out among the beds of flowers, all across the fields, all across the courtyard, in and out of classrooms. Except for me, no one seemed a stranger to anything or anyone. Hearing the way they greeted each other, I couldn't be sure that they hadn't all come out of the same woman's belly, and at the same time, too. Looking at them, I was suddenly glad that because I had wanted to avoid an argument with my mother I had eaten all my breakfast, for now I surely would have fainted if I had been in any more weakened a condition.

2   I knew where my classroom was, because my mother and I had kept an appointment at the school a week before. There I met some of my teachers and was shown the ins and outs of everything. When I saw it then, it was nice and orderly and empty and smelled just scrubbed. Now it smelled of girls milling around, fresh ink in inkwells, new books, chalk and erasers. The girls in my classroom acted even more familiar with each other. I was sure I would never be able to tell them apart just from looking at them, and I was sure that I would never be able to tell them apart from the sound of their voices.

3 When the school bell rang at half past eight, we formed ourselves into the required pairs and filed into the auditorium for morning prayers and hymn-singing. Our headmistress gave us a little talk, welcoming the new students and welcoming back the old students, saying that she hoped we had all left our bad ways behind us, that we would be good examples for each other and bring greater credit to our school than any of the other groups of girls who had been there before us. My palms were wet, and quite a few times the ground felt as if it were seesawing under my feet, but that didn't stop me from taking in a few things. For instance, the headmistress, Miss Moore. I knew right away that she had come to Antigua from England, for she looked like a prune left out of its jar a long time and she sounded as if she had borrowed her voice from an owl. The way she said, "Now, girls . . ." When she was just standing still there, listening to some of the other activities, her gray eyes going all around the room hoping to see something wrong, her throat would beat up and down as if a fish fresh out of water were caught inside. I wondered if she even smelled like a fish. Once when I didn't wash, my mother had given me a long scolding about it, and she ended by saying that it was the only thing she didn't like about English people: they didn't wash often enough, or wash properly when they finally did. My mother had said, "Have you ever noticed how they smell as if they had been bottled up in a fish?" On either side of Miss Moore stood our other teachers, women and men—mostly women. I recognized Miss George, our music teacher; Miss Nelson, our homeroom teacher; Miss Edward, our history and geography teacher; and Miss Newgate, our algebra and geometry teacher. I had met them the day my mother and I were at school. I did not know who the others were, and I did not worry about it. Since they were teachers, I was sure it wouldn't be long before, because of some misunderstanding, they would be thorns in my side.

4 We walked back to our classroom the same way we had come, quite orderly and, except for a few whispered exchanges, quite silent. But no sooner were we back in our classroom than the girls were in each other's laps, arms wrapped around necks. After peeping over my shoulder left and right, I sat down in my seat and wondered what would become of me. There were twenty of us in my class, and we were seated at desks arranged five in a row, four rows deep. I was at a desk in the third row, and this made me even more miserable. I hated to be seated so far away from the teacher, because I was sure I would miss something she said. But, even worse, if I was out of my teacher's sight all the time, how could she see my industriousness and quickness at learning things? And, besides, only dunces were seated so far to the rear, and I could not bear to be thought a dunce. I was now staring at the back of a shrubby-haired girl seated in the front row—the seat I most coveted, since it was directly in front of the teacher's desk. At that moment, the girl twisted herself around, stared at me, and said, "You are Annie John? We hear you are very bright." It was a good thing Miss Nelson walked in right then, for how would it have appeared if I had replied, "Yes, that is completely true"—the very thing that was on the tip of my tongue.

5 As soon as Miss Nelson walked in, we came to order and stood up stiffly at our desks. She said to us, "Good morning, class," half in a way that someone must have told her was the proper way to speak to us and half in a jocular way, as if we secretly amused her. We replied, "Good morning, Miss," in unison and in a respectful way, at the same time making a barely visible curtsy, also in unison. When she had seated herself at her desk, she said to us, "You may sit now," and we did. She opened the roll book, and as she called out our names each of us answered,

"Present, Miss." As she called out our names, she kept her head bent over the book, but when she called out my name and I answered with the customary response she looked up and smiled at me and said, "Welcome, Annie." Everyone, of course, then turned and looked at me. I was sure it was because they could hear the loud racket my heart was making in my chest.

6   It was the first day of a new term, Miss Nelson said, so we would not be attending to any of our usual subjects; instead, we were to spend the morning in contemplation and reflection and writing something she described as an "autobiographical essay." In the afternoon, we would read aloud to each other our autobiographical essays. (I knew quite well about "autobiography" and "essay," but reflection and contemplation! A day at school spent in such a way! Of course, in most books all the good people were always contemplating and reflecting before they did anything. Perhaps in her mind's eye she could see our futures and, against all prediction, we turned out to be good people.) On hearing this, a huge sigh went up from the girls. Half the sighs were in happiness at the thought of sitting and gazing off into clear space, the other half in unhappiness at the misdeeds that would have to go unaccomplished. I joined the happy half, because I knew it would please Miss Nelson, and, my own selfish interest aside, I liked so much the way she wore her ironed hair and her long-sleeved blouse and box-pleated skirt that I wanted to please her.

7   The morning was uneventful enough: a girl spilled ink from her inkwell all over her uniform; a girl broke her pen nib and then made a big to-do about replacing it; girls twisted and turned in their seats and pinched each other's bottoms; girls passed notes to each other. All this Miss Nelson must have seen and heard, but she didn't say anything—only kept reading her book: an elaborately illustrated edition of The Tempest, as later, passing by her desk, I saw. Midway in the morning, we were told to go out and stretch our legs and breathe some fresh air for a few minutes; when we returned, we were given glasses of cold lemonade and a slice of bun to refresh us.

8   As soon as the sun stood in the middle of the sky, we were sent home for lunch. The earth may have grown an inch or two larger between the time I had walked to school that morning and the time I went home to lunch, for some girls made a small space for me in their little band. But I couldn't pay much attention to them; my mind was on my new surroundings, my new teacher, what I had written in my nice new notebook with its black-all-mixed-up-with-white cover and smooth lined pages (so glad was I to get rid of my old notebooks, which had on their covers a picture of a wrinkled-up woman wearing a crown on her head and a neckful and armfuls of diamonds and pearls—their pages so coarse, as if they were made of cornmeal). I flew home. I must have eaten my food. I flew back to school. By half past one, we were sitting under a flamboyant tree in a secluded part of our schoolyard, our autobiographical essays in hand. We were about to read aloud what we had written during our morning of contemplation and reflection.

Analyzing the writer's strategies

1. Although a great deal is discussed among teachers and students on this first day of class, the selection contains only a few direct quotations. Why do you think the writer avoids the use of much dialogue in the piece? What is the effect of this on the reader?

2. Throughout the selection, the narrator shows how isolated she feels in this new situation. Starting with the first sentence of the selection, in how many places does she reveal this sense of isolation?

3. The narrator is a close observer of people and things around her. Choose five or six examples from the selection that demonstrate this ability to observe. Why do these examples strike you as outstanding?

4. In the selection, the writer's emphasis is on what happens to the young girl on the first day of school. However, we have more than one indication of her life at home. Based on details in the selection, what can you tell about the young girl's life at home and about her relationship with her mother?

Writing the essay using narration

> *Narration* is the oldest and best-known form of verbal communication. It is, quite simply, the telling of a story.

Choose a story and a point for that story

1. My worst (or best) classroom experience

2. A parent who listened (or did not listen)

3. My first _____

4. My experience with an aggressive salesperson

5. The day when nothing went right

6. A mix-up with a friend

7. Trouble at the _____

8. A day that changed my life

9. A memorable event from my childhood

10. A perfect evening

Using the list of ten topics, or using ideas of your own, jot down two or three different topics that appeal to you.

_____

_____

_____

From these two or three topics, select the one you think would give you the best opportunity for writing an interesting story. Which one do you feel strongest about? Which one is most likely to interest your readers? Which topic is most suitable for a college essay?

_____

_____

_____

Selected topic: _____

Good narration should have a point. Think about your story. What is the point you could make by telling this story? In a story, a writer does not usually come right out and state the point of the story, but the reader should understand the point by the time he or she reaches the end.

Point of your story: _____

_____

_____

The introductory paragraph for a story usually sets the scene. What will be the time (time of year, time of day), place, and mood that you would like set in your introductory paragraph?

Time: _____

Place: _____

Mood: _____

Gather the information using brainstorming techniques

Take at least fifteen minutes to jot down the sequence of events for your story as you remember it. Try to remember the way things looked at the time, how people reacted (what they did, what they said), what you thought as the event was happening. If you can go to the actual spot where the event took place, you might go there and take notes of the details of the place. Later on you can sort through the material and pick out what you want to use.

_____

_____

_____

_____

_____

_____

_____

_____

_____

_____

_____

Select and organize material

Review your brainstorming list and cross out any details that are not appropriate. Prepare to build on the ideas that you like. Put these remaining ideas into an order that will serve as your temporary guide.

_____

_____

_____

_____

_____

_____

_____

_____

_____

_____

_____

_____

Write the rough draft

Find a quiet place where you will not be interrupted for at least one hour. With the plan for your essay in front of you, sit down and write the story that is in your mind. Do not try to judge what you are putting down as right or wrong. What is important is that you let your mind relax and allow the words to flow freely. Do not worry if you find yourself not following your plan exactly. Keep in mind that you are free to add parts, drop sections of the story, or rearrange details at any point. Sometimes just allowing your thoughts to take you wherever they will lead results in new ideas. You may like these inspirations better than your original plan. Writing a rough draft is a little like setting out on an expedition; there are limitless possibilities, so it is important to be flexible.

Keep in mind that in a narrative essay, details are usually ordered according to a *time sequence*. One way to make the time sequence clear is to use transitional words that will signal a time change.

TRANSITIONAL EXPRESSIONS FOR NARRATION

A few carefully chosen transitional words will help the reader move smoothly from one part of a story to the next. Some examples are:

in December of 1980 . . .	after a little while
the following month	then
soon afterward	meanwhile
at once	next, the next day
suddenly	several weeks passed
immediately	later, later on
now, by now	at the same time
in the next month	finally

Revise the rough draft

As you work on your rough draft, you may work alone, with a group, with a peer tutor, or directly with your instructor. If you are working on a computer, making changes is so easy that you will feel encouraged to explore alternatives. Working on a computer to insert or delete material is a simple matter, unlike making changes using traditional pen and paper.

Here are some of the basic questions you should consider when the time comes to revise your narration.

1. Does the rough draft satisfy the conditions for the essay form? Is there an introductory paragraph? Are there at least three well-developed paragraphs in the body of the essay? Is there a concluding paragraph? Remember that one sentence is not a developed paragraph. One exception to this rule is when you use dialogue. When you write a story, you often include the conversation between two people. In this case, the writer makes a new paragraph each time a different person speaks. This often means that one sentence could be a separate paragraph.

2. Is your essay a narration? Does it tell the story of one particular incident that takes place in a specific time and location? Sometimes writers make the mistake of talking about incidents in a general way, and commenting on the meaning of the incidents. Be careful. This would not be considered a narration. You must be a story teller. Where does the action take place? Can the reader see it? What time of day, week, or season is it? What is your main character in the story doing?

3. Have you put the details of the essay in a certain time order? Find the expressions you have used that show the time sequence.

4. Can you think of any part of the story that is missing and should be added? Is there any material that is irrelevant and should be omitted?

5. Are there sentences or paragraphs that seem to be repetitious?

6. Find several places where you can substitute stronger verbs or nouns. Add adjectives to give the reader better sensory images.

7. Find at least three places in your draft where you can add details. Perhaps you might add an entire paragraph that will more fully describe the person or place that is central to your story.

8. Can you think of a more effective way to begin or end?

9. Does your story have a point? If a person just told you everything he did on a certain day, that would not be a good story. A good story needs to have a point.

10. Show your rough draft to at least two other readers and ask for suggestions.

Prepare the final copy, print, and proofread it

The typing of the final version should follow the traditional rules for an acceptable submission.

CHECKLIST FOR THE FINAL COPY

Use only 8½-by-11 inch paper (never paper torn out of a spiral bound notebook).

Type on one side of the paper only.

Double space.

Leave approximately 1½-inch margins on each side of the paper.

Center the title at the top of the page. Do not put quotation marks around the title and do not underline it.

Do not hyphenate a word at the end of a line unless you are willing to consult a dictionary to check on the acceptable division of the word into syllables.

You may put your name, the date, and the title of your paper on a separate title page. Ask your instructor for specific advice on what information to include.

Indent each paragraph five spaces.

Leave two spaces after each period.

If your paper is more than one page, number the pages and staple the pages together so they will not get lost.

Do not forget to make a copy before you submit the paper.

Note: In most cases, college teachers will not accept handwritten work. However, if you are submitting handwritten work, you must be sure to write on every other line and have good legible handwriting. Begin today to learn to type on the computer. You will be at a disadvantage if you cannot use the current technology.

Once you have typed your final version and printed it out, an important step still remains. This step can often mean the difference of an entire letter grade. You must *proofread* your paper. Even if you have used a spellcheck feature available on your word processing program, there still could be errors in your paper. The spellcheck feature only finds groupings of letters that are not words. For example, if you typed the word *van* when you meant to type *ban,* the spellcheck would not catch this error.

The secret of good proofreading is to look at each word and sentence construction by itself without thinking about the paper's contents.

CHECKLIST FOR PROOFREADING

Study each sentence: One way to proofread is to read backwards, starting with the last sentence and examining every sentence, one at a time. First, check that the sentence is really complete and not a fragment or a run-on. Then check the punctuation. Go on to the next sentence and do the same. In this way, you will develop a critical eye for spotting any problems with sentence level errors.

Study each word: Read the paper again, this time studying each word in every sentence. Look at the letters of the words. Have you transposed any letters or have you left off an ending such as the *-ed* or the *-s*? If there are any words you are not sure how to spell, do not forget to check for the correct spelling. Is there any word you have omitted?

Working Together

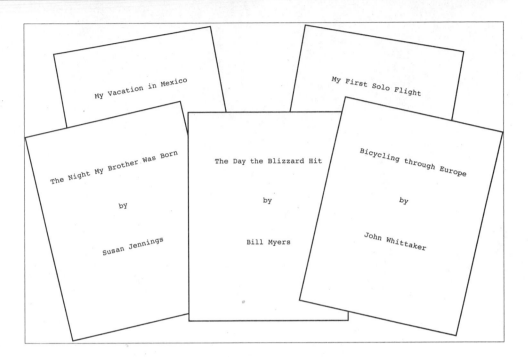

In this chapter, each student has written a narrative essay. This essay will be a writing project to keep in your portfolio. At some later time, you may want to return to the essay and work on it again, or use it as the basis for another piece of writing.

Divide into groups and share these narrative essays with each other. Attach a sheet of paper to each essay so that each person who reads the essay can answer the following questions:

1. In your opinion, what is one aspect of the essay that you feel is a strength?

2. In your opinion, what is one aspect of the essay that still needs improvement?

If some writers are willing to read their essays out loud to the entire class, the class would enjoy listening to a few of them, not for criticism but just for enjoyment.

Chapter 6

Writing an Essay Using Process

Exploring the topic: Following and giving instructions

It is your sister's birthday. You have bought her a gift that tells you that "some assembly is required." You follow the instructions carefully as you try to put the item together, but something is wrong. No matter what you try, it does not work. You feel frustrated and angry and rip up the instructions in disgust.

At one time or another, all of us have found ourselves in such a situation. When we do, we understand the misery caused by poorly written instructions. Providing directions or instructions takes careful thought. These writers must be able to put themselves in the shoes of the persons following the directions. These readers may have no special background in or skill for performing the procedure. Careful writers are sensitive to those places in the directions where the readers could go wrong. Clarity and accuracy is absolutely essential.

1. Think of a time when you had to put something together, but you were not given good directions. Describe the process that was involved and what happened when you tried to accomplish it.

   _____

   _____

   _____

2. When people write instructions or give directions, what do they often leave out? Looking back on the situation you described above, why do you think you were not able to assemble the item?

   _____

   _____

   _____

3. Recall a time when you had to explain a process to someone. You might have had to show someone how to get somewhere, or you might have had to write a detailed description of how you performed a science experiment in a chemistry class. What was the process? Was it hard to explain? Why or why not?

_____

_____

_____

4. What was your worst experience in trying to follow a process? You could have been trying to work something out yourself, or you could have been trying to follow someone else's directions. How did you overcome your difficulty?

_____

_____

_____

Reading a model essay to discover steps in a process

Some of the most commonly seen examples of process writing occur in books and articles on cooking. In order to be understood, a writer describing a process like cooking must be clear, accurate, and complete. In the following selection, the famous nutritionist and health expert Gayelord Hauser first gives background information on the right approach to cooking vegetables, and then takes us through the actual process of cooking them.

How to Short-Cook Vegetables

GAYELORD HAUSER

1   In lean vegetable cookery, just remember that the quicker vegetables are prepared and cooked, the better your family will like them. Also, the less is the loss of vitamins B, C, P. These vitamins, like salt, dissolve in water; therefore we never pour off any vegetable water. Better still, we short-cook vegetables in such a way that all the goodness and nutrients remain. I have said it a thousand and one times and I'll say it again—when vegetables are cooked half an hour or more in pots full of water, you'd be wiser to throw out the dead vegetables and drink the water they were cooked in, for that's where the precious vitamins and minerals have gone.

2   Any vegetable can be short-cooked in a matter of minutes. All you need is a heavy cooking utensil, preferably heavy enamelware, and one of those handy vegetable cutters, or "snitzlers" as they are called. Or use an ordinary shredder (the coarse one). Or cut vegetables into thin slivers. Do your shredding or slivering as quickly as possible to prevent vitamin C loss.

3   Have your cooking pot piping hot; use a small one so it will be filled to the top; the less space for air, the better. In the bottom of the pot have three tablespoons of water; when this boils and the pot is filled with steam, put in your

cut-up vegetables and cover the pot tightly. Let the vegetables cook on low flame for two minutes; then shake the pot (without lifting the lid) so there is no possible chance of sticking. After about four minutes, remove the cover and taste of the vegetable slivers; if it is soft but still a bit chewy, as the vegetables are in Chinese restaurants, it is at its best. Now all you add is a sprinkle of vegetable salt, some herbs, and a bit of vegetable oil; or, if you prefer, you may use half vegetable oil and half butter as my Italian students do. Such short-cooked vegetables have a wonderful, natural flavor and keep their attractive color. When you use vegetable salt last, the juices are not extracted during cooking.

4   For *extra* lean short-cooking, here is a trick: Instead of water, we steam the sliced vegetables in flavorsome broth—left-over "pot likker," Hauser broth, canned or dehydrated vegetable broth, or chicken or beef broth made with bouillon cubes. Cooked this way, with the addition of vegetable salt and sprinkled with herbs, short-cooked vegetables can be enjoyed without the addition of extra fat. You'll be amazed how soon you and your family will begin to like, and even prefer, the nutty flavor of these vegetables short-cooked *extra* lean.

5   Here are three easily remembered pointers for successful vegetable cookery: (1) do not peel; just wash thoroughly, or scrub with a vegetable brush; (2) boil or bake whole vegetables in their skins; (3) short-cook sliced or shredded vegetables in the smallest amount of water or broth, and add a bit of vegetable salt *after* they are done. If your family insists on a "buttery" taste, add a pat of sunbutter just before serving.

Analyzing the writer's strategies

1. What is the writer's purpose, as he states it in the first paragraph?

2. Often a process requires specialized tools. What paragraph in the Hauser selection describes the needed cooking utensils? What are those utensils?

3. Which paragraph describes the process? How many steps are there in the process? Make a list of the steps and number each of them.

4. What is the author's purpose in writing paragraph 4?

5. How does the writer's last paragraph provide a useful conclusion to the essay?

Writing the essay using process (how to . . .)

> *Process* is one method of development that shows a step-by-step progression in the accomplishment of a goal. It can be directional (explaining how to do something readers might try themselves), or it can be strictly informational (explaining how something was done or how something works, with no expectation that the readers will actually try the process).

The "how to" section of every library and bookstore is usually a busy area. People come to find books that will help them perform thousands of different tasks—from plumbing to flower arranging. If you want to learn how to cook

Chinese dishes, assemble a child's bicycle, start your own business, or even remodel your bathroom, you can find a book that will tell you how to do it. Thousands of books and articles have been written that promise to help people accomplish their goals in life. What do you think are the best selling "how to" books in America? Perhaps you have guessed the answer: how to lose weight! In the essay that you write, be sure to choose a process with which you are already familiar.

Choose the topic and the purpose of the information for the thesis statement

1. How to get good grades in college

2. How to do well in a job interview

3. How to plan a budget

4. How to buy a used car

5. How to study for a test

6. How to change a tire

7. How to redecorate a room

8. How to buy clothes on a limited budget

9. How to find the right place to live

10. How to make new friends

Using the above list of ten topics or using ideas of your own, jot down two or three processes with which you are familiar.

_____

_____

_____

From these two or three topics, select the one you think would give you the best opportunity for writing. Which process do you feel strongest about? Which one is most likely to interest your readers? For which topic do you have the most first-hand experience?

Selected topic: _____

Your next step is to decide your purpose in writing. Which of the two types of process writing will you be doing? Do you want to give directions on how to carry out each step in a process so that your readers can do this process themselves? For instance, would you provide directions on how to change a tire, perhaps suggesting that your readers keep these directions in the glove compartments of their cars? On the other hand, do you want to provide information as to how a certain process works because you think your readers might find the process interesting? For instance, you might explain the process involved in getting an airplane off the ground. Not many of us understand how this works, and very few of us will actually ever pilot a plane. Perhaps you know a lot about an unusual process that might amuse or entertain readers.

Directional _____ or informational _____

Now put your topic and controlling idea together into your thesis statement.

Thesis statement: _____

_____

Gather the information (use brainstorming techniques)

Take at least fifteen minutes to list as many steps or stages in the process as you can. If the process is one that others in your class or at home already know, consult with them for any additional steps that you may have overlooked. You may also need to think of the precise vocabulary words associated with the process (such as the names of tools used for building or repairing something). The more specific you can be, the more helpful and interesting the process will be for your readers. List the steps or stages in the process:

_____

_____

_____

_____

_____

_____

_____

_____

_____

_____

_____

_____

_____

_____

_____

_____

Select and organize material

Review your brainstorming list and ask yourself if you now have a complete list. Have you left out any step that someone who is unfamiliar with this process might need to know? Is there some extra information you could provide along the way that would be helpful and encouraging? Do you have a special warning about something that the reader should *not* do? You might consider telling your readers exactly where in the process most people are likely to make mistakes.

Make an outline giving each stage a heading. Underneath each heading, list all of the different ideas or vocabulary words that you should keep in mind as you begin to write. In a process essay, the most essential elements for judging its success are the order, the accuracy, and the completeness of all the steps.

_____

_____

_____

_____

_____

_____

_____

_____

_____

_____

_____

Write the rough draft

Follow your outline and write your rough draft, keeping in mind that this outline is only a guide. As you write, you will find yourself reevaluating the logic of your ideas, a perfectly natural step that may involve making some changes from your outline. You may think of some special advice that would help the reader, and if you do, feel free to add these details. Your main goal is to get the process down on paper as completely and accurately as possible.

Achieving coherence in the process essay

When you buy a product and read the instructions that go with it, the form of writing in those instructions usually consists of a list of numbered items, each telling you what to do. In an essay, you do not usually number the steps. Instead, you can signal the movement from one step to another by changing to a new paragraph and/or by using a transitional expression. As in other methods for developing ideas, *process* has its own special words and expressions that can be used to signal movement from one step to the next.

TRANSITIONAL EXPRESSIONS FOR PROCESS

the first step	while you are	the last step
in the beginning	as you are	the final step
to start with	next	finally
to begin with	then	at last
first of all	the second step	eventually
	after you have	

Revise the rough draft

A space of time if very helpful to allow you to think about your written ideas; this allows you to judge your work more objectively than you can immediately after writing. Therefore, if you can put aside your draft for a day or two before you need to revise it, your work will benefit.

When you revise, you may work alone, with a group, with a peer tutor, or directly with your instructor. Here are some of the basic questions you should consider during this most important stage of your work:

1. Does the rough draft satisfy all the conditions for the essay form? Is there an introductory paragraph? Are there at least three well-developed paragraphs in the body of the essay? Have you written a concluding paragraph? Remember that a single sentence is not a developed paragraph.

2. Does the essay describe the process, one that is either directional or informational?

3. Are the steps in the process in the correct order? In a process essay, the sequence of the steps is crucial. A step that is placed out of order could result in a disaster of major proportions.

4. Are the directions accurate and complete? Check more than once that no important piece of information has been left out. Have you considered the points where some special advice might be helpful? Are there any special tools that would be useful?

5. Is any of the material not relevant?

6. Are there sentences or words that seem to be repetitious?

7. Find several places where you can substitute more specific verbs, nouns or adjectives. Always try to use vocabulary that is appropriate for the process being described.

8. Can you think of a more effective way to begin or end?

9. Does the essay flow logically from one idea to the next? Could you improve this flow with better use of transitional expressions?

10. Show your draft to at least two other readers and ask for suggestions.

Prepare the final copy, print it, and proofread it

The typing of the final version should follow the traditional rules for an acceptable submission.

CHECKLIST FOR THE FINAL COPY

Use only 8½-by-11 inch paper (never paper torn out of a spiral bound notebook).

Type on one side of the paper only.

Double space.

Leave approximately 1½-inch margins on each side of the paper.

Center the title at the top of the page. Do not put quotation marks around the title and do not underline it.

Do not hyphenate a word at the end of a line unless you are willing to consult a dictionary to check on the acceptable division of the word into syllables.

You may put your name, the date, and the title of your paper on a separate title page. Ask your instructor for specific advice on what information to include.

Indent each paragraph five spaces.

Leave two spaces after each period.

If your paper is more than one page, number the pages and staple the pages together so they will not get lost.

Do not forget to make a copy before you submit the paper.

Note: In most cases, college teachers will not accept handwritten work. However, if you are submitting handwritten work, you must be sure to write on every other line and have good legible handwriting. Begin today to learn to type on the computer. You will be at a disadvantage if you cannot use the current technology.

Once you have typed your final version and printed it out, an important step still remains. This step can often mean the difference of an entire letter grade. You must *proofread* your paper. Even if you have used a spellcheck feature available on your word processing program, there still could be errors in your paper. The spellcheck feature only finds groupings of letters that are not words. For example, if you typed the word *van* when you meant to type *ban,* the spellcheck would not catch this error.

The secret of good proofreading is to look at each word and sentence construction by itself without thinking about the paper's contents.

CHECKLIST FOR PROOFREADING

Study each sentence: One way to proofread is to read backwards, starting with the last sentence and examining every sentence, one at a time. First, check that the sentence is really complete and not a fragment or a run-on. Then check the punctuation. Go on to the next sentence and do the same. In this way, you will develop a critical eye for spotting any problems with sentence level errors.

Study each word: Read the paper again, this time studying each word in every sentence. Look at the letters of the words. Have you transposed any letters or have you left off an ending such as the *-ed* or the *-s*? If there are any words you are not sure how to spell, do not forget to check for the correct spelling. Is there any word you have omitted?

Working Together

1. The students in the class should list and discuss some of the current problems on their campus today. Then the members of the class should divide into groups of three or four, each group choosing one of the problems discussed. After discussion, each group then draws up a list of steps needed to be taken in order to improve the situation.

2. Each group chooses a secretary. The group uses the list from the first activity to create sentences that will go into a letter to be sent to the appropriate college official, suggesting what could be done to solve the problem. The secretary will write the finished letter. Be sure there is an introductory paragraph which presents the problem and a conclusion which thanks the official for his or her attention.

Writing an Essay Using Comparison or Contrast

Exploring a topic: Computers and the human brain

Computer technology is advancing so rapidly that scientists are already discussing the possibility of creating *artificial intelligence*—a computer that will be able to duplicate the thinking process of the human mind. Scientists in this country and abroad are making progress in designing such a computer. While many people are skeptical that any machine could ever replace a person's mind, many jobs are certainly changing or disappearing because of the work that computers are now able to do.

1. What are some of the jobs computers can already do better and faster than human beings can?

   _____

   _____

   _____

2. What are some of the jobs you have to do now that you would like a computer to do for you? How many of these jobs do you think a computer will take over in your lifetime?

   _____

   _____

   _____

3. Do you think a computer could ever be programmed to be as creative as the human mind? Why or why not?

   _____

   _____

   _____

4. In your opinion, what are the dangers in the sophisticated computer technology we see today?

_____

_____

_____

Reading a model essay to discover how a writer uses comparison or contrast to develop a topic

In the following selection from his book *Please Explain*, science writer Isaac Asimov compares the workings of the modern computer with the workings of the human mind.

The Computer and the Brain
ISAAC ASIMOV

1   The difference between a brain and a computer can be expressed in a single word: complexity.

mammalian: having the characteristics of animals that produce milk for their young

2   The large mammalian brain is the most complicated thing, for its size, known to us. The human brain weighs three pounds, but in that three pounds are ten billion neurons and a hundred billion smaller cells. These many billions of cells are interconnected in a vastly complicated network that we can't begin to unravel as yet.

intricacy: having complex parts

3   Even the most complicated computer man has yet built can't compare in intricacy with the brain. Computer switches and components number in the thousands rather than in the billions. What's more, the computer switch is just an on-off device, whereas the brain cell is itself possessed of a tremendously complex inner structure.

4   Can a computer think? That depends on what you mean by "think." If solving a mathematical problem is "thinking," then a computer can "think" and do so much faster than a man. Of course, most mathematical problems can be solved quite mechanically by repeating certain straightforward processes over and over again. Even the simple computers of today can be geared for that.

5   It is frequently said that computers solve problems only because they are "programmed" to do so. They can only do what men have them do. One must remember that human beings also can only do what they are "programmed" to do. Our genes "program" us the instant the fertilized ovum is formed, and our potentialities are limited by that "program."

6   Our "program" is so much more enormously complex, though, that we might like to define "thinking" in terms of the creativity that goes into writing a great play or composing a great symphony, in conceiving a brilliant scientific theory or a profound ethical judgment. In that sense, computers certainly can't think and neither can most humans.

7   Surely, though, if a computer can be made complex enough, it can be as creative as we. If it could be made as complex as a human brain, it could be the equivalent of a human brain and do whatever a human brain can do.

8   To suppose anything else is to suppose that there is more to the human brain than the matter that composes it. The brain is made up of cells in a certain arrangement and the cells are made up of atoms and molecules in certain arrangements. If anything else is there, no signs of it have ever been detected. To duplicate the material complexity of the brain is therefore to duplicate everything about it.

9   But how long will it take to build a computer complex enough to duplicate the human brain? Perhaps not as long as some think. Long before we approach a computer as complex as our brain, we will perhaps build a computer that is at least complex enough to design another computer more complex than itself. This more complex computer could design one still more complex and so on and so on and so on.

10   In other words, once we pass a certain critical point, the computers take over and there is a "complexity explosion." In a very short time thereafter, computers may exist that not only duplicate the human brain—but far surpass it.

11   Then what? Well, mankind is not doing a very good job of running the earth right now. Maybe, when the time comes, we ought to step gracefully aside and hand over the job to someone who can do it better. And if we don't step aside, perhaps Supercomputer will simply move in and push us aside.

Analyzing the writer's strategies

1. An essay of comparison usually emphasizes the similarities between two subjects, while an essay of contrast emphasizes the differences. With this in mind, is the essay you have just read an essay of comparison or contrast?

2. How does this essay help to explain why a human can still beat a computer in a game of chess?

3. Does the writer provide an equal number of details that relate to both computers and the human brain or does he concentrate mostly on one part of the two-part topic? Go through the essay and underline each comparison or contrast that is made.

4. Specifically, how does the writer demonstrate the complexity of a computer and the complexity of the human brain?

5. Study the conclusion. How serious is the author's final suggestion?

Writing the essay using comparison and contrast

> *Comparison* or *Contrast,* a method for developing ideas, is the careful look at the similarities and/or differences between people, objects, or ideas, usually in order to reach some conclusion or make a judgment.

Find a topic and controlling idea for the thesis statement

1. High school classes and college classes

2. Studying with a friend or studying alone

3. Male and female stereotypes

4. Your best friend in childhood with your best friend now

5. Using public transportation versus using a car

6. Our current president with any previous chief executive

7. Two items you have compared when shopping

8. Two apartments or houses where you have lived

9. Cooking dinner at home versus eating out

10. Watching television versus reading a book

Using the above list of ten topics or using ideas of your own, jot down a few two-part topics that appeal to you.

_____

_____

_____

From your list of two-part topics, select the one you think would give you the best opportunity for writing. Which one of these do you feel most strongly about? Which one is most likely to interest your readers? For which topic do you have the greatest first-hand experience?

Selected topic: _____

Your next step is to decide what your controlling idea should be. What is your main purpose in comparing or contrasting these two topics? Do you want to show that although people think two topics are similar, they actually differ in important ways? Do you want to show one topic is better in some ways than the other topic? Do you want to analyze how something has changed over the years (a "then-and-now" essay)?

Controlling idea: _____

At this point, combine your two-point topic and controlling idea into one thesis statement.

Thesis statement: _____

_____

Gather the information (use brainstorming techniques)

Take at least fifteen minutes to brainstorm (use listing or clustering) as many comparison or contrasting points as you can on your chosen topic. You will probably want to think of at least three or four points. Under each point, brainstorm as many details as come to mind. For instance, if you are comparing two friends and the first point covers the interests you have in common, recall as much as you can about the activities you share together. If you are brainstorming a topic that other classmates or family members might know something about, ask them to help you think of additional points to compare. If any special vocabulary comes to mind, jot that down as well. The more specific you can be, the more helpful and interesting you will make your comparison or contrast for your readers.

Points that could be compared or contrasted

_____

_____

_____

_____

_____

_____

_____

_____

_____

_____

_____

_____

_____

_____

_____

Select and organize material

As a method of developing ideas, comparison or contrast involves a two-part topic. For instance, you might compare the school you attend now with a school you attended in the past. Often we need to make choices or judgments, and we can make better decisions if we can compare and/or contrast the two items in front of us. Since this is a two-part topic, there is a choice in organizing the essay:

1. **The block method:** This is when you write entirely about one item or idea, and then in a later paragraph or paragraphs you write entirely about the other topic. If you choose this method, you must be sure to bring up the same points and keep the same order as when you discussed the first topic.

2. **The point-by-point method:** This is when you discuss one point and show both topics relating to this in one paragraph. Then, in a new paragraph, you discuss the second point and relate it to both topics, and so forth.

Which method will be best for the topic you have selected, the block method or point-by-point method?

At this stage, review your brainstorming list and ask yourself if you have a list that is complete. Have you left out any point that might need to be considered? Do you have at least three points, and do you have enough material to develop both parts of the topic? You do not want the comparison or contrast to end up one-sided with all the content about only one part of the topic.

Make an outline, choosing one of the formats below, depending on whether you selected the block method or point-by-point method.

The example shown is the contrast between high school classes and college classes.

Outline for Block Method

I.	Topic 1	High School Classes
	A. First Point	meet 5 days a week
	B. Second Point	daily homework
	C. Third Point	no research papers
	D. Fourth Point	disciplinary problems in the class
II.	Topic 2	College Classes
	A. First Point	meet only 2 or 3 days a week
	B. Second Point	long term assignments
	C. Third Point	research papers required
	D. Fourth Point	no discipline problems

Outline for point-by-point method

I.	First Point	How often classes meet
	A. Topic 1	high school classes
	B. Topic 2	college classes
II.	Second Point	Homework
	A. Topic 1	high school classes
	B. Topic 2	college classes
III.	Third Point	Research papers
	A. Topic 1	high school classes
	B. Topic 2	college classes
IV.	Fourth Point	Discipline
	A. Topic 1	high school classes
	B. Topic 2	college classes

_____

_____

_____

_____

_____

_____

_____

_____

_____

_____

_____

_____

_____

_____

_____

_____

_____

_____

_____

_____

_____

_____

_____

_____

_____

_____

Write the rough draft

Follow your outline and write your rough draft. Remember the outline is a guide. Most writers find new ideas occur to them at this time, so if you have new thoughts, you should feel free to explore these ideas along the way. As you write, you will be constantly re-evaluating the logic of your ideas.

Coherence in the comparison or contrast essay

As in other methods of developing ideas, the comparison and contrast essay has its particular words and expressions which can be used to signal the movement from one point to the next.

COMMON TRANSITIONAL EXPRESSIONS		
Transitions for Comparison	**Transitions for Contrast**	
similar to	on the contrary	though
similarly	on the other hand	unlike
like	in contrast with	even though
likewise	in spite of	nevertheless
just like	despite	however
just as	instead of	but
furthermore	different from	otherwise
moreover	whereas	except for
equally	while	and yet
again	although	still
also		
too		
so		

Revise the rough draft

If you can have an interval of time between the writing of the rough draft and your work on revising it, you will be able to look at your work with a greater objectivity. Ideally, you should put aside your first draft for a day or two before you approach it again for revision.

When you revise, you may work alone, with a group, with a peer tutor, or directly with your instructor. Here are some of the basic questions you should consider during this most important stage of your work:

1. Does the rough draft satisfy the conditions for the essay form? Is there an introductory paragraph? Are there at least three well-developed paragraphs in the body of the essay? Is there a concluding paragraph? Remember that one sentence is not a developed paragraph.

2. Does the essay compare or contrast a two-part topic and come to some conclusion about the comparison or contrast?

3. Did you use either the point-by-point method or the block method to organize the essay?

4. Is any important point omitted? Is any of the material included irrelevant?

5. Are there sentences or paragraphs that are repetitious?

6. Find several places where you can substitute more specific verbs, nouns or adjectives. Try to use the vocabulary appropriate for the topic being discussed.

7. Can you think of a more effective way to begin or end?

8. Does the essay flow logically from one idea to the next? Could you improve this flow with better use of transitional devices?

9. Show your draft to at least two other readers and ask for suggestions.

Prepare the final copy, print, and proofread it

The typing of the final version should follow the traditional rules for an acceptable submission.

CHECKLIST FOR THE FINAL COPY

Use only 8½-by-11 inch paper (never paper torn out of a spiral bound notebook).

Type on one side of the paper only.

Double space.

Leave approximately 1½-inch margins on each side of the paper.

Center the title at the top of the page. Do not put quotation marks around the title and do not underline it.

Do not hyphenate a word at the end of a line unless you are willing to consult a dictionary to check on the acceptable division of the word into syllables.

You may put your name, the date, and the title of your paper on a separate title page. Ask your instructor for specific advice on what information to include.

Indent each paragraph five spaces.

Leave two spaces after each period.

If your paper is more than one page, number the pages and staple the pages together so they will not get lost.

Do not forget to make a copy before you submit the paper.

Note: In most cases, college teachers will not accept handwritten work. However, if you are submitting handwritten work, you must be sure to write on every other line and have good legible handwriting. Begin today to learn to type on the computer. You will be at a disadvantage if you cannot use the current technology.

Once you have typed your final version and printed it out, an important step still remains. This step can often mean the difference of an entire letter grade. You must *proofread* your paper. Even if you have used a spellcheck feature available on your word processing program, there still could be errors in your paper. The spellcheck feature only finds groupings of letters that are not words. For example, if you typed the word *van* when you meant to type *ban,* the spellcheck would not catch this error.

The secret of good proofreading is to look at each word and sentence construction by itself without thinking about the paper's contents.

CHECKLIST FOR PROOFREADING

Study each sentence: One way to proofread is to read backwards, starting with the last sentence and examining every sentence, one at a time. First, check that the sentence is really complete and not a fragment or a run-on. Then check the punctuation. Go on to the next sentence and do the same. In this way, you will develop a critical eye for spotting any problems with sentence level errors.

Study each word: Read the paper again, this time studying each word in every sentence. Look at the letters of the words. Have you transposed any letters or have you left off an ending such as the *-ed* or the *-s?* If there are any words you are not sure how to spell, do not forget to check for the correct spelling. Is there any word you have omitted?

Working Together

The selection that follows is from a journalist's contrast of President Carter with President Clinton. A person in the class should read the selection out loud while students make a list of the areas being contrasted (such as education or place of birth). Following the reading, put on the chalkboard the areas that have been contrasted along with the specific examples. With these general areas in mind, choose two other presidents from the same party (perhaps Reagan and Bush or Kennedy and Johnson) and brainstorm to see what information class members can contribute. Like most writers, you will probably discover you need to do some additional research in the library to gather more information. Work together in small groups to see what you can find out in the library. Then work individually to write an essay of comparison or contrast. Remember, since there is an endless number of points that could be compared, limit yourself to those points that seem most significant in the light of history.

Clinton's No Carter

DAVID BRODER

1 Is there any reason to believe that Clinton will be another Carter, either in the opposition he draws from his party's congressional wing or in the economic mess he creates?

2 The differences between the two men are far more striking and significant than their similarities.

3 The main parallels include their background as Southern governors, devoid of national government experience. Both beat establishment Republican presidents by exploiting public disenchantment with Washington insiders and using the rhetoric of reform to suggest that they were not conventional Democrats.

4 That is more than casual kinship. But the differences are more vivid—and consequential.

5 Carter was a Naval Academy graduate and an engineer. His model of policy-making was rational, efficient, and introspective. Governing to him was an exercise in problem-solving. Congress did not respond well to that approach. And Carter did not react well when legislators tinkered with his solutions. Soon they were at odds.

6   Clinton is a lawyer, not an engineer. His instinct is to be consultative and inclusive. He is as flexible as Carter was rigid—some would say, almost too ready to compromise.

7   In temperament, too, the two men are strikingly dissimilar. Carter regarded politics as the price you paid for the privilege of public service. But to him, politics in itself was a rather tawdry arena of ego, ambition, and selfish interests, and he did his best to keep it at bay.

8   Clinton, by contrast, loves politics. He gets joy out of the bickering and dickering and he clearly is renewed by the hours he spends with voters and politicians of all kinds. The schmoozing and shop-talk that Carter found a burden, Clinton craves.

9   The third difference is that Carter came to Washington wearing his Georgia parochialism as a badge of honor. He made a point of saying in his 1976 campaign that he had never met a Democratic president.

10   Clinton is a polar opposite. He celebrates the moment of his meeting with John F. Kennedy, when Kennedy was president and Clinton an awe-struck high schooler. And he has had a connection to every Democratic president and presidential contender for the past 20 years.

11   Indeed, Clinton comes to the job as the most thoroughly "networked" politician of his era. He has been part of every major movement in his party from the McGovern campaign on the left to the Democratic Leadership Council on the right.

12   And he has never given up one set of relationships or alliances when he has moved on to another. Every one of those people has a claim on Clinton, and Clinton has a claim on their loyalty in return.

13   Indeed, it is the fact that Clinton has been so many things to so many people on his climb to the presidency that makes the selection of his Cabinet and White House staff so vital—and so fascinating. This is the first time that he will have to disappoint the hopes of many who have a personal or political claim on him. As he does that, we will get our first clues on who Clinton really is.

14   But I don't think we will learn much by trying to fit him into the Jimmy Carter mold. They are so unlike, I'd be willing to bet that Clinton's performance—and his problems—will bear little resemblance to those of the last Democratic president.

THE ESSAY

Chapter 8

Writing an Essay Using Persuasion

What is persuasion?

From one point of view, all writing is persuasion since the main goal of any writer is to convince a reader to see, think, or believe in a certain way. There is, however, a more formal understanding of persuasive writing. Anyone who has ever been a member of a high school debate team knows there are techniques that the effective speaker or writer uses to present a case successfully. Learning how to recognize these techniques of persuasion and discovering how to use them in your own writing is the subject of this chapter.

An essay of *persuasion* presents evidence intended to convince the reader that the writer's viewpoint is valid.

Guide to writing the persuasive essay

1. **State a clear thesis.** Use words such as *must, ought,* or *should*. Study the following three sample thesis statements:

   The United States must reform its prison system.

   All states ought to have the same legal drinking age.

   We should not ban all handguns.

2. **Give evidence or reasons for your beliefs.** Your evidence is the heart of the essay. You must show the wisdom of your logic by providing the best evidence available.

3. **Use examples.** Well-chosen examples are among the best types of evidence for an argument. People can identify with a specific example from real life in a way that is not possible with an abstract idea. Without examples, essays of persuasion would be flat, lifeless, and unconvincing.

4. **Use opinions from recognized authorities to support your points.** One of the oldest methods of supporting an argument is to use one or more

93

persons of authority to support your particular position. People will usually believe what well-known experts claim. However, be sure that your expert is someone who is respected in the area you are discussing. For example, if you are arguing that we must end ocean dumping, your argument will be stronger if you quote a respected scientist who can accurately predict the consequences of this approach to waste disposal. A famous movie star giving the same information might be more glamorous and get more attention, but he or she would not be as great an authority as the scientist.

5. **Answer your critics in advance.** When you point out, beforehand, what your opposition is likely to say in answer to your argument, you will be writing from a position of strength. You are letting your reader know that there is another side to the argument you are making. By pointing out this other side and then answering its objections in advance, you are strengthening your own position.

6. **Point out the results.** Here, you help your reader see what will happen if your argument is (or is not) believed or acted upon as you think it should be. You should be very specific and very rational when you point out results, making sure that you avoid exaggerations of any kind. For example, if you are arguing against the possession of handguns, it would be an exaggeration to say that if we don't ban handguns, "everyone will be murdered."

As in other methods of developing the essay, the essay using persuasion has its own special words that signal parts of the argument. The chart below can help you choose transitional expressions that will move you from one part of your argument to the next.

WORDS AND PHRASES THAT SIGNAL PARTS OF AN ARGUMENT

To signal the thesis of an argument

    I agree (disagree) that

    I support (do not support) the idea that

    I am in favor of (not in favor of)

    I propose

    ———— must be (must not be) changed

    ———— should be (should not be) adopted

To signal a reason

    because, just because, since, for

    in the first place

    in view of

    can be shown

    The first reason is . . .

    An additional reason is . . .

    Another reason is . . .

    The most convincing piece of evidence is . . .

To suggest another way to think about something

    Most people assume that . . .

    One would think that . . .

    We have been told that . . .

    Popular thought is that . . .

    Consider the case of . . .

    There is no comparison between . . .

To signal a conclusion

    therefore, thus, consequently, so

    as a result

    We can conclude that . . .

    This proves that . . .

    This shows that . . .

    This demonstrates that . . .

    This suggests that . . .

    This leads to the conclusion that . . .

    It follows that . . .

Be careful not to fall into the following traps, both of which are poor ways to try to win over an opponent to your position:

1. Appeals to fear or pity:
   If we don't double the police force this year, a child in our neighborhood might be killed.

2. Sweeping or false generalizations:
   All women belong in the kitchen.

It's Time We Helped Patients Die

DR. HOWARD CAPLAN

Howard Caplan is a medical doctor who specializes in geriatrics, that branch of medicine that deals with the care of older people. He is also the medical director of three nursing homes in Los Angeles, California.

As you read Dr. Caplan's essay, look for all of the elements of an effective argument. Where does the writer give his thesis statement? Where are his major examples? At what point does he use authorities to support his point of view? In addition, look for the paragraphs where he answers those who do not agree with him and be sure to find that section of the essay where he predicts the future of

euthanasia, commonly known as "mercy killing." As you read the essay, do you see any weaknesses in the writer's argument?

aneurysm: a sac formed by the swelling of a vein or artery

astrocytoma: a tumor made up of nerve cells

nasogastric: relating to a tube inserted through the nose and into the stomach

1   For three years, the husband of one of my elderly patients watched helplessly as she deteriorated. She'd burst an *aneurysm* and later had an *astrocytoma* removed from her brain. Early in the ordeal, realizing that she'd never recover from a vegetative state, he'd pleaded with me to pull her *nasogastric* tube.

2   I'd refused, citing the policy of the convalescent hospital. I told him I could do it only if he got a court order. But he couldn't bring himself to start such proceedings, although the months dragged by with no signs of improvements in his wife's condition. He grieved as her skin broke down and she developed terrible bedsores. She had to have several courses of antibiotics to treat the infections in them, as well as in her bladder, which had an indwelling catheter.

3   Finally I got a call from a lawyer who said he'd been retained by the family to force me to comply with the husband's wishes.

4   "I'm on your side," I assured him. "But you'll have to get that court order just the same."

5   I went on to suggest—though none too hopefully—that we ask the court to do more than just let the patient starve to death. "If the judge will agree to let her die slowly, why won't he admit that he wants death to happen? Let's ask for permission to give her an injection and end her life in a truly humane manner."

6   The lawyer had no answer except to say, "Aw, come on, Doc—that's euthanasia!"

7   Frankly, I'd have been surprised at any other reaction. Although most states have enacted living-will laws in the past decade, none has yet taken the next logical step—legalizing euthanasia. But I believe it's time they did. Ten years of practice in geriatrics have convinced me that a proper death is a humane death, either in your sleep or being *put* to sleep.

8   I see appropriate patients every day in the extended-care facilities at which I practice. About 50 of the 350 people under my care have already ended their biographical lives. They've reached the stage in life at which there's no more learning, communicating, or experiencing pleasure. They're now simply existing in what is left of their biological lives.

demented: having lost normal brain function

9   Most of these patients are the elderly *demented*. A typical case is that of a woman in her 80s or 90s, who speaks only in gibberish and doesn't recognize her family. She has forgotten how to eat, so she has a feeding tube coming from her nose. She is incontinent, so she has an indwelling catheter. She can no longer walk, so she is tied into a wheelchair. She's easily agitated, so she gets daily doses of a major tranquilizer. Why shouldn't I, with the concurrence of her family and an independent medical panel, be allowed to quickly and painlessly end her suffering?

aphasic triplegic: a person who has lost the ability to express or comprehend language, and who has paralysis of three limbs

10   I think of another patient, a woman in her 50s, with end-stage multiple sclerosis, unable to move a muscle except for her eyeballs and her tongue. And younger patients: I have on my census a man in his early 40s, left an *aphasic triplegic* by a motorcycle accident when he was 19. For nearly a quarter of a century, while most of us were working, raising children, traveling, reading, and otherwise going about our lives, he's been vegetating. His biographical life ended with that crash. He can't articulate—only make sounds to convey that he's hungry or wet. If he were to become acutely ill, I would prefer not to try saving him. I'd want to let pneumonia end it for him.

11   Of my remaining 300 patients, there are perhaps 50 to 100 borderline functional people who are nearing the end of their biographical lives and—were euthanasia legal—would probably tell me: "I'm ready to go. My bags are packed. Help me."

12   Anyone who's had front-line responsibility for the elderly has been asked if there wasn't "something you can give me" to end life. Such requests are made by patients who clearly see the inevitability of their deterioration and dread having to suffer through it. For these people, there is no more pleasure, let alone joy—merely misery. They want out.

13   What is their fate? Chances are they'll be referred for psychiatric consultation on the grounds that they must be seriously depressed. The psychiatrist, usually decades younger than the patient, does indeed diagnose depression and recommends an antidepressant.

14   But if such patients lived in the Netherlands, odds are they'd get assistance in obtaining a release from the slow dying process to which our modern technology condemns them. While euthanasia is not yet legal there, it's openly practiced. On a segment of the CBS show "60 Minutes" not long ago, I heard a Dutch *anesthesiologist* describe how doctors in his country help 5,000 terminal patients slip away peacefully each year. Isn't that a promising indication of how well euthanasia would work in this country?

anesthesiologist: a medical specialist who administers anesthesia, or pain killers, to people about to undergo operations

15   I realize that there are those who vigorously oppose the idea. And there are moral issues to confront—how much suffering is too much, the one-in-several-million chance that a person given no hope of improving will beat the odds. But it's time for society to seriously reconsider whether it is immoral to take the life of someone whose existence is nothing but irreversible suffering. Euthanasia ought to be treated the same way the abortion issue has been treated: People who believe it a sin to take a life even for merciful reasons would not be forced to do so. What I'm pleading for is that doctors and their patients at least have the choice.

16   I doubt that we'll get congressional action on such an emotionally charged issue during my lifetime. Action may have to come at the state level. Ideally, legislatures should permit each hospital and each nursing home to have a panel that would approve candidates for euthanasia. Or it might be more practical to have one panel serve several hospitals and nursing homes in a geographic area. Made up of one or two physicians and a lawyer or judge, plus the attending doctor, the panel would assess the attending's findings and recommendations, the patient's wishes, and those of the immediate family. This would ensure that getting a heart-stopping injection was truly in the patient's best interests, and that there was no ulterior motive—for example, trying to hasten an insurance payout. Needless to say, members of the board would be protected by law from liability claims.

17   Then, if the patient had made it known while of sound mind that under certain circumstances he wanted a deadly substance administered, the process would be easy for everyone. But in most cases, it would be up to the attending to raise the question of euthanasia with the patient's relatives.

18   I'd start with those who've been part of the patient's recent life. If there are relatives who haven't seen the patient for years, it really shouldn't be any of their business. For instance, I'd try involving a son who's just kept in touch by phone. I'd say to him, "If you really want to stop this from happening, then you'd better come out here to see firsthand what's going on."

19   However, if he said, "Well, I can't really get away, Doctor, but I violently disagree," my answer would be, "Well, not violently enough. Everyone here can see

what shape your mother's in. We're quite sure what she'd want if she could tell us, and we're going to help her."

20   Before any of this can happen, though, there's going to have to be widespread public education. The media will have to do a better job of discussing the issues than it has with living wills. Among my patients who are nearing death, there aren't more than a half-dozen with living wills attached to their charts. Patients' families often haven't even heard of them, and even when large institutions encourage families to get these things taken care of while the patient is still alert, it's hardly ever done.

21   Not knowing about living wills, unaware of no-code options, many families plunge their loved ones—and themselves—into unwanted misery. How many rapidly deteriorating patients are rushed from a nursing home to a hospital to be intubated, simply because that's the facility's rigid policy? How many families impoverish themselves to keep alive someone who's unaware of himself and his surroundings?

22   For that matter, how many people themselves suffer heart attacks or ulcers—not to mention divorces or bankruptcies—from the stresses involved in working to pay where Medicare and Medicaid leave off?

23   Every day in my professional life, I encounter illogical, irrational, and inhumane regulations that prevent me, and those with whom I work, from doing what we know in our souls to be the right thing. Before high technology, much of this debate was irrelevant. There was little we could do, for example, when a patient *arrested*. And what we could do rarely worked.

arrested: died

24   But times have changed. Now we have decisions to make. It helps to understand that many of the elderly infirm have accepted the inevitability—and, indeed, the desirability—of death. We who are younger must not mistake this philosophical position for depression. We need to understand the natural acceptance of death when life has lost its meaning.

25   About 28 percent of our huge Medicare budget is spent providing care during the last year of life. Far too little of that money goes to ensure that dying patients' last months are pain-free and comfortable. Far too much is wasted on heroic, pain-inducing measures that can make no difference. It's time to turn that ratio around—and to fight for the right to provide the ultimate assistance to patients who know their own fight to prolong life is a losing one.

Analyzing the writer's strategies

Because Dr. Caplan deals with a very sensitive subject, many people might find his position to be dangerous and even frightening. Even before we examine his essay, the title of the piece and the writer's medical background gain our attention. When a doctor writes on matters of life and death, we tend to pay more attention than we ordinarily might; the fact that Dr. Caplan works so closely with older people tends to give his views even more authority. For example, the facts and figures he gives in paragraphs eight and eleven go a long way toward strengthening his point of view. In addition, the writer uses both his own experience and his close observation of people in other countries to convince us that his stand on this controversial topic is a valid one.

The writer's position is also supported by the fact that he is so precise in paragraphs three to seven, when he deals with the law; almost from the beginning, Dr. Caplan is seen as a careful and caring professional. We notice too that in paragraphs twelve and thirteen he points out what happens under our present system, and in paragraphs sixteen to eighteen he gives practical suggestions that would help put his own system into operation. Finally, we see that in paragraph fifteen he pays attention to the other side's arguments and then answers those same arguments.

It is clear that Dr. Caplan's argument is carefully written and complete; it has all of the parts needed for a good argument. After you have studied each part of the essay, are you able to find any weaknesses in the writer's presentation?

Responding to the writer's argument

Take a position either for or against one of the following topics and write an argumentative essay supporting your position. Use the "Guide to Writing the Persuasive Essay" (pp. 93–95) to help construct the essay. Be sure to include all of the important points needed for a good argument.

1. All medical care should be free in our society.

2. Doctors should not be burdened by outrageously high malpractice insurance payments.

3. If a person wishes to commit suicide, for any reason, society should not try to interfere with that decision.

4. Doctors should always work to preserve life; they must never cooperate in any effort to end life.

5. New medical technology has created more problems than it has solved.

6. Permitting euthanasia would create a dangerous precedent that could easily lead to government sponsored murder of people it considers "undesirable."

7. People should always leave instructions (a living will) as to what should be done if they are terminally ill and are unable to respond to their surroundings.

8. A person's family has the responsibility to support decisions for life, not death, when a person is gravely ill, no matter how much money and effort it might cost that family.

9. In the case of a hopeless medical situation, no human being—including the person who is ill—has the right to make decisions that would lead to immediate death (euthanasia).

10. A husband or wife who helps a terminally ill spouse die should not be prosecuted by the law since the decision for euthanasia was made out of love, not from a desire to commit murder.

EXERCISE 1   Using Research Material to Write the Persuasive Essay

Who would make the life-and-death decisions if mercy killings were to be permitted? The following pieces of information are on this controversial topic of mercy killing. Use this information as the basis for your own essay on the topic. You may select as many of the items as you want, or you may adapt the items to agree with your own way of thinking. After selecting the material to be used, be sure to organize your major points before starting the rough draft.

1. The idea of suicide has been rejected by society for many centuries.

2. Some societies discourage suicide by enacting strict laws against it.

3. In the famous Karen Anne Quinlan case, when the life-support system was turned off, she remained alive for nearly ten years.

4. As our technical ability to extend life increases, the pressure on us to make life and death decisions will also increase.

5. If we had laws that encouraged mercy killing, we would not have the lives of such people as Helen Keller to show the world what handicapped people can do.

6. The general reaction to mercy killing will change as people realize that life should not always go on no matter what the cost may be.

7. In 1973 the American Medical Association stated that "mercy killing . . . is contrary to the policy of the American Medical Association."

8. The worst tragedy in life is to live without dignity.

9. Years ago, people seldom spoke openly about suicide; now there are organizations that openly advocate it.

10. A very common form of mercy killing occurs when parents and doctors agree not to give retarded newborn children needed medical attention, eventually causing their deaths.

Why Not Unconcealed Guns?

SAM HOWE VERHOVEK

Just when we feel we have heard every possible argument for or against the use of guns in our society, a new twist on an old topic is presented to us. The following selection by Sam Howe Verhovek appeared in the *New York Times* and argues for what some people might think is a strange point of view: he openly wonders why, if guns are legally owned, they could not also be carried openly by their owners. As the writer pictures what it would be like to live in such a society, he is also careful to maintain a steady tone, one that avoids unnecessary emotion in a debate that is already filled with strong opinions and beliefs.

1 In a move that Gov. George W. Bush declared would make his state "a better and safer place to live," Texas last week overturned a 125-year-old law that banned its private citizens from carrying guns. A new law will allow any adult Texan without a history of mental illness or felony convictions to secure a permit to wear a concealed weapon.

2   Texas thus becomes the ninth state in the past two years and the 28th overall to make carrying concealed weapons a basic right of the citizenry. But with the surge in these new laws, many a result of increasing fears of crime and Republican

takeovers of state legislatures, one question has been strangely absent from the often emotional debate over their passage:

3   Just why should the weapons be concealed?

4   It is a question that genuinely seems to take many of the laws' proponents aback. "We want to maintain some modicum of social decorum here," said Ron Wilson, a state representative from Houston who was a chief sponsor of the new Texas law. "It never was my purpose to have folks running around intimidating one another with an open weapon. We are operating in what we like to call a civilized society."

5   Guns used to be not only openly displayed, but viewed almost benignly—perhaps the most famous gun in the West, after all, was dubbed the Colt Peacemaker. In the 19th Century, the right to wear a gun in a holster was widespread. On the other hand, many states had strong prohibitions against concealed weapons, which basically arose from the societal belief that only a miscreant or a coward bent on sneaking up on someone would have reason to carry a hidden gun.

6   Today, of course, with guns killing more than 100 Americans a day in real life and wreaking almost unfathomable violence on screen, simply the sight of a gun puts many people on edge. (Hunting rifles and police revolvers are possible exceptions.) And so, even as society is becoming more permissive on carrying guns, it literally doesn't want people to have to face that fact.

7   "For a significant minority of the population, guns are a frightening, awful, immoral thing and looking at them is simply very disturbing," said David B. Kopel, research director for the Independence Institute, a nonpartisan research group in Golden, Colo. "That we have concealed-carry laws is a reflection of some deference to their sensibilities." Mr. Kopel, the author of a study of right-to-carry legislation, likened this approach to guns to the approach to legal pornography, which is not openly displayed in stores.

8   So perhaps the new gun laws are being driven by a popular sense of aesthetics, or, as others suggest, only by a sense of fashion. "In modern society a gun doesn't go with the attire," said Stephen Hallbrook, a Virginia attorney who is the author of a litigation manual on gun laws. "You don't wear a cowboy hat with a gun on your hip. You wear a business suit or a lady wears a dress, and you're not going to strap a six-shooter around that."

9   But just whether the concealed-carry approach is logical is an entirely different question. For one thing, if, as many proponents contend, allowing people to carry guns is a deterrent to crime, what is the point of keeping the guns hidden? Wouldn't an openly displayed gun be a far more powerful deterrent?

10   At the moment of a perceived criminal assault, a gun could of course be drawn in a last-minute bid to defuse the situation. Bob Ross, an Arizona man who testified in favor of the Texas law, described an encounter with young men armed with aluminum baseball bats outside his neighborhood video store. As the toughs approached, Mr. Ross said, he drew his gun from a shoulder holster inside his coat.

11   "Fortunately for me and for them," he told Texas lawmakers, "they jumped back 10 feet and I convinced them it was a good night for them to go home." Still, if Mr. Ross had had a gun on his hip, the episode might never have escalated to the brink of confrontation.

12   As it turns out, there is a serious debate over whether open or concealed weapons are the greater deterrent. "Open versus concealed is really a trade-off of one kind of deterrence for another," says Mr. Kopel. "A guy carrying a gun, certainly that is a really powerful specific deterrence. On the other hand, if you have

2 percent of the population carrying a gun and nobody knows who the 2 percent is, you may have a broader general deterrent effect."

13　　Many argue the debate is frighteningly beside the point. "The issue is not whether people are carrying concealed or unconcealed," said Richard M. Aborn, president of Handgun Control, Inc. "It's that they're carrying them at all. More guns means more death."

14　　Surprisingly, while many police officials staunchly oppose more guns on the streets, some openly wonder whether open-carry legislation would be the lesser of two evils. "If we had the exact same kind of licensing requirements either way but the law said you had to carry it openly, I think we actually would be more in favor of that," said Kenneth R. Yarbrough, president of the Texas Police Chiefs Association, which lobbied against the new Texas law. "Then at least we would know immediately, visually, by sight, that a person was carrying a weapon. But I don't know that our society would be willing to accept that kind of a law."

15　　While the public sighting of a gun did not provoke wide terror a century or so ago, no one seems to agree on just when things changed. Some experts trace the shift in perceptions back to 1903 and the screening of one of the first movies ever, Edwin S. Porter's "The Great Train Robbery."

16　　In one scene, a bad buy with a pistol stares directly at the audience, revolver pointed straight outward. He fires, disappearing in a cloud of smoke. News accounts at the time had members of the audience screaming, fainting, even ducking for cover. Other experts say revulsion over guns has been more recent, as murder rates climbed and movies became far more violent.

17　　"An armed society is a polite society," writes Jim Wilson, the "Gun Smoke" columnist in the current issue of *Shooting Times,* a magazine for gun aficionados. People with guns, he says, "treat others with respect, tolerance and consideration. And they expect to be treated the same way in return. The handguns that they pack are for those who just don't get the message until they look down the bore and get a little glimpse of those pearly gates."

Analyzing the writer's strategies

Sam Howe Verhoverk's essay is a provocative combination of current events and lessons from history. After opening with a report on the latest gun law from Texas (where people will be allowed to carry concealed weapons), the writer asks a startling question: Why do the guns have to be concealed? Why not carry guns openly? The question causes discomfort among lawmakers, even those who proposed and supported the new Texas law, and it leads the writer to bring up some well-known historical facts, among them the widespread right in the nineteenth century "to wear a gun in a holster . . ." This use of history is further strengthened when he adds that many states even had specific laws "against concealed weapons," a fact that only seems to make the idea of carrying guns openly even more logical and correct. If lawmakers a century ago passed laws against concealed weapons, why should lawmakers now be *in favor* of concealed weapons?

As the writer goes beyond the law in his search for answers to his original question, the information he receives has some odd twists: The head of one research group says that it disturbs people when they see guns, while a Virginia attorney who is very familiar with gun laws makes a statement about fashion when he observes that people would not "strap a six-shooter" around suits or dresses.

After giving the extended example of a man from Arizona who protected himself with a gun, and after quoting relevant figures such as a Texas police official and the president of Handgun Control, Inc., the writer again turns to history for an answer. This time he uses popular culture to try to find out "when things changed" in terms of public reactions to guns carried openly. His analysis of the famous 1903 movie *The Great Train Robbery* may well be correct, but he concludes the piece without any definite answer for why people are not comfortable when they see guns. By asking this provocative question and by using current authorities and historical events, the writer makes us ask the question of ourselves and, without saying it directly, leads us to examine a situation that is even more remarkable because it is so obvious, but so unaddressed.

Responding to the writer's argument

Take a position either for or against one of the following topics and write an argumentative essay supporting your position. Use the "Guide to Writing the Persuasive Essay" (pp. 93–95) to help construct the essay. Be sure to include all of the important points needed for a good argument.

1. The use of guns on television and in the movies is a terrible influence on young people and must be reduced or eliminated.

2. Some states allow children as young as twelve to use hunting rifles, and some people feel that it is all right for these young people to handle guns. This law should be repealed because it adds to the level of violence in our society.

3. If a person is threatened or assaulted and that person has a gun, the fact that the person is able to show a gun will help to prevent violence from happening.

4. People who sell or distribute stolen or illegal guns should receive very long prison sentences with no possibility of parole.

5. If we want to reduce violence from guns in our society, we should allow everyone to carry guns if they want to and display them openly if they wish.

6. Two kinds of gun laws should be enacted: One for sport and the other for people who need guns for protection.

7. If more people in our society have guns, these people should be able to help the police catch criminals; therefore, policy officers should be in favor of more guns in the hands of the public.

8. At least one town in the United States requires each family to own a gun and be able to use it. If every town and city in this country had such a law, the crime rate in our society would certainly go down.

9. We now have metal detectors in places such as airports and schools. We should also have such detectors in factories, offices, and other public places.

10. In our society, having more guns leads to more death.

EXERCISE 1   Using Research Material to Write the Persuasive Essay

Should there be a national law that more strictly regulates the possession and use of guns? The following pieces of information are on this controversial topic of *gun control.* Use this information as the basis for your own essay on the topic. You may select as many of the items as you want, or you may adapt the items to agree with your own way of thinking. After selecting the material to be used, be sure to organize your major points before starting the rough draft.

1. More than half of the people who kill themselves each year do so with handguns.

2. More than half of the murders committed in the United States each year are committed with handguns.

3. Robert Digrazia, the chief of police of Montgomery County, Maryland, states that "No private citizen, whatever his claim, should possess a handgun."

4. Anybody can purchase machine guns by mail order.

5. There are forty million handguns in this country, and every year two and a half million more handguns are sold.

6. Since 1963, guns have killed over 400,000 Americans.

7. There are over 20,000 state and local gun laws on the books, but they are obviously ineffective.

8. It has been estimated that simply to track down and register all of the handguns in this country would cost four or five billion dollars.

9. The state of California has a law which requires a jail sentence for a person who is convicted of a gun-related felony.

10. Members of the National Rifle Association often assert that people, not guns, kill people.

Writing the persuasive essay: Additional topics

Choose one of the fifteen topics listed and write an essay of at least five paragraphs. Use the six points discussed on pages 93–94 and repeated below as a guide for your writing.

- Write a strong thesis statement.
- Give evidence or reasons for your beliefs.
- Provide examples for each of your reasons.
- Use at least one authority to support your thesis.
- Admit that others have a different point of view.
- Indicate the results or make predictions in the conclusion.

Essay topics   Argue for or against:

1. Legalized prostitution

2. Gambling casinos

3. Stricter immigration laws

4. Prayer in the public schools

5. Abortion

6. Tax exemption for religious organizations

7. Capital punishment

8. Single-parent adoption

9. Continuation of the manned space program

10. Females playing on male sports teams

11. Required courses in college

12. Tenure for teachers

13. Expense accounts for business people

14. Canceling a driver's license for drunk driving

15. Random drug testing in the workplace

EXERCISE 1   Using Research Material to Write the Persuasive Essay

The following pieces of information are on the controversial topic of *violence in the movies and on television.* To what extent is the violence we see in films and on television programs responsible for the degree of violence in our society? Use this information as the basis for your own essay on the topic. You may select as many of the items as you want, or you may adapt the items to agree with your way of thinking. As you study the list, decide which of your paragraphs could make use of these facts or opinions.

1. The National Coalition on Television Violence estimates that up to half of all violence in our country comes from the violent entertainment we are exposed to every day.

2. In 1984, violence in Hollywood movies contained an average of 28.5 violent acts per hour.

3. Hollywood spends over $300 million dollars each year advertising movies that are extremely violent.

4. Sixty-six percent of Americans interviewed think that violent entertainment increases crime in the streets.

5. Television violence has increased by 65 percent since 1980.

6. Mark Fowler, the former head of the Federal Communications Commission (FCC), stated openly that he did not want an investigation of the whole question of violence in the media.

7. Horror, slasher, and violent science fiction movies have increased from 6 percent of box office receipts in 1970 to over 30 percent today.

8. In some years, more than half of the films produced by Hollywood have content that is intensely violent.

9. Over 900 research studies on violent entertainment give overwhelming evidence that violent films and other programs are having a harmful effect on the American people.

10. A proposal has been made that every cable TV company offering violent movie channels should also be required to offer a nonviolent channel.

EXERCISE 2 Using Research Material to Write the Persuasive Essay

To what extent can a society permit its people to read, write, and say whatever they want? The following pieces of information are on this controversial topic of *censorship and free speech.* Use this information as the basis for your own essay on the topic. You may select as many of the items as you want, or you may adapt the items to agree with your own way of thinking. After selecting the material to be used, be sure to organize your major points before starting the rough draft.

1. In Anchorage, Alaska, the *American Heritage Dictionary* was banned from the schools.

2. In 1961, the American Nazi leader George Lincoln Rockwell was denied the right to speak in New York City, but the courts upheld his right to express his views.

3. Such literary works as D.H. Lawrence's *Lady Chatterly's Lover,* James Joyce's *Ulysses,* and J.D. Salinger's *The Catcher in the Rye,* have been denounced as pornographic.

4. The Supreme Court has stated that the government may prohibit materials that "portray sexual conduct in a patently offensive way."

5. In ancient Rome, the Censor was a powerful official who judged people's morals and who could even remove government officials from office.

6. *MS* magazine was banned from a number of high school libraries because it was judged to be obscene.

7. The researcher and writer Gay Talese believes that we should not allow law enforcement officials "to deny pornography to those who want it."

8. Jerry Falwell, the founder of Moral Majority, has stated that "basic values such as morality, individualism, respect for our nation's heritage, and the benefits of the free-enterprise system have, for the most part, been censored from today's public-classroom textbooks."

9. In 1983, when the United States invaded the Caribbean island of Grenada, newspaper and television reporters were not told there would be an invasion. When they did find out, they were not permitted to go to the island and report on the invasion.

10. Some psychologists believe that being able to enjoy pornography helps people deal with their frustrations without having to commit criminal or anti-social acts.

Working Together

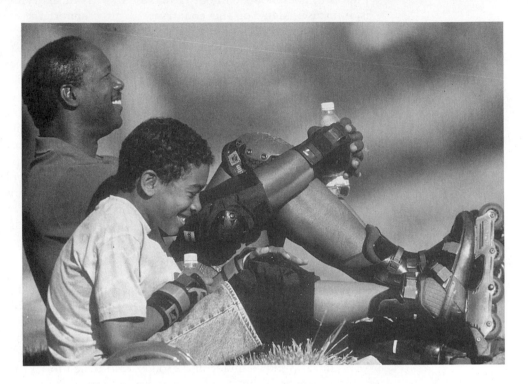

The following editorial appeared in the *Chicago Tribune* on June 18, 1995.

Where Have All the Fathers Gone?

1   Today is Father's Day, so let's talk about dads. Not the ones who cheer their sons and daughters at baseball and soccer games or the ones who fix dinner for the family every night or the ones who come home dead tired after a day at the Merc or McDonald's but still have time for a little family conversation.

2   No, let's talk about the invisible dads, the ones who don't marry mom, don't support their kids and don't hang around for hugs, kisses and helping with homework. There are millions of them in the United States, and their numbers are growing.

3   In 1950, 14 of every 1,000 unmarried women had babies. By 1992, 45 of every 1,000 did. In fact, almost one-third of the children born in the United States in 1992 were born to unwed parents, a 54 percent increase over 1980, according to figures released this month by the National Center for Health Statistics.

4   And though the figures generally are compiled in terms of unmarried women and the resulting handwringing is done in the name of unwed mothers, the facts of life are that for every one of those unmarried mothers there is an unmarried father.

5   The moms are a lot more visible though, because in the overwhelming number of cases, they are the ones raising the kids. So who's the real problem here? And why should we care?

Merc: The Chicago Mercantile Exchange

6 We *must* care because the social and financial costs of children growing up in households without fathers is immense. Many of the country's most troublesome social problems poverty, poor performance in schools, gang activity, juvenile crime, mounting welfare costs—have their roots in families where a father has abdicated responsibility for his children.

7 Women who do not marry before having their first child are three times more likely to wind up on welfare for 10 years or more than those who do marry. And census figures indicate that an intact mother-father household has a far better chance for financial security than a single-parent family.

8 Moreover, children who have little or no contact with their fathers are robbed of a crucial role model for fashioning their own lives.

9 What's to be done? For starters, parents, grandparents, churches and schools must hammer home the lesson that a man who conceives a child without marrying and being prepared to support the child for 18 years unfairly burdens his family and his community. He must understand that his action will be met by community disapprobation, not the respect and awe of his peers.

10 And while government can't legislate morality, it can encourage responsibility. Legislators should make that a priority by providing tax incentives for couples to marry and by requiring every woman to name her child's father on the birth certificate. Law enforcement officers can (and are beginning to) go after the fathers for child support.

11 Fatherhood, like motherhood, is its own reward—as most dads have found. Sadly, for the others, the invisible ones, it is a gift foolishly squandered.

1. The class should divide into groups, read the editorial together, conduct a discussion, and then individually write the answers to the following questions.

   a. What is the thesis of the editorial?

   b. What supporting evidence for the thesis is given in the editorial?

   c. Were any outside sources used to support the thesis? If so, provide the sources.

   d. Does the editor say what will or will not happen if nothing is done?

   e. Does the editorial propose a solution to the problem?

   f. Does the editorial seem reasonable to you?

   g. State why or why not you believe this is an effective argument.

2. Write a letter to a vanished father, trying to persuade him to become involved in the lives of his children.

3. If you could gather ten of these "vanished" fathers in a room, what would their arguments be for not participating in the raising of their children?

4. As a class, gather material on this topic of deadbeat dads (or on another topic that particularly interests the majority of students). Whenever a news story appears or an idea comes to mind, share it with the class. This material could become the research for a future essay or research paper that the class could work on together or in groups.

THE ESSAY

Chapter 9

Writing under Pressure

Most people prefer to do their writing when they are not under the pressure of a time limit. However, many situations demand that a piece of writing be finished by a certain time. One situation is the writing of a story for a newspaper that constantly works under a very tight deadline. Another pressured situation is writing an essay exam that must be handed in by the end of a class period. This chapter will review some of the techniques for writing successful essays under pressure.

How to write well under pressure

The first rule of doing well in any test is to come to the test well rested and well prepared. Research proves that reviewing notes and reading assignments systematically throughout the semester is much more effective than cramming for a test the night before. You'll be greatly satisfied if you learn to use your time efficiently and wisely.

Coming to an exam well prepared

1. Study the textbook chapters and your notes. In your textbook, review headings and bolded words as well as information you have highlighted or underlined. Look for both chapter reviews and summaries at the ends of chapters. If you have already made an outline, study that too.

2. Avoid having to face any surprises when the exam is distributed. When the test is first announced in class, ask if it will include material from the textbook in addition to notes taken in class. Also, find out the format of the test. How many essay questions will there be, and how many points will each question be worth? How much time will you have to complete the test?

3. Form a study group if you can. One way a study group can work is the following: each person comes to the study group prepared to present at least one major question that he or she thinks the instructor will ask. Also, be prepared to give any information needed to answer that question. The other students

take notes and add whatever additional information they can. Each person in turn presents a different question along with the information needed for the answer. Members of the group can quiz each other on the information that is to be covered by the exam. For an essay exam, some material needs to be memorized. If you are unable to be part of a study group, you should still try to predict what questions will be on the exam. Prepare an outline for study and then memorize your outline.

Remember that an essay test, unlike a multiple-choice test, requires more than simply recognizing information. In an essay exam, you must be able to recall ideas and specific details and present them quickly in your own words. This ability to memorize not only concepts but also factual information is quite demanding.

Strategies for answering timed in-class essay questions

The smart test taker does not begin to answer the first question immediately. Instead, he or she takes a few moments to look over the test and form a strategy for the best way to tackle it. The following pointers will help you become "test smart."

1. When you receive the exam, *read over each essay question twice*. How many points is each question worth? The way in which you budget your time will depend heavily on the importance of each question. A well-written test should tell you how many points each question is worth. If, for example, one essay question is worth 50 points, you should spend approximately half your time planning and answering this question. However, if the test consists of ten shorter essay questions and you have a class period of 100 minutes, you should spend no more than ten minutes on each question, keeping a careful watch on your time. Tests composed of several shorter essays can be disastrous to people who do not watch their time. Students often write too much for the first four or five questions and then panic because they have very little time left to answer the final questions.

2. When you read an essay question, ask yourself *what method of development is being asked for*? We all know stories of people who failed tests because they misunderstood the question.

3. *Use key words from the test question itself* to compose your thesis statement, which in a test should be your first sentence. Don't try to be too clever on a test. State your points as directly and clearly as possible.

4. Answer the question by stating your basic point and then *using as many specific details as you have time or knowledge to give*. The more specific names, dates, and places (all spelled correctly) that you can provide will add points to your grade.

5. Since a question can have more than one part, be sure you *answer all the parts*. Check over the question to be sure your answer includes all parts.

Study the question to determine exactly what is being asked for.

Sample essay question

What were the changes that contributed to the rise of the feminist movement in the 1960s in the United States? Be specific.

If the question given were one of ten short essay questions on a 1½ hour final examination, the following answer would probably be adequate:

Sample essay question answer

The feminist movement grew out of many changes happening in the 1960s in the United States. In 1961, the President's Commission on the Status of Women documented discrimination against women in the work force. The result of the Commission's report was a growing public awareness which soon led to the enactment of two pieces of legislation: the Equal Pay Act of 1963 and the Civil Rights Act of 1964. In addition, the development of the birth-control pill brought the discussion of sexuality out into the open. It also lowered the birth rate, leaving more women looking to the world of work. A high divorce rate as well as delayed marriages further contributed to more women being concerned with feminist issues. Finally, in 1966 the National Organization for Women was formed which encouraged women to share their experiences with each other and to organize in an effort to lobby for legislative change.

Notice that the first sentence uses the key words from the question to state the thesis. The answer gives not one but four examples of the changes that were taking place in the 1960s. Moreover, the answer is very specific, naming legislation, organizations, and dates whenever significant. Can you spot the transitional expressions the writer uses to signal the movement from one example to the next?

Frequently used terms in essay questions

Define: A definition is the precise meaning of a word or term. When you define something in an essay you usually write an *extended definition,* in which you select an appropriate example or examples to illustrate the meaning of a term.

Comparison or Contrast: When you *compare* two people or things, you point out the similarities between them. When you *contrast* two items, you point out the differences. Sometimes you may find yourself using both comparison and contrast in an essay.

Narration: Narration is the telling of a story by the careful use of a sequence of events. The events are usually (but not always) told in chronological order.

Summary: When you write a summary, you are supplying the main ideas of a longer piece of writing.

Discussion: This is a general term that encourages you to analyze a subject at length. Inviting students to discuss some aspect of a topic is a widely used method of asking examination questions.

Classification: When you *classify* items of any kind, you place them into separate groups so that large amounts of material can be more easily understood.

Cause and Effect: When you deal with causes, you answer the question *why;* when you deal with effects you show *results* or *consequences.*

EXERCISE 1   Methods of Development

Each of the following college essay questions deals with the single topic of computers. Use the above list of explanations to decide which method of development is being called for in each case. In the space provided after each question, identify the method being required.

1. Trace the development of the computer, beginning in 1937. Be sure to include all significant developments discussed in class.

    Method of development: _____

2. Choose two of the word processing programs practiced in class and discuss the similarities and differences you encountered. What in your opinion were the advantages and disadvantages of each?

    Method of development: _____

3. Explain the meaning of each of the following terms: *hard disk, memory, directory, menu,* and *software.*

    Method of development: _____

4. We have discussed many of the common business applications for the computer. Select ten applications and group them according to the functions they perform.

    Method of development: _____

5. Discuss the problems that have resulted in the typical office as a result of computer technology.

    Method of development: _____

EXERCISE 2   Methods of Development/Parts of a Question

Each of the following is an example of an essay question that could be asked in different college courses. In the spaces provided after each question, indicate: (a) what method of development (definition, comparison or contrast, narration, summary, or discussion) is being called for, and (b) how many parts there are to the question. This indicates how many parts there will be in your answer.

1. What does the term *sociology* mean? Include in your answer at least four different meanings the term *sociology* has had since this area of study began.

    Method of development: _____

    The different parts of the question: _____

    _____

    _____

2. Compare the reasons the United States entered the Korean War with the reasons it entered the Vietnam War.

   Method of development: _____

   The different parts of the question: _____

   _____

   _____

3. Trace the history of our knowledge of the planet Jupiter, from the time it was first discovered until the present day. Include in your answer at least one nineteenth-century discovery and three of the most recent discoveries that have been made about Jupiter through the use of unmanned space vehicles sent near that planet.

   Method of development: _____

   The different parts of the question: _____

   _____

   _____

4. In view of the dramatic increase in cases of contagious diseases, describe the types of precautions now required for medical personnel. What changes are likely to be required in the future?

   Method of development: _____

   The different parts of the question: _____

   _____

   _____

5. Explain the three effects of high temperatures on space vehicles as they reenter the earth's atmosphere.

   Method of development: _____

   The different parts of the question: _____

   _____

   _____

6. What was the complete process of restoring the Statue of Liberty to its original condition? Include in your answer six different aspects of the restoration, from the rebuilding of the inside supports to the treatment of the metal surface.

   Method of development: _____

   The different parts of the question: _____

   _____

   _____

7. Trace the history of the English language from its beginning to the present day. Divide the history of the language into at least three different parts, using Old English, Middle English, and Modern English as your main divisions.

   Method of development: _____

   The different parts of the question: _____

   _____

   _____

8. Discuss the events that led up to World War II. Be sure to include both the political and social problems of the time that directly and indirectly led to the war.

   Method of development: _____

   The different parts of the question: _____

   _____

   _____

9. Summarize the four theories that have been proposed as to why dinosaurs became extinct sixty-five million years ago.

   Method of development: _____

   The different parts of the question: _____

   _____

   _____

10. Define the term *monarchy* and discuss the relevance or irrelevance of this form of government in today's world.

    Method of development: _____

    The different parts of the question: _____

    _____

    _____

Using the thesis statement for timed in-class essay questions

One of the most effective ways to begin an essay answer is to write a thesis statement. Your thesis statement should include the important parts of the question and should also give a clear indication of the approach you intend to take in your answer. Writing your opening sentence in this way gives you a real advantage: as your professor begins to read your work, it is clear what you are going to write about and how you are going to treat your subject.

For example, suppose you were going to write an essay on the following topic:

Agree or disagree that a woman president could handle the demands of the most stressful job in the country.

An effective way to write your opening sentence would be to write the following thesis sentence:

I agree that a woman president could handle the demands of the most stressful job in the country.

The reader would then know that this was indeed the topic you had chosen and would also know how you intended to approach that topic.

EXERCISE 3   Writing Thesis Statements

Rewrite each of the following essay questions in thesis statement form. Read each question carefully and underline the important words or phrases in it. Then decide on the approach you would take in answering that question. An example has been done for you.

Essay question: How does one learn another language?

Thesis statement: The process of learning another language is complicated but usually follows four distinct stages.

1. Essay Questions: Discuss Thorstein Veblen's theory of the leisure class.

   Thesis statement: _____

   _____

2. Essay Question: What are the effects of TV violence on children?

   Thesis statement: _____

   _____

3. Essay Question: Trace the development of portrait painting from the Middle Ages to today.

   Thesis statement: _____

   _____

4. Essay Question: What are the major causes for the economic crisis facing the African nations today?

   Thesis statement: _____

   _____

5. Essay Question: What have we recently learned from ocean exploration, and what remains to be done?

   Thesis statement: _____

   _____

6. Essay Question: Is it harmful or beneficial to adopt a child from one culture and raise that child in another culture?

   Thesis statement: _____

   _____

7. Essay Question: In what ways does the new Japan differ from the old Japan?

   Thesis statement: _____

   _____

8. Essay Question: What four countries depend on tourism for the major part of their national income and why is this so?

   Thesis statement: _____

   _____

9. Essay Question: What factors should a college use when judging the merits of a particular student for admission?

   Thesis statement: _____

   _____

10. Essay Question: What is Alzheimer's disease, its sequence of characteristic symptoms, and the current methods of treatment?

    Thesis statement: _____

    _____

Working Together

The following passage on the consequences of the shift of human society from nomadic to agricultural is taken from *Biology*, by Helena Curtis:

Whatever its causes, the change to agriculture had profound consequences. Populations were no longer nomadic. Thus they could store food not only in silos and granaries, but in the form of domesticated animals. In addition to food stores, other possessions could be accumulated to an extent far beyond that previously possible. Even land could be owned and accumulated and passed on by inheritance. Thus the world became divided into semipermanent groups of haves and have-nots, as it is today.

Because the efforts of a few could produce enough food for everyone, the communities became diversified. People became tradesmen, artisans, bankers, scholars, poets, all the rich mixture of which a modern community is composed. And these people could live much more densely than ever before. For hunting and food-gathering economies, 2 square miles, on the average, are required to provide enough for one family to eat.

One immediate and direct consequence of the agricultural revolution was an increase in populations. A striking characteristic of hunting groups is that they vigorously limit their numbers. A woman on the move cannot carry more than one infant along with her household baggage, minimal though that may be. When simple means of birth control—often just abstention—are not effective, she resorts to abortion or, more probably, infanticide. In addition, there is a high natural mortality, particularly among the very young, the very old, the ill, the disabled, and women at childbirth. As a result, populations dependent on hunting tend to remain small.

1. After you have studied the selection, construct an essay question that a professor in a biology or anthropology course could ask as part of a mid-term or final examination. At the same time, your present instructor could also make up a question based on the selection. When everyone has finished, your instructor could read his or her question first. Is it the question you had expected? How many students in the class came close to the instructor's choice of question?

2. List the questions discussed in the activity above, and use the following checklist to analyze each question.

   a. Does the question seem to be fair?
      (Some questions might be too vague or too general to be a fair test of what the student has learned.)

   b. How many parts does the question have?

   c. Does the question call for a specific method of development (for example, definition and analysis)?

   d. What are the key terms that should be used in the answer?

   e. What would be an effective opening sentence for the answer?

The College Report: Using Summary and Direct Quotation

Using outside sources for college writing

Most of the required writing in composition courses is done without the use of outside sources. However, during your semesters in college, you will be asked to produce reports or term papers for other courses, papers that will require you to do research using *outside sources.*

> An *outside source* is any material that provides you with facts or perceptions that are not your own.

When you use outside sources, special skills are required to incorporate the ideas of others and to give credit to the original authors. In this chapter, you will study three selections, all related to the theme of valuable items people have stolen or misused. One selection describes Egypt's struggle to recover its world-famous portrait statue of the legendary Queen Nefertiti; another excerpt reports on Allied soldiers looting in war-torn Europe in 1945; a third selection gives us insight into the problem of theft that plagues many college and public libraries today. With each selection, you will have the opportunity to practice *summarizing, quoting,* and *expressing your reactions* to the ideas of others.

Before we get started, however, we need to consider a very serious problem that can occur when students use source material incorrectly. Often a student comes across material written by someone else, material that seems to be just what the student wants to say. The temptation is to copy the exact words, ideas, facts, or opinions from the other writer and present those words as if they were the student's own thoughts. This can happen when a student lacks the confidence or the experience to use material properly from other writers. The name for this dishonest practice is called *plagiarism.*

> *Plagiarism* is the use of someone else's words, ideas, facts, or opinions without proper documentation.

If an idea is not your own original thought, you must give credit to the source. Plagiarism is a very serious offense, sometimes resulting in failure in a course or, in extreme cases, expulsion from school. This does not mean you should be afraid to use the ideas of others; you may do so, but everything depends on how you present the material. As long as you cite your sources, you may summarize and quote from the work of others to produce your own report or research paper.

Direct quotations: Using quotation marks around the exact words of another writer

When you quote a source directly in your own writing, your work gains authority by using material from that published source. Occasionally you will come across phrases or sentences that are so relevant to your work and so well-expressed that you will want to use those words exactly, to strengthen your own conclusions or point of view. Using quotations is one of the most effective ways to add authority to your own work. However, a few words of caution:

1. When you decide to quote, you may not add any words of your own or change any words of the original. Whatever appears within the quotation marks must be exactly the same words that appear in the original source.

2. Sometimes students use too many quotations, often because they do not feel secure enough with their own writing. Be selective in choosing your quotations. Too many quotations will ruin your report.

3. Be cautious about inserting a very long quotation into your paper. Unless every part of that quotation relates directly to what you are saying, the quotation will seem out of place.

4. In a formal paper, you will be required to provide a citation to show the source of every quotation. Every student should have the MLA Stylesheet, or a similar guide to writing a research paper, as a resource tool that is always at hand during the writing of a paper needing citations. With the use of computer technology, the task of including this information in your paper has become much easier than it used to be.

5. Some typical ways of introducing a quote are the following:

   In the words of one noted authority, . . .

   One authority has said, . . .

   As one well-known expert has observed, . . .

How to write a summary

At the heart of education is the task of extracting the main ideas from a reading selection, or taking notes of the main ideas on lectures given in class. Learning how to summarize is perhaps the most important skill needed for this kind of college work. Summaries become the basis for further study and consideration, and are constantly used by writers as they research material for reports. For example, a student writing a report on a certain topic may read ten or eleven articles on that topic. Some articles, of course, will be more useful than others, but the researcher should summarize each of the articles so that when the actual writing is done, these summaries can provide information as needed.

A summary should include only main ideas. Only a few examples or supporting details from the original text will find their way into the summary because in a summary it is always necessary to reduce the amount of material. You will probably need to read and review the material more than once in order to separate the main idea statements from the details and examples. The summary will be significantly shorter than the original text, but you must be careful not to leave out any main ideas or add any of your own ideas.

Suggestions for reacting to the ideas of others

In most reports, it is not enough to summarize the ideas others have about a topic; you will be expected to make points of your own. Since students often feel unqualified to make their own judgments, the following suggestions may be helpful when it comes to reacting to the material of others:

1. Make a suggestion of your own for further work to be done in the field.

2. Use examples from different articles to support one of your major points.

3. Make the purpose of your report a survey of the existing information on the topic.

4. Contrast the ways different writers see the same event or subject.

5. Suggest an idea that has been overlooked, or underestimated.

6. Give your own opinion about the matter.

7. Conduct a survey of your own to determine how those around you think about some aspect of your topic.

8. Use your own experience to provide examples for added interest in the material.

Practicing skills for writing research papers

REPORT 1   The Controversy over the Statue of Nefertiti

The story of the circumstances surrounding the discovery of the famous portrait statue of Nefertiti could easily be a detective novel. In 1912, in the ancient Egyptian royal city of Amarna, German archaeologists uncovered the portrait statue of Queen Nefertiti. This beautiful image, which had not been seen for over 3,000 years, finally gave reality to the mystery that had always surrounded this legendary queen. Under the terms of the excavating agreement between Egypt and Germany, the discovery should have remained in Egypt, but the archaeologists distracted the Egyptian government by having another discovery, made at the same time, seem to be a more desirable item. This they gave to the Egyptian government. Later, after the Germans had taken the statue to Berlin, they claimed that when it had been dug up, it was in pieces and could not have been recognized for what it was.

A storm of protest broke out in Egypt, as government officials demanded the return of the statue. Newspaper stories appeared all over the world, and throughout Europe many people pressured the German government to give back the treasure. Still the Germans refused. Even when the Egyptians announced the cancellation of any further permits for German archeological teams to dig in Egypt, the Germans would not budge. The Egyptians even offered to exchange the Nefertiti for renewed digging rights and two rare statues of ancient Egyptian kings, but this offer was also refused. Finally, all negotiations stopped, and no German archaeological team was allowed back into Egypt.

During World War II, the German authorities hid the Nefertiti, along with other works of art they did not want the approaching Allied Armies to find, in a salt mine. At the end of the war, American troops did find all of the hidden items, and when this discovery was announced, officials in Egypt once more called for the return of their national treasure. They were to be disappointed again: The Allies allowed the Germans to keep Nefertiti, and to this day she remains on display in Berlin.

Quote: What two statements would you select from the text that you feel are important enough for possible quotation in a research paper? Copy those sentences below, word for word.

1. _____

_____

_____

2. _____

_____

_____

Summarize the material: In your own words, write down the main ideas of the text. Do not forget that a summary should always be a good deal shorter than the original text.

_____

_____

_____

_____

_____

_____

_____

_____

_____

_____

_____

_____

_____

React: What are two of your own reactions to this material, reactions that could eventually become part of your research paper?

1. _____

_____

2. _____

_____

Write a paragraph for your research paper: As you write, incorporate your summary, one of the quotations you copied, and a reaction of your own to the material.

_____

_____

_____

_____

_____

_____

_____

_____

_____

_____

_____

_____

_____

_____

_____

_____

REPORT 2   Looting in Wartime

The Spoils of World War II
KENNETH D. ALFORD

All the occupying forces looted, and the army made it easy. Looting was done without shame or hesitation and was not regarded as stealing. Bankers, clergymen—persons who were normally honest—did not hesitate to dip into an unlimited treasure trove. There were no effective rules to control the game. The army permitted personnel to mail home captured enemy equipment provided that there was no "military need" for it. Technically, soldiers were forbidden to mail home items taken from German homes and public buildings. The ruling was admirable but rarely enforced. An occasional commanding officer attempted to apply the law, but even in respectable outfits it was possible for an enlisted man to have an officer censor his package without inspecting it, or even let it go after inspecting it. An officer's signature on a parcel was only as honest or dishonest as he was, and officers' personal baggage was not even examined.

unmitigated:
constant

Especially, there was the bold, unmitigated theft of motorcycles, pistols, rifles, knives, cameras, and binoculars, as these were the items most desired by the average soldier. Many of these items were expensive and beautiful, the best in the world. Once in the possession of an American, a camera, pistol, or pair of binoculars might change hands twenty times before reaching the United States. The guns included military Lugers, finely crafted civilian pistols, beautiful shotguns, and superb hunting rifles. Also into the mail pouch went priceless collections of antique ornamental swords.

Destroyed vacated towns were the most fruitful hunting grounds. The conquering American would pop through a hole in the side of a house and survey the ruins. Whatever he wanted he took. Eager hands were waiting to relieve him of his prize; if he was wounded, he was almost certain to lose the booty to ambulance drivers, medics, or hospital attendants.

Quote: What two statements would you select from the text that you feel are important enough for possible quotation in a research paper? Copy those sentences below, word for word.

1. _____

_____

_____

2. _____

_____

_____

Summarize the material: In your own words, write down the main ideas of the text. Do not forget that a summary should always be a good deal shorter than the original text.

_____

_____

_____

_____

_____

_____

_____

_____

_____

_____

_____

_____

_____

React: What are two of your own reactions to this material, reactions that could eventually become part of your research paper?

1. _____

   _____

2. _____

   _____

Write a paragraph for your research paper: As you write, incorporate your summary, one of the quotations you copied, and a reaction of your own to the material.

_____

_____

_____

_____

_____

_____

_____

_____

_____

_____

_____

_____

_____

_____

_____

_____

_____

_____

REPORT 3   To Catch a Thief

Libraries everywhere experience thefts of their valuable materials including expensive books and manuscripts that cannot be replaced. Most of the time these items are never recovered, but a few years ago librarians and archivists across the country were able to celebrate a real victory for their professions: one of the nation's worst library thieves was finally caught and convicted for his crimes.

The thief's name is Stephen Blumberg, and over the years he was able to rob libraries and archives of over nineteen tons of material with a market value of more than twenty million dollars. The investigator who traced Blumberg's criminal career was a Washington State University Campus police officer named Stephen Huntsberry. Huntsberry had worked as a security officer, but his profession took a new turn when a librarian showed him an example of the type of material thieves liked to take. It was a book printed in 1463, and the officer remembered his emotions when he saw the volume. "I thought to myself," he later recalled, "'Christopher Columbus could have held this book.'" This dramatic experience led Huntsberry to want to know more about such thefts, and soon he was doing his own reading about library thefts that had occurred earlier. He also conducted his own research into robberies that had never been solved. It was not long before he was sending information bulletins about these unsolved cases, distributing them to towns and cities throughout the West.

One of the cases involved an incident at the University of California's Riverside Campus. In 1988, Stephen Blumberg was arrested for theft in that college's library, an arrest that resulted directly from one of Stephen Huntsberry's alerts to librarians. Blumberg was released on bail and then fled; the fact that he had been caught frightened him so much that he stopped stealing material for over two years. Then an informant reported him to the FBI as the man responsible for stealing from one hundred and forty libraries throughout forty-five states and Canada. At the same time, Stephen Huntsberry had sent the FBI a file he had researched on Blumberg's complete criminal record. When FBI officials put all of these facts together, they identified Blumberg as the probable culprit in the long series of unsolved library crimes.

A search warrant was issued and officers entered Blumberg's Ottumwa, Iowa, home. What they found astonished them. There in room after room, were the results of his years of crime. The officers saw shelf after shelf of valuable books (three shelves alone were filled with works printed before 1500), and there was even a Bible that had been produced in 1480. The rooms were also filled with priceless manuscripts, most of them unique.

Officer Huntsberry received a promotion as the result of his work on the case, the one he considers the most exciting and rewarding he has been associated with so far. He wants to continue to investigate library thefts, and he has begun to conduct workshops for libraries on how to achieve increased security. In the meantime, as one observer has remarked, no library in the country should charge Officer Huntsberry for an overdue book.

Quote: What two statements would you select from the text that you feel are important enough for possible quotation in a research paper? Copy those sentences below, word for word.

1. _____
   _____
   _____

2. _____
   _____
   _____

Summarize the material: In your own words, write down the main ideas of the text. Do not forget that a summary should always be a good deal shorter than the original text.

_____
_____
_____
_____
_____
_____
_____
_____
_____
_____

_____

_____

React: What are two of your own reactions to this material, reactions that could eventually become part of your research paper?

1. _____

   _____

2. _____

   _____

Write a paragraph for your research paper: As you write, incorporate your summary, one of the quotations you copied, and a reaction of your own to the material.

_____

_____

_____

_____

_____

_____

_____

_____

_____

_____

_____

_____

_____

_____

_____

_____

_____

_____

Working Together

The following biographical information reports on the life of Nellie Cashman, an Irish-American woman who was a pioneer in many of our Western mining towns in the late nineteenth and early twentieth centuries. The brief biography you are about to read covers the first thirty years of Nellie Cashman's adventurous life and takes us from her birth in 1845 in Ireland to one of her famous adventures in British Columbia in 1875.

Nellie was born in Midleton, in Ireland's County Cork, to Patrick Cashman and Frances "Fanny" Cronin in 1845. When she was about five years old, Nellie, her younger sister Fanny, and their now-widowed mother arrived in the United States, refugees from Ireland's potato famine. After 13 or 14 years in Boston, the Cashmans headed west in the late 1860s, settling in the vibrant community of San Francisco, where Irishmen were numerous and influential.

In 1872, Nellie and her elderly mother traveled to the new silver-mining district of Pioche, Nevada, opening a boarding house about ten miles from the camp. At Pioche, they found a wild environment, with thousands of boisterous miners and millmen—most of them Irish—living in a situation where filth, gun fights, and altercations between owners and employees were commonplace. The throbbing life of this mining and milling center must have appealed to Nellie; in the coming decades, she would consistently move to similar communities.

There is no evidence that Nellie engaged in mining during her first experience at living near a mining camp. But during her two years at Pioche, she did become very involved in the affairs of the local Catholic church, participating in bazaars and other money-raising efforts.

When Nellie moved from Pioche, she left her mother with her sister Fanny in San Francisco and traveled alone to northern British Columbia. There, for a few years in the mid-1870s, she operated a boarding house in the Cassiar District, on the Stikine River, not far from modern Juneau. She also worked gold-placer ground, becoming familiar with elementary mining geology.

In the winter of 1874–75, Nellie's reputation as an "angel of mercy," for which she is best known today, was born. While on a trip to Victoria, Nellie heard that a severe winter storm had hammered her fellow miners in the Cassiar diggings and that no one could get through. She immediately purchased supplies and sleds, hired six men, sailed to Fort Wrangell, Alaska, and headed inland through heavy snows. Her success at reaching the miners with the needed medicines and food became the talk of the West, as hundreds of miners considered her their savior.

The Victoria *Daily British Colonist* of February 5, 1875, in describing the rescue attempt, compared it to other efforts by famous prospectors and woodsmen, and declared that "Her extraordinary feat of attempting to reach the diggings in midwinter and in the face of dangers and obstacles which appalled even the stouthearted Fannin and thrice drove him back to Wrangell for shelter is attributed by her friends to insanity." If Nellie had done nothing else for the rest of her career, that incident alone would have guaranteed her place in mining lore and tradition.

Imagine you are writing a report on pioneer women in American history. This piece is one of your sources. Discuss the piece and then write a paragraph that could be a part of your final report. In the paragraph you write, summarize what you believe is significant about Nellie Cashman's life giving one quote from the piece and at the end of the paragraph providing your own commentary on her life. Begin your summary with the following words:

Another pioneer woman of the period was Nellie Cashman.

_____

_____

_____

_____

_____

_____

_____

_____

_____

_____

_____

_____

_____

Step 3

CREATING EFFECTIVE SENTENCES

CONTENTS

THE SENTENCE

Chapter 11

Finding Subjects and Verbs in Simple Sentences

Why should we use complete sentences when we write?

We do not always speak in complete sentences. Sometimes we abbreviate a thought into a word or two, knowing that the person to whom we are talking will understand our meaning. We all do this occasionally in our conversations with friends and family.

For example, if a friend walked up to you around lunch time and said, "Lunch?" you would assume that your friend was asking to have lunch with you. While the word "lunch" is not a complete thought, the situation and the way the word was spoken allowed you to guess the probable meaning.

In writing down thoughts, however, a reader (your audience) is not likely to be totally familiar with the thoughts or the circumstances surrounding your words. The reader often cannot interpret or fill in the missing parts. Therefore, *one characteristic of good writing is that the ideas are expressed in complete sentences.*

What is a complete sentence?

A c*omplete sentence* must contain a subject and a verb, as well as express a complete thought.

In this chapter, we will practice finding the subjects and the verbs in some basic sentences. These basic sentences are called *simple sentences* because they each have only one subject and verb group. (Later we will practice with compound and complex sentences in which two or more ideas are combined giving the sentence more than one subject and verb group.)

How do you find the subject of a sentence?

For most simple sentences, you can find the subject by keeping five points in mind.

1. The subject often answers the question, "Who or what is the sentence about?"

2. The subject often comes early in the sentence.

3. The subject is usually a noun or a pronoun.

4. Noun or pronoun subjects can be modified by adjectives.

5. The subject can be compound.

Understanding parts of speech: Nouns, pronouns, adjectives

A *noun* is a word that names persons, places, or things.
A *noun* can function as a subject, an object, or a possessive in a sentence.

The *Ford* is parked outside.

We parked the *Ford* outside.

The *Ford's* hood is dented.

Nouns can be either *common* nouns or *proper* nouns. Most nouns in our writing are common nouns. They are not capitalized. Proper nouns name particular persons, places, or things. They are always capitalized.

NOUNS	
Common	*Proper*
cousin	Cousin Bill
state	Nebraska
car	Ford

Another way to categorize nouns is into *concrete* or *abstract* nouns. Concrete nouns are all the things we can see or touch, such as *desk, car,* or *friend*. Abstract nouns are the things we cannot see or touch, such as *justice, honesty,* or *friendship*

NOUNS	
Concrete	*Abstract*
store	commerce
crowd	pleasure
book	knowledge

A *pronoun* is a word used to take the place of a noun. Just like a noun, a pronoun can be used as the subject, the object, or in some cases to show possession.

It is parked outside.

We parked *it* outside.

Its hood is dented.

Pronouns can also be categorized or divided into groups: personal, indefinite, relative, or demonstrative.

PRONOUNS

Personal Pronouns (refer to people or things)

Personal pronouns have three forms depending on how they are used in a sentence: as a subject, an object, or a possessive.

	Subjective		*Objective*		*Possessive*	
	Singular	**Plural**	**Singular**	**Plural**	**Singular**	**Plural**
1st person	I	we	me	us	my (mine)	our (ours)
2nd person	you	you	you	you	your (yours)	your (yours)
3rd person	he	they	him	them	his (his)	their (theirs)
	she		her		her (hers)	
	it		it		its (its)	

Relative Pronouns	*Demonstrative Pronouns*	*Indefinite Pronouns*			
(can introduce noun clauses and adjective clauses)	(can point out the antecedent)	(refer to non-specific persons or things)			
who, whom, whose	this	**Singular**			
which	that	everyone	someone	anyone	no one
that	these	everybody	somebody	anybody	nobody
what	those	everything	something	anything	nothing
whoever		each	another	either	neither
whichever		**Singular** or **Plural** (depending on meaning)			
whatever		all	more	none	
		any	most	some	
		Plural			
		both	few	many	several
					others

Noun or pronoun subjects can be modified by **adjectives.**

An *adjective* is a word that modifies (describes or limits) a noun or a pronoun.

　　young Robert

　　one boy

Adjectives usually come directly in front of the nouns they modify, but they can also appear later in the sentence and refer back to the noun.

The boy is *young*.

The subject can be *compound.*

A *compound subject* is made up of two or more nouns or pronouns joined together by *and, or, either/or,* or *neither/nor.*

Robert and his *dog*

• PRACTICE

The different kinds of subjects you will encounter in this chapter are illustrated in these seven sentences. Examine each of the sentences and ask yourself who or what each sentence is about. Draw a line under the word (or words) you think is the subject in each sentence. Then on the line to the right, write what kind of subject you have underlined. Be as specific as possible: *concrete noun* or *personal pronoun,* for example.

1. The young boy walked. _____

2. Young Robert Worthing walked. _____

3. He walked. _____

4. The road became dark. _____

5. The trees swayed. _____

6. An idea crossed his mind. _____

7. His parents and his dog would be sleeping. _____

Note: Not every noun or pronoun in a sentence is necessarily the subject for a verb. Nouns and pronouns function as subjects and as objects. In the following sentence, which noun is the subject and which noun is the object?

Helen drank the water.

For some students, the following exercises will seem easy. However, for many, analyzing the structure of a sentence is unfamiliar. As you practice, get into the habit of referring back to the definitions, charts, and examples. You can, with a little patience, develop an understanding for those words that serve as the subjects of sentences.

EXERCISE 1 Finding the Subject of a Sentence

Underline the subject in each of the following sentences. An example follows:

The Saturday paper had the movie listings.

1. We were a little late.

2. A long line had already formed.

3. Tickets cost six dollars.

4. The concession stand was doing a brisk business.

5. I wanted popcorn and a soda.

6. My date bought a hot dog and candy.

7. Ticket holders had already taken the best seats.

8. The movie began on time.

9. My date and I could only find front row seats.

10. The lights suddenly dimmed.

EXERCISE 2   Finding the Subject of a Sentence

Underline the subject in each of the following sentences. An example follows:

The old <u>friends</u> went shopping together.

1. Shoppers waited outside the glass doors.

2. The department store opened early.

3. The sale would last only three hours.

4. Many household items and electrical appliances were greatly reduced.

5. I needed new dinner dishes.

6. The kitchenware department was crowded.

7. I spotted my favorite dishes immediately.

8. The customers hurridly grabbed items.

9. Sales people worked feverishly.

10. This day would be exhausting.

How do you find the subject in sentences with prepositional phrases?

The sentences in Exercises 1 and 2 were short and basic. If we wrote only such sentences, our writing would sound choppy. Complex ideas would be difficult to express. One way to expand the simple sentence is to add prepositional phrases.

> **Example:** The athlete was injured *on the ice*.
> *On* is the preposition.
> *Ice* is a noun used as the object of the preposition.
> The prepositional phrase is *on the ice*.

> A *prepositional phrase* is a group of words containing a preposition and an object of the preposition with its modifiers. Prepositional phrases contain nouns or pronouns, but these nouns and pronouns are never the subject of the sentence.

In sentences with prepositional phrases, the subject may be difficult to spot. What is the subject of the following sentence?

> In the locker room, the conversation was boisterous.

In this sentence, *in the locker room* is a prepositional phrase. Since the subject can never be found within a prepositional phrase, a good idea is to cross out the prepositional phrase before you look for the subject.

> ~~In the locker room~~, the conversation was boisterous.

Now the subject, *conversation,* is easier to identify.

> When you are looking for the subject of a sentence, do not look for it within the prepositional phrase.

You can easily recognize a prepositional phrase because it always begins with a preposition. Study the following list so that you will be able to quickly recognize all of the common prepositions.

COMMON PREPOSITIONS

about	below	in	since
above	beneath	inside	through
across	beside	into	to
after	between	like	toward
against	beyond	near	under
along	by	of	until
among	down	off	up
around	during	on	upon
at	except	outside	with
before	for	over	within
behind	from	past	without

In addition to these common prepositions, English has a number of prepositional combinations that together with other words also function as prepositions.

COMMON PREPOSITIONAL COMBINATIONS

ahead of	in addition to	in reference to
at the time of	in between	in regard to
because of	in care of	in search of
by means of	in case of	in spite of
except for	in common with	instead of
for fear of	in contrast to	on account of
for the purpose of	in the course of	similar to
for the sake of	in exchange for	

EXERCISE 1   Finding Subjects in Sentences with Prepositional Phrases

Remember that you will never find the subject of a sentence within a prepositional phrase. In each of the following sentences, cross out any prepositional phrases. Then underline the subject of each sentence. An example follows:

~~In spite of the fear of earthquakes,~~ <u>tourists</u> throng ~~to San Francisco~~.

1. On Monday morning, we arrived in San Francisco.

2. Out hotel was near Fisherman's Wharf.

3. From the window, you could see Golden Gate Bridge.

4. Both of us enjoyed the view.

5. It seemed a perfect day for sightseeing.

6. On the trolley, we rode to Lombardi Street, "the crookedest street in the world."

7. After a boat ride, the two of us ate lunch at a restaurant on Nob Hill.

8. By that time, the suggestion of a nap appealed to us both.

9. Toward the end of a busy day, some San Francisco sidewalks seem much too steep.

10. Back in our room, two tired sightseers went to sleep.

EXERCISE 2 Finding Subjects in Sentences with Prepositional Phrases

Remember that you will never find the subject of a sentence within a prepositional phrase. In each of the following sentences, cross out any prepositional phrases. Then underline the subject of each sentence. An example follows:

~~At some time or another,~~ all ~~of us~~ must go ~~without a good night's sleep~~.

1. For those of us without a good night's sleep, herbal remedies can provide a cure to a haggard appearance.

2. Instead of preparing for the day, some of us roll over and go back to bed.

3. At the last minute in a panic, we jump out of bed and rush to our jobs.

4. A better approach for the sleep-deprived involves herbal remedies.

5. For those awful black circles under the eyes, chamomile tea bags can come to the rescue.

6. The tea bags should rest on the eyelids for at least ten minutes.

7. In addition to our physical appearance, our mental state may need some attention on these days.

8. A good wake-up call for a sleepy brain is a sniff of rosemary.

9. The ancient Greeks and Romans wore laurels of rosemary for mental alertness during exams.

10. Of course, the ideal solution is proper rest.

What are the other problems in finding subjects?

Sentences with a change in the normal subject position

Some sentences begin with words that indicate that a question is being asked. Such words as *why, where, how,* and *when* give the reader the signal that a question will follow. Such opening words are not the subjects. The subjects will be found later in the sentences. The following sentences begin with question words:

Why did Steffi speak softly?

How did the fans react to the news?

Notice that in each sentence the subject is not found in the opening part of the sentence. By answering questions or changing the question into a statement, the subject is easier to spot.

Steffi spoke softly because . . .

The *fans* reacted to the news by . . .

Using *there* or *here*

Such words as *there* or *here* can never be the subjects of sentences.

> There have been many stories about the event.

> Here is one of the stories.

Who or what is the subject of the first sentence? The answer is *stories*. What is the subject of the second sentence? Remember to cross out the prepositional phrase *of the stories*. The answer is *one*.

Commands

Sometimes a sentence contains a verb that gives an order:

> *Play* ball.

> *Stay* alert.

In sentences that give orders, the subject *you* is not written, but understood to be the subject. This is the only case where the subject of a sentence may be left out.

> (You) play ball.

> (You) stay alert.

Sentences that contain appositive phrases

> An *appositive phrase* is a group of words in a sentence that gives us extra information about a noun in the sentence. It is always separated from the rest of the sentence by commas.
>
> Steffi Graf, *the German tennis player,* has returned to the game.

In this sentence, the words *the German tennis player* make up the appositive phrase. These words give you extra information about Ms. Graf. Notice that commas separate the appositive phrase from the rest of the sentence. If you leave out the appositive phrase when you read this sentence, the thought will still be complete.

> Steffi Graf has returned to the game.

Now the subject is clear: Steffi Graf.

> When you are looking for the subject of a sentence, you will not find it within an appositive phrase.

EXERCISE 1   Finding Hidden Subjects

Each of the following sentences contains an example of a special problem in finding the subject of a sentence. First cross out any prepositional phrases or appositive phrases. Then underline the subject of each sentence. An example follows:

What will this new <u>job</u> be like?

1. Why was the bus on my route late?

2. There was no sign of its arrival.

3. In the middle of rush hour, the bus stop was crammed with people.

4. Luckily, I had plenty of time.

5. My job, a temporary data entry position, would last for six weeks.

6. Would I make a good impression on the manager?

7. Here is some good advice for a person with a new job.

8. Arrive on time.

9. Be ready to work.

10. In this economy, good work habits at one job may lead to another better job.

EXERCISE 2   Finding Hidden Subjects

Each of the following sentences contains an example of a special problem in finding the subject of a sentence. First cross out any prepositional phrases or appositive phrases. Then underline the subject of each sentence. An example follows:

<s>In many cases,</s> <u>people</u> are lactose intolerant.

1. Do you have an allergy?

2. A food intolerance, the body's inability to digest some part of a particular food, is different from an allergy.

3. Here is the best known food intolerance: milk.

4. With a food allergy, the immune system mistakes a harmless food as a dangerous invader and attacks it with irritating chemicals usually within the first 45 minutes of eating the food.

5. How can a person control an allergy or intolerance?

6. Keep a daily record of your diet for two weeks.

7. Record any adverse reactions after meals.

8. In most cases, people can pinpoint the troublesome foods.

9. There is some good news.

10. By avoidance of the offending food for a year or two, you may be able to outgrow your adverse reactions.

How do you find the verb of a sentence?

Every sentence must have a verb. Verbs can be divided into three classes.

Action: An *action verb* tells what the subject is doing.

Isaac Stern *played* a violin solo.

Linking: A *linking verb* indicates a state of being or condition.

The violinist *seemed* confident.

Helping: A *helping verb* combines with a main verb to form a verb phrase and gives the main verb a special time or meaning.

The musician *may* perform again tomorrow.

Verbs tell time. Use this fact to test for a verb. If you can put the verb into different tenses in the sentence, that word is a verb.

Present: (Today) she *performs.*
Past: (Yesterday) she *performed.*
Future: (Tomorrow) she will *perform.*

Action verbs

> *Action verbs* tell us what the subject is doing and when the subject does the action.

The student *practiced* the trumpet.

What was the student doing?   practicing
What is the time of the action?   past (*-ed* is the past tense ending)

ACTION VERBS

Most verbs are **action verbs.** Here are a few examples:

arrive	learn	open	watch
leave	forget	write	fly
enjoy	help	speak	catch
despise	make	teach	wait

EXERCISE 1   Finding Action Verbs

Each of the following sentences contains an action verb. Find the action verb by first underlining the subject of the sentence. Then circle the verb (the word that tells what the subject is doing). An example follows:

My childhood friend (visited) me this spring.

1. Friendship teaches patience and understanding.

2. You learn respect.

3. Friends enjoy one another's company.

4. They help each other through good and bad times.

5. Good friends watch out for one another.

6. Best friends often speak honestly to one another.

7. We forget the occasional arguments.

8. Sometimes good friends move away from each other.

9. They write and call frequently.

10. Good friends give life fuller meaning.

EXERCISE 2   Finding Action Verbs

Each of the following sentences contains an action verb. Find the action verb by first underlining the subject of the sentence. Then circle the verb (the word that tells what the subject is doing). An example follows:

In our house, family members (share) the housework equally.

1. Housework requires a system of organization.

2. A plan of action saves time.

3. Some people, myself included, collect all the cleaning products first.

4. Others clean in a haphazard fashion.

5. We always start with the kitchen.

6. Bathrooms and bedrooms receive our attention next.

7. The den, the most heavily used room, gets special treatment.

8. The dining and living rooms take the least amount of time.

9. Dusting, polishing, and vacuuming keep us busy every Saturday morning.

10. With help from everyone, the work goes fast.

Linking verbs

> A *linking verb* is a verb that links the subject of a sentence to one or more words that describe or identify the subject.

For example:

The social worker (is) my cousin.

She (seems) qualified.

We (feel) proud of her.

In each of these examples, the verb links the subject to a word that identifies or describes the subject. In the first example, the verb *is* links *worker* with *cousin*. The verb *seems* links the pronoun *she* with *qualified*. Finally, in the third example, the verb *feel* links the pronoun *we* with *proud*.

COMMON LINKING VERBS	
act	feel
appear	grow
be (am, is, are, was,	look
were, have been)	seem
become	taste

EXERCISE 1   Finding Linking Verbs

Each of the following sentences contains a linking verb. Find the linking verb by first underlining the subject of the sentence. Then draw an arrow to the word or words that identify or describe the subject. Finally, circle the linking verb. An example follows:

Home economics (was) a required course in my high school.

1. Sewing is a creative act.

2. It has become a less popular activity in the past decade.

3. The cost of clothing is quite expensive.

4. Homemade clothes will usually be less costly.

5. Sewing looks difficult to many people.

6. I was happy about my sewing project.

7. The finished skirt looks wonderful.

8. It felt perfectly tailored.

9. I grow more confident with each new project.

10. I feel satisfied with my sewing efforts.

EXERCISE 2   Finding Linking Verbs

Each of the following sentences contains a linking verb. Find the linking verb by first underlining the subject of the sentence. Then draw an arrow to the word or words that identify or describe the subject. Finally, circle the linking verb. An example follows:

Brain teasers (were) popular games among my friends.

1. Puzzles are tests of logic.

2. Sometimes they appear deceptively simple.

3. Most people become absorbed in a puzzle.

4. Almost everyone seems eager to find the answer.

5. Unfortunately, some people grow frustrated with the passage of time.

6. The process is fun to other people.

7. I become especially excited at the final step.

8. I feel victorious.

9. Be patient.

10. With persistence, a solution is possible.

Helping verbs (also called auxiliary verbs)

Some verbs can be used to help the main verb express a special time or meaning.

Sentence using auxiliary verb	Time expressed by auxiliary verb
He is reading.	right now
He might read.	maybe now or in the future
He should read.	ought to, now or in the future
He could have been reading.	maybe in the past

COMMON HELPING VERBS

can, could

may, might, must

shall, should

will, would

forms of the irregular verbs *be, do,* and *have.*

Remember that *be, do,* and *have* are also used as the main verbs of sentences. In such cases, *be* is a linking verb while *do* and *have* are action verbs. All the other helping verbs are usually used only as helping verbs.

Watch out for adverbs that may come in between the helping verb and the main verb.

> *Adverbs* are words that can modify verbs, adjectives, or other adverbs.

In the following sentence, the word *often* is an adverb coming between the verb phrase *can frighten*. For a list of adverbs, see Appendix B: Parts of Speech (pp. 331–338).

A good book can *often* leave a strong impression on the reader.

EXERCISE 1   **Finding Helping Verbs**

Each of the following sentences contains a helping verb in addition to the main verb. In each sentence, first underline the subject. Then circle the entire verb phrase. An example follows:

People today are living longer lives and are enjoying those lives more fully.

1. Growing old can frighten some people.

2. Aging well will depend on your physical health and your outlook on life.

3. Adolescents do sometimes leave their teen years behind with pleasure.

4. Forty year olds will often worry about entering their fifties.

5. Attitudes about aging have changed dramatically.

6. People are taking much better care of themselves.

7. Regular exercise can insure your aging with fewer health problems.

8. You should remain physically active in later years.

9. Aging may bring unexpected pleasure to your life.

10. You might gain new insights and discover new interests.

EXERCISE 2   **Finding Helping Verbs**

Each of the following sentences contains a helping verb in addition to the main verb. In each sentence, first underline the subject. Then circle the entire verb phrase. An example follows:

Did you wake from your dreams refreshed?

1. Dreams should tell us something about ourselves.

2. You may dream in black and white or in color.

3. Your dreams can seem real.

4. Did the event really happen or not?

5. Dreams can often be frightening.

6. Some people might dream of falling off a tall building.

7. The heart may race.

8. Other dreams will be delightful.

9. Have you ever had a repeating dream?

10. Do you ever try to continue your dream after waking up?

11. That, unfortunately, will rarely happen.

Parts of Speech

In this chapter you have learned how most of the words in the English language function. These categories for words are called *parts of speech*. You have learned to recognize and understand the functioning of *nouns, pronouns, adjectives, verbs, adverbs* and *prepositions*. (In later chapters you will learn how the *conjunction* functions.) You can review your understanding of these parts of speech as you practice identifying them in the exercises provided here. You may also refer to Appendix B (at the back of the book) for a quick summary whenever you want to refresh your memory.

EXERCISE 1   Identifying Parts of Speech

In the sentences below, identify the part of speech for each underlined word. Choose from the following list.

a. noun
b. pronoun
c. adjective
d. verb
e. adverb
f. preposition

_____ 1. Chubby Checker taught the <u>world</u> how to twist.

_____ 2. Dick Clark, host of American Bandstand, <u>decided</u> he liked "The Twist" and showcased it.

_____ 3. The song shot up to number one <u>on</u> the pop charts in September of 1960.

_____ 4. Twisting became the biggest <u>teenage</u> fad.

_____ 5. At first, <u>it</u> was considered strictly kid stuff.

_____ 6. Then it became <u>respectable</u> among older groups.

_____ 7. Liz Taylor and Richard Burton were seen twisting in the fashionable night spots of <u>Rome</u>.

_____ 8. The dance set the pace <u>for</u> a decade.

_____ 9. The "beautiful people" were seen <u>breathlessly</u> twisting at the Peppermint Lounge in New York.

_____ 10. The 60s were going to be a reckless and unruly <u>time</u>.

EXERCISE 2   Identifying Parts of Speech

In the sentences below, identify the part of speech for each underlined word. Choose from the following list.

  a. noun
  b. pronoun
  c. adjective
  d. verb
  e. adverb
  f. preposition

_____ 1. "The Grand Ole Opry" is a <u>famous</u> radio program.

_____ 2. <u>It</u> began more than seventy years ago in Nashville, Tennessee.

_____ 3. By the 1930s, the <u>program</u> was the best source of country music on the radio.

_____ 4. In 1943, the program <u>could</u> be heard in every home in the nation.

_____ 5. <u>Many</u> people traveled to Nashville.

_____ 6. <u>They</u> wanted to see the performers for themselves.

_____ 7. The existing old concert hall, <u>poorly</u> constructed in the nineteenth century, was not an ideal place for modern audiences.

_____ 8. Television came in during the 1950s, and with it the demand <u>for</u> a new hall.

_____ 9. Now the Nashville hall is <u>modern</u> and air-conditioned.

_____ 10. Three million people <u>visit</u> Nashville every year.

Mastery and editing tests

TEST 1   Finding Subjects and Verbs in Simple Sentences

After reading the paragraph, use the lines that follow to write the subject and verb of each sentence.

[1]The field of red stretched out before us. [2]Red, round berries bobbed slightly in the breeze. [3]Our range of vision was filled with the sight of ripening cranberries. [4]Cranberries are symbolic of the autumn. [5]They

conjure up images of cornucopias with their fruits of the harvest, or of Thanksgiving tables with their feasts of meats and pies. [6]The Cranberry, one of the native American fruits, got its name from the earliest European settlers in the area. [7]To the Indians, cranberries were known as *sassamanash,* a source of color for dyes, or as *pemican,* their survival cake of dried deer meat and cranberries. [8]The European settlers noticed the delicately curved pink blossoms in the spring. [9]These blossoms resemble the head and bill of the sand hill crane. [10]This explains the name *crane berry.*

	Subject	Verb
Sentence 1	_____	_____
Sentence 2	_____	_____
Sentence 3	_____	_____
Sentence 4	_____	_____
Sentence 5	_____	_____
Sentence 6	_____	_____
Sentence 7	_____	_____
Sentence 8	_____	_____
Sentence 9	_____	_____
Sentence 10	_____	_____

TEST 2   Finding Subjects and Verbs in Simple Sentences

After reading the paragraph, use the lines that follow to write the subject and verb of each sentence.

[1]On Friday the thirteenth, Jason attended his first baseball game. [2]He and his father arrived two hours early at the stadium. [3]In that way, they could watch batting practice. [4]Before the game, some of the players signed autographs. [5]With the signatures of his three favorite players, Jason accompanied his dad to their seats for the game. [6]Their seats were on field level, behind home plate. [7]During the first inning, Jason's dad bought him a frank, a soda, and a souvenir program. [8]Jason sat between his dad and a white-haired gentleman. [9]Within moments, Jason's father recognized the gentleman. [10]The man, a Hall of Fame pitcher, gladly signed his name on Jason's program.

	Subject	Verb
Sentence 1	_____	_____
Sentence 2	_____	_____
Sentence 3	_____	_____
Sentence 4	_____	_____

Sentence 5 _____ _____

Sentence 6 _____ _____

Sentence 7 _____ _____

Sentence 8 _____ _____

Sentence 9 _____ _____

Sentence 10 _____ _____

TEST 3 Finding Subjects and Verbs in Simple Sentences

After reading the paragraph, use the lines that follow to write the subject and verb of each sentence.

[1]A large number of people are afraid of flying. [2]What can those of us with a fear of flying do about our fear? [3]How can a person change irrational thought patterns? [4]Until recently, I had always preferred the train for vacations or business trips. [5]With the right therapy, most fearful fliers can be helped. [6]In the months after my participation in a seminar for people like me, I took three flights. [7]Here is the strange fact. [8]During the flights, I slept comfortably. [9]There are ways for gaining control of your symptoms. [10]Try behavioral approaches before medications like Xanex or Prozac.

	Subject	**Verb**
Sentence 1	_____	_____
Sentence 2	_____	_____
Sentence 3	_____	_____
Sentence 4	_____	_____
Sentence 5	_____	_____
Sentence 6	_____	_____
Sentence 7	_____	_____
Sentence 8	_____	_____
Sentence 9	_____	_____
Sentence 10	_____	_____

THE SENTENCE

Chapter 12

Making Subjects and Verbs Agree

The fact that a complete sentence must have a subject for its verb, leads us to a related problem: making that subject agree with its verb.

What is subject-verb agreement?

> A verb must agree with its subject in number (singular or plural).
> When the subject is a singular noun, the verb takes an *s* in the present tense.
>
>   The athlete *rests*.
>
> When the subject is a plural noun, the verb does <u>not</u> take an *s* in the present tense.
>
>   The athletes *rest*.

Notice that when you add *s* or *es* to an ordinary noun, you form the plural of that noun. However, when you add an *s* to a verb, and you want the verb to be in the present tense, you are writing a singular verb. This causes a lot of confusion because not everyone follows this rule when speaking or writing. However, all of us must use this standard form in school and in the world of business. Mastering the material contained in this chapter is therefore of real importance to your success in college and beyond.

Pronouns can also present problems for subject-verb agreement

The following chart shows personal pronouns used with the verb *rest*. After you have studied the chart, what can you tell about the ending of a verb when the subject of that verb is a personal pronoun?

PERSONAL PRONOUNS	
Singular	*Plural*
I rest	we rest
you rest	you rest
he, she, it rests	they rest

• PRACTICE

Underline the correct verb in the following sentences.

1. The florist (arranges, arrange) the centerpiece.

2. The arrangement (includes, include) tulips and baby's breath.

3. I (likes, like) the effect of fresh flowers on a table.

4. The flowers (arrives, arrive) the day of the party.

5. The evening (promises, promise) to be a great success.

Pay special attention to the verbs *do* and *be*

Though you may have heard someone say, *it don't matter* or *we was working*, these expressions are not correct standard English usage.

THE VERB *TO DO*		
Singular	**Plural**	
I do	we	
you do	you	} do
he	they	
she } does		
it		
(never *he don't, she don't, it don't*)		

THE VERB *TO BE*			
Present Tense		**Past Tense**	
Singular	**Plural**	**Singular**	**Plural**
I am	we	I was	we
you are	you } are	you were	you } were
he	they	he	they
she } is		she } was	
it		it	
(never *we was, you was,* or *they was*)			

• PRACTICE

Underline the verb that agrees with the subject.

1. We (was, were) meeting to discuss the youth retreat.

2. The leader (was, were) concerned about the accommodations.

3. He (doesn't, don't) want boys and girls on the same floor.

4. Ann (doesn't, don't) want to chaperone unruly teenagers.

5. It (doesn't, don't) matter if some of the youth bring extra money.

EXERCISE 1   Making the Subject and Verb Agree

In the blanks next to each sentence, write the subject of the sentence and the correct form of the verb.

	Subject	Verb
1. A mystery writer (lives, live) in our town.	_____	_____
2. He (was, were) nominated for the Edgar Award for best paperback of the year.	_____	_____
3. He (doesn't, don't) live too far from me.	_____	_____
4. Sometimes we (sees, see) him out walking.	_____	_____
5. He always (wears, wear) an old wide-brimmed hat.	_____	_____
6. I (thinks, think) he enjoys his work.	_____	_____
7. His books always (centers, center) around a sports theme.	_____	_____
8. The latest book (is, are) about a murder at the US Open Tennis Tournament.	_____	_____
9. We (doesn't, don't) know yet if he will win the award.	_____	_____
10. The mystery writers of America (presents, present) an award called the Edgar, named for Edgar Allan Poe.	_____	_____

EXERCISE 2   Making the Subject and Verb Agree

In the blanks next to each sentence, write the subject of the sentence and the correct form of the verb.

	Subject	Verb
1. Clair (was, were) at home all summer.	_____	_____
2. She (doesn't, don't) mind being at home.	_____	_____
3. Clair's parents (doesn't, don't) have the opportunity to go on vacation very often.	_____	_____
4. Next summer, however, they (plans, plan) to drive across the country.	_____	_____

	Subject	Verb
5. It (is, are) fun to anticipate the places they will visit.	_____	_____
6. Her brother (lives, live) in Ohio.	_____	_____
7. He (has, have) a little baby boy.	_____	_____
8. He (doesn't, don't) care how long they stay.	_____	_____
9. They also (does, do) plan to drive south through Tennessee and Kentucky.	_____	_____
10. Clair (dreams, dream) about the Rocky Mountains and the Sonora Desert.	_____	_____

Subject-verb agreement with hard-to-find subjects

As we learned in Chapter 11, a verb does not always immediately follow the subject. Other words or groups of words called phrases (prepositional phrases or appositive phrases, for example) can come between the subject and verb. Furthermore, subjects and verbs can be inverted as they are in questions or sentences beginning with *there* or *here*.

When looking for subject-verb agreement in sentences where the subjects are more difficult to find, keep in mind two points:

- Subjects are not found in prepositional phrases or appositive phrases.
- Subjects can be found after the verb in sentences that are questions and in sentences that begin with *there* or *here*.

EXERCISE 1   Agreement with Hidden Subjects

Circle the correct verb in each sentence.

1. Sometimes there (is, are) an amazing spectacle in some European countries.

2. (Does, Do) the thought of seeing thousands of lemmings make you queasy?

3. An abundance of these little rodents (makes, make) many people afraid.

4. In "Lemming years," most individuals in their pathway (has, have) cause for concern.

5. Here (is, are) some of the things lemmings do: eat everything in sight, move in large groups, and travel in straight lines.

6. These creatures with their strange obsession (has, have) been known to run right into a lake or river and drown.

7. An automobile, unable to put on the brakes fast enough, often (runs, run) lemmings down by the hundreds.

8. (Is, Are) there other dangers with lemmings?

9. In many cases, the presence of dead lemmings in lakes and rivers (poisons, poison) the water.

10. Lack of caution on the part of many people (leads, lead) to numerous illnesses.

EXERCISE 2   Agreement with Hidden Subjects

Circle the correct verb in each sentence.

1. Every family member (needs, need) to know about first aid.

2. In what cases (is, are) the resuscitation of a loved one required?

3. Local hospitals in your town certainly (teaches, teach) resuscitation techniques.

4. Where in our homes (does, do) we keep the well-stocked first aid kit?

5. In the kit there (is, are) bandages, gauze, and antiseptic.

6. Neighbors on our street (does, do) not seem prepared for their children's accidental injuries.

7. Children with a calm, prepared parent usually (fares, fare) much better in an emergency.

8. Readiness for first aid assistance (reduces, reduce) the risk of long-term damage and can save lives.

9. Lack of preparedness often (leads, lead) to serious consequences.

10. There (is, are) too many sad cases as a result of inaction.

Special problems with subject-verb agreement

1. **Subject-verb agreement with group nouns.** Look at the list of group nouns given in the chart. Do you think a group noun should be considered singular or plural? In American English, the answer to that question depends on whether the group acts as a single unit, or if the individuals in the group are acting separately.

   - A group noun takes a singular verb if the noun acts as a unit. To test this, substitute the pronoun *it* for the noun.

     The orchestra is performing today.

     Test: *It is* performing today.

   - A group noun takes a plural verb if the members of the group act as individuals. To test this, substitute the pronoun *they* for the noun.

     The orchestra are tuning their instruments.

     Test: *They are* tuning their instruments.

COMMON GROUP NOUNS		
audience	council	jury
assembly	crowd	number
board	faculty	orchestra
class	family	panel
club	group	public
committee	herd	team

EXERCISE 1   Subject-Verb Agreement with Group Nouns

Circle the correct verb in each sentence.

1. Every season the Navy (wants, want) to win a special swim meet.

2. The Navy team (trains, train) all year for the big event.

3. A crowd (gathers, gather) near the water to see the race.

4. The public (enjoys, enjoy) watching athletes who are also in the military.

5. The number of spectators (varies, vary) every year.

6. Sometimes, the police (is, are) called if the crowd becomes too large.

7. The family of each team member (is, are) not always able to be there.

8. Occasionally a school of fish (gets, get) in the way of the swimmers.

9. A crew (stands, stand) ready with a rescue boat in case of emergencies.

10. Often the panel of judges (disagrees, disagree) about issues concerning disqualification.

EXERCISE 2   Subject-Verb Agreement with Group Nouns

Circle the correct verb in each sentence.

1. The crew of carpenters (travels, travel) throughout the state looking for special old homes in disrepair.

2. A number of houses (is, are) always under review.

3. The group (forms, form) into several different committees to consider the purchase of the houses.

4. One committee (considers, consider) the cost of restoring the house in question.

5. Another committee (determines, determine) a likely selling price for the restored home.

6. A team (arrives, arrive) to plan the restoration.

7. A crowd sometimes (gathers, gather) to disagree with the plan.

8. The historical society in the town (is, are) sometimes distrustful.

9. Sometimes a town zoning board (rules, rule) what features of a particular house must be preserved.

10. Sometimes a local club of a small town (decides, decide) to save unique and crumbling old homes in the area.

2. **Subject-verb agreement with indefinite pronouns.** Care should be taken with indefinite pronouns to learn which ones are considered singular and which are considered plural.

INDEFINITE PRONOUNS

Indefinite Pronouns Taking a Singular Verb:

everyone	someone	anyone	no one
everybody	somebody	anybody	nobody
everything	something	anything	nothing
each	another	either	neither

Nobody *is* telling the truth.

Indefinite Pronouns Taking a Plural Verb:

both	few	many	several

Both a*re* telling the truth.

Indefinite Pronouns Taking a Singular or Plural Verb Depending on the Meaning in the Sentence:

any	all	more	most
none	some		

The books are gone. All of them were very popular.

The sugar is gone. All of it was spilled.

EXERCISE 1   Agreement with Indefinite Pronouns

Circle the correct verb in each sentence.

1. Everyone (wants, want) a stable job.

2. Some (trains, train) for a specific job without the guarantee of a future job.

3. One of the realizations (is, are) the change in the job market.

4. Most (acknowledges, acknowledge) the importance of flexibility and a wide range of skills.

5. Both (helps, help) to adapt to the changing market.

6. Nobody (is, are) able to exactly predict the jobs of the future.

7. All of the experts (agrees, agree) on the need for computer skills.

8. All of the training for computer skills (is, are) time well invested.

9. Anybody with an interest in technical repairs (has, have) an opportunity to find employment.

10. None of the training programs (promises, promise) you success without your individual determination.

EXERCISE 2   Agreement with Indefinite Pronouns

Circle the correct verb in each sentence.

1. Few (has, have) not heard of MTV.

2. Nothing (has, have) saturated television more than the MTV style of quick cuts and extravagant imagery.

3. Several of the rules for pop music (has, have) changed.

4. Each of the pop songs now (requires, require) interesting visuals as well.

5. Everybody (sees, see) the combination of music and video as unique entertainment.

6. All of the ads (is, are) geared to be hip.

7. Someone (has, have) counted the number of violent videos.

8. Another (has, have) described the presentation of women as nothing more than brainless trollops.

9. Many (does, do) not like the social message MTV gives.

10. Neither of my parents ever (watches, watch) MTV.

3. **Subject-verb agreement with compound subjects**

   • If the conjunction used to connect the compound subjects is *and*, the verb is usually plural.

        Frank and Cynthia *are* helpful neighbors.

   The exception to this is if the two subjects together are thought of as a single unit.

        Bacon and eggs *is* my favorite breakfast.

- If the conjunction used to connect the compound subjects is *or, nor, either, either/or, neither, neither/nor, not only/but also,* you need to be particularly careful. The verb is singular if both subjects are singular.

> Frank or Cynthia *is* watching the children tomorrow.

The verb is plural if both subjects are plural.

> My neighbors or my parents *are* watching the children tomorrow.

The verb agrees with the subject closest to the verb if one subject is singular and one subject is plural.

> My neighbors or my mother *is* watching the children tomorrow.

EXERCISE 1   Subject-verb Agreement with Compound Subjects

Circle the correct verb in each sentence below.

1. Ham and eggs (is, are) a breakfast dish too high in cholesterol for most people to eat every day.

2. My mother and father always (sits, sit) down to a large breakfast of eggs, sausage, toast, and potatoes.

3. My husband and children often (runs, run) out of the house without so much as a glass of orange juice.

4. Half a grapefruit or a banana on cereal (makes, make) a good breakfast.

5. Whole grained breads or cooked cereal (is, are) better than white bread with jam or sugared cereals.

6. Not only the adults but also the children (needs, need) energy for the day's activities.

7. A nutritious breakfast and hot lunch (has, have) a proven effect on the ability of children to concentrate in school.

8. Today, neither the busy schedules of working parents nor their interest (encourages, encourage) the cooking of large family meals.

9. A donut, a cookie, or a sweet roll (is, are) a terrible choice for breakfast.

10. Fruits and vegetables (does, do) keep a family healthy.

EXERCISE 2   Subject-verb Agreement with Compound Subjects

Circle the correct verb in each sentence below.

1. Pen and paper (is, are) the traditional image of a writer's tools.

2. These days, both traditional tools and added supports (helps, help) people become published writers.

3. Workshops and an experienced teacher (has, have) become necessary for the ambitious writer.

4. Novelists and poets (seems, seem) to benefit most from small seminars.

5. Not only commercial publishers but also non-profit organizations (wants, want) the work of up-and-coming writers.

6. Neither the readers nor the publisher (desires, desire) a dull book.

7. Lack of interesting content or poor style (results, result) in disappointing sales.

8. Computer skills and familiarity with the most commonly used word processing programs (continues, continue) to be important.

9. Either an agent or an editor (is, are) always an asset.

10. Good advice and a little luck (gives, give) the promising new writer a better chance for success.

4. **Subject-verb agreement with certain nouns.** Don't assume that every noun ending in *s* is plural, or that all nouns that do not end in *s* are singular. There are some exceptions. Here are a few of the most common.

Some nouns are always singular but end in *s*.

mathematics	diabetes	United States
economics	measles	Kansas

Some nouns are always plural.

clothes	scissors	fireworks
headquarters	tweezers	pants

Some nouns have an irregular plural form that does not end in *s* or *es*.

people	feet	men	data
children	mice	women	alumni (masculine)
			alumnae (feminine)

Mastery and editing tests

TEST 1   Making the Subject and Verb Agree

In the blanks next to each sentence, write the subject of the sentence and the correct form of the verb. An example follows:

	Subject	Verb
Fried chicken dishes (is, are) most popular in the South.	*dishes*	*are*

1. The most common sandwich in the United States (is, are) ham with mayonnaise.

2. No city except Philadelphia (sells, sell) pepperpot soup.

3. Salsa and ketchup (is, are) in a competition throughout the country for the most popular condiment.

4. French fries (is, are) the most popular way of eating potatoes.

5. A candy called Goo Goo Clusters (remains, remain) a favorite in Tennessee but is not sold anywhere else.

6. Both the East and Middle West with its German descendants (consumes, consume) more hot dogs.

7. Throughout the fifty states, steaks (is, are) the dinner of choice in an increasing number of restaurants.

8. In 1995, over seventy pounds of chicken (was, were) consumed by the average person.

9. That number (has, have) been growing every year.

10. One of the most popular fast foods in the North Central region of the country (is, are) frozen pizza.

TEST 2   Making the Subject and Verb Agree

Complete each of the following sentences being sure that the verb in each sentence agrees with the subject of that sentence. Use verbs in the present tense.

1. The board of health _____

_____

2. One of the issues _____

_____

3. The reports on the blood drive _____

_____

4. Either the reporters or the editor _____

_____

5. Neither the teacher nor the tutors _____

_____

6. How _____

_____

7. During this week, there _____

_____

8. Everyone _____

_____

9. The judge and jury _____

_____

10. All of the _____

_____

TEST 3   Making the Subject and Verb Agree

Complete each of the following sentences being sure that the verb in each sentence agrees with the subject of that sentence. Use verbs in the present tense.

1. The committee of citizens _____

_____

2. When _____

_____

3. The significance of the findings _____

_____

4. The park or the sidewalks _____

_____

5. The work of a few committed persons _____

_____

6. One of the speakers _____

_____

7. In the spring, there _____

_____

8. Nobody in the class _____

_____

9. The team of volunteers _____

_____

10. Neither the residents nor the visitors _____

_____

Chapter 13

Correcting the Fragment in Simple Sentences

Fragments in everyday conversations

The fragment is a major problem for many student writers. A thought may be clear in a writer's mind, but on paper this same idea may turn out to be incomplete because it does not include a subject, a verb, or express a complete thought. In this section, you will improve your ability to spot incomplete sentences or fragments, and you will learn how to correct them. This practice will prepare you to avoid such fragments in your own writing. Here, for example, is a typical conversation between two people. It is composed entirely of fragments, but the two people who are speaking have no trouble understanding each other.

> *Betty:*   Going to the concert?
> *Veronica:* Later.
> *Betty:*   Want to meet me?
> *Veronica:* Sure.

If we use complete sentences to rewrite this brief conversation, the result might be the following:

> *Betty:*   Are you going to the concert?
> *Veronica:* I plan to go later.
> *Betty:*   Do you want to meet me there?
> *Veronica:* Sure I do.

In the first conversation, misunderstanding is unlikely since the two speakers stand face to face, see each other's gestures, and hear the intonations of each other's voice in order to help figure out the meaning. These short phrases may be enough for communication since the speakers are using more than just words to convey their thoughts. They understand each other because each one is able to complete the thoughts that are in the other person's mind.

In writing, however, readers cannot be present at the scene to observe the situation for themselves. They cannot be expected to read the author's mind. Only the words grouped into sentences and the sentences grouped into paragraphs provide the clues to the meaning. Since writing often involves thoughts that are abstract and even complex, fragments cause great difficulty and sometimes total confusion for the reader.

KVCC KALAMAZOO VALLEY COMMUNITY COLLEGE LIBRARY

EXERCISE 1   Putting a Conversation into Complete Sentences

The following conversation is one that a couple of students might have at school registration. Rewrite the conversation in complete thoughts or standard sentences. Remember the definition of a sentence.

> A *complete sentence* has a subject and a verb and expresses a complete thought.

Scott: What a disaster.
Carol: Same every year.
Scott: Get all your classes?
Carol: Hardly.
Scott: Biology still open?
Carol: Hope so.
Scott: Took it last year.
Carol: Tough course?
Scott: Guess so. Had worse.

1. _____
2. _____
3. _____
4. _____
5. _____
6. _____
7. _____
8. _____
9. _____
10. _____

Remember, when you write in complete sentences, this writing may be somewhat different from the way you would express the same idea in everyday conversation with a friend.

Although you will occasionally spot incomplete sentences in professional writing, you may be sure the writer is using these fragments intentionally. In such cases, the fragment may capture the way a person thinks or speaks, or it may create a special effect. A student developing his or her writing skills should be sure to use only standard sentence form so that thoughts will be communicated effectively. Nearly all the writing you will do in your life—letters to friends, business correspondence, papers in school, or reports in your job—will demand standard sentence form. Fragments will be looked upon as a sign of ignorance rather than creative style!

What is a fragment?

> A *fragment* is a piece of a sentence.

A fragment is not a sentence for one of the following reasons:

a. The subject is missing:

> covered the roads

b. The verb is missing:

> the bus to the school

c. Both the subject and verb are missing:

> to the school

d. The subject and verb are present but the words do not express a complete thought:

> the bus reached

EXERCISE 2   Understanding Fragments

Each of the following groups of words is a fragment. In the blank to the right of each fragment, identify what part of the sentence is missing and needs to be added to make the fragment into a sentence.

   a. Add a subject.
   b. Add a verb.
   c. Add a subject and a verb.
   d. The subject and verb are already present, but the sentence needs to express a complete thought.

An example is done for you.

Fragment	Add
1. melted in the streets	_____
2. the ice on the roofs	_____
3. from the roofs to the ground	_____

Fragment	Add
4. the skiers across the fields	_____
5. crows and other birds against the sky	_____
6. built on the branches of the tallest trees	_____
7. young birds in each of the nests	_____
8. the skiers found	_____
9. goes down behind the hills	_____
10. deep into the night	_____

How do you correct a fragment?

1. **Add the missing part or parts.**

   Example: Fragment: through the park
   Add: subject and verb
   Sentence: I walked through the park.

   Note: The prepositional phrase *through the park* is a fragment because a prepositional phrase cannot function as the subject or the verb in a sentence. Furthermore, the words do not express a complete thought.

2. **Join the fragment to the sentence that precedes it or to the sentence that follows it, depending on where it belongs.**

   If a writer examines a text that includes a fragment, the writer will see that a complete thought may already exist. The writer did not immediately realize that the thought belonged to the sentence that came before or just after the fragment. Study the example below.

   Wrong: In the early morning, I walked. Through the park. The day was going to be unbearably hot.

   Correct: In the early morning, I walked through the park. The day was going to be unbearably hot.

There can be more than one reason for fragments in a writer's work. A writer may be careless for a moment, or a writer may not fully understand the necessary parts of a sentence. Also, if the writer does not have a clear idea of what he or she is trying to say, fragments and other errors are more likely to occur. Sometimes further thought or another try at expressing the same idea may produce a better result.

In the following two exercises, practice correcting both kinds of fragments.

EXERCISE 3   Making Fragments into Sentences

Change the fragments of Exercise 2 into complete sentences by adding the missing part or parts that you have already identified.

1. melted in the streets

   _____

2. the ice on the roofs

   _____

3. from the roofs to the ground

   _____

4. the skiers across the fields

   _____

5. crows and other birds against the sky

   _____

6. built on the branches of the tallest trees

   _____

7. young birds in each of the nests

   _____

8. the skiers found

   _____

9. goes down behind the hills

   _____

10. deep into the night

   _____

EXERCISE 4   Finding Fragments That Belong to Other Sentences

Each of the following passages contains a fragment or two. First, read each passage. Then locate the fragment in each passage. Circle the fragment and draw an arrow to the sentence to which it should be connected. An example follows:

> The students washed the cars. They worked hard. After the carwash They decided to have a picnic.

Passage 1   People in elevators sometimes can act strangely. And can behave rudely. Most elevator passengers stare at the light above the door. Not looking at each other. Others go directly into a corner and stay there. Some people do not wait for others to leave an elevator. They just rush out the door when the elevator stops.

Passage 2   Many of the life forms that exist in the woods are never noticed. Millions of ants, invisible to us. Live, work and fight in their underground nests. Beetles hide under nearly every rock and fallen tree. Up in the highest branches, owls and hawks of many species. Hunt for food day and night. The woods are teeming with life, even if we cannot see it.

Passage 3   Mark Twain wrote his autobiography over a period of several years. In 1873, he wrote a brief personal sketch for a friend. A few years later he wrote a recollection of his earliest days. In Missouri, his boyhood home. Toward the end of the century, he wrote another sketch of himself. For his nephew. Twain's autobiography is really a series of pieces written over many years and for different purposes.

What is a phrase?

> A *phrase* is a group of words that go together but that lacks one or more of the elements necessary to be classified as a sentence.

Fragments are usually made up of phrases. These phrases are often mistaken for sentences because they are words that go together as a group. However, they do not fit the definition of a sentence. *Do not confuse a phrase with a sentence.*

How many kinds of phrases are there?

The English language has six phrases (three of which you have already studied in Chapter 11). You should learn to recognize each of these phrases. Remember that a phrase is never a sentence.

1. **Noun phrase:** a noun plus its modifiers

   small pink house

2. **Prepositional phrase:** a preposition plus its object and modifiers

   above the garage

3. **Verb phrase:** the main verb plus its helping verbs

   was dancing
   might have danced
   should have been dancing

The three remaining phrases are formed from *verbs*. However, these phrases do not function as verbs in the sentence. Study carefully how to use them.

4. **Participial phrase:**
   How is the participial phrase formed?

   a. the present form of a verb ending in *-ing* and any other words necessary to complete the phrase

   > walking downtown
   > appearing quite healthy

   b. the past form of a verb usually ending in *-ed* and any other words necessary to complete the phrase

   > extremely depressed
   > explained carefully

   How does the participial phrase function? Participial phrases function as ***adjectives*** in a sentence. Study how the above phrases could be made into complete sentences. These phrases will function as adjectives for the noun or pronoun that follows.

   > *Walking downtown,* the child looked for amusement.
   > *Appearing quite healthy,* she returned to work.
   > *Extremely depressed,* the man looked for medical help.
   > *Explained carefully,* the directions became clear.

   > Do not confuse a participle that is used as an adjective with a participle that is used as part of the main verb of a sentence. A participle requires a helping verb when it is used as the main verb of the sentence.

   Participial phrase: *Walking downtown,* the child felt carefree.

   Verb phrase: The child *is walking* downtown.

5. **Gerund phrase:** the present form of a verb ending in *-ing,* and any other words necessary to complete the phrase.

   The gerund phrase functions as a noun. It can be the subject or the object of the sentence.

   a. subject of the sentence:

   > *Walking downtown* was good exercise.

   b. direct object of the sentence:

   > He liked *walking downtown.*

6. **Infinitive phrase:** *to* plus the verb and any other words necessary to complete the phrase

He decided *to walk downtown.*

Note: The word *to* can also function as a preposition.

I walked *to school.*

EXERCISE 1   Identifying Phrases

Identify each of the underlined phrases in the following sentences.

1. <u>Becoming a professional athlete</u> takes hard work and some luck.   _____

2. The story of Roberto Clemente is known <u>to baseball fans</u> around the world.   _____

3. Coming <u>from a modest home</u> in Puerto Rico, Roberto Clemente wanted to be a professional baseball player.   _____

4. <u>His hardworking father</u> was a foreman on a large sugar plantation and also ran a grocery store for the workers.   _____

5. At twenty, Clemente <u>was spotted</u> by the major leagues and drafted by the Pittsburgh Pirates.   _____

6. He became one of the most honored baseball players <u>of all time.</u>   _____

7. Finding success in major league baseball <u>could have been</u> his life's ambition.   _____

8. However, in addition to his success in sports, Roberto Clemente was also <u>a great humanitarian.</u>   _____

9. By 1971, he had decided to use part of his money <u>to build a "sports city"</u> for young people in his native Puerto Rico.   _____

10. Tragically, in 1972, on his way <u>to aid earthquake victims</u> in Nicaragua, Clemente was killed in a plane crash.   _____

EXERCISE 2   Identifying Phrases

Identify each of the underlined phrases in the following sentences.

1. In the morning, the rain became sleet. _____

2. Then snow began to fall steadily, covering the hills in a thick blanket. _____

3. Shouting and laughing together, the boys and girls ran to the barn. _____

4. The first job of the morning was to find the skis and other equipment. _____

5. Meanwhile, the parents worked over the stove in the farmhouse kitchen. _____

6. They were preparing a good breakfast for the young skiers. _____

7. Smells of bacon and pancake syrup mixed in the morning air. _____

8. The skiers chatted happily about their plans for the day. _____

9. Finding hats, gloves, and boots was the next major task. _____

10. Before long the children were racing out the door. _____

Understanding the uses of the present participle

The present participle causes a good deal of confusion for students working with the fragment. Because the participle can be used sometimes as a verb, sometimes as an adjective, and sometimes as a noun, you will want to be aware of which of these uses you intend.

EXERCISE 1   Using the Participle in a Verb Phrase

Below are five present participles. Use each of them as part of a verb phrase in a sentence. An example has been done for you.

Present participle: jumping

Verb phrase: was jumping

Sentence: The boy was jumping on the sofa.

1. singing _____

2. buying _____

3. climbing   _____

4. forgetting   _____

5. fixing   _____

EXERCISE 2   Using the Participle Phrase as an Adjective

Each of the underlined words below is a present participle. Use the word along with the phrase provided to compose sentences in which the phrase functions as an adjective. An example has been done for you.

Present participle: jumping

Participial phrase: jumping on the sofa

Participial phrase used as an adjective phrase in the sentence: Jumping on the sofa, the boy laughed with glee.

1. Singing in the shower

_____

_____

2. Buying the tickets

_____

_____

3. Climbing the steps

_____

_____

4. Forgetting the address

_____

_____

5. Fixing the window

_____

_____

EXERCISE 3 Using the Participle Phrase as a Noun (Gerund)

Each of the underlined words below is a present participle. Use the word along with the phrase provided as a noun phrase in a sentence. An example has been done for you.

Present participle:	jumping
Participial phrase:	jumping on the sofa
Participial phrase used as a noun phrase in a sentence:	Jumping on the sofa was fun.

1. Singing in the shower

   _____

   _____

2. Buying the tickets

   _____

   _____

3. Climbing the steps

   _____

   _____

4. Forgetting the address

   _____

   _____

5. Fixing the window

   _____

   _____

How do you make a complete sentence from a fragment that contains a participle?

Fragment: She wishing for winter to end.

1. Add a helping verb to the participle:

   She is wishing for winter to end.

2. Change the participle to a different form of the verb:

   She wishes for winter to end.

3. Use the participle as an adjective, being sure to provide a subject and verb for the sentence.

<u>Wishing for winter to end</u>, she read her gardening magazine.

4. Use the participle as a noun:

<u>Wishing for winter to end</u> is understandable.

EXERCISE 1   Correcting the Fragment That Contains a Participle

Make four complete sentences from each of the following fragments. Use the following example as your model.

Fragment: designing silver jewelry

a. He <u>is designing</u> silver jewelry.

b. He <u>designs</u> silver jewelry.

c. <u>Designing the silver jewelry</u>, he hummed and whistled all afternoon.

d. <u>Designing silver jewelry</u> is his greatest pleasure in life.

1. saving money for a computer

a. _____

b. _____

c. _____

d. _____

2. working out every morning

a. _____

b. _____

c. _____

d. _____

3. reading comic books

a. _____

b. _____

c. _____

d. _____

EXERCISE 2 Correcting the Fragment That Contains a Participle

Make four complete sentences from each of the following fragments. Use the following example as your model.

Fragment: working as a lifeguard

a. He is working as a lifeguard.

b. He works as a lifeguard.

c. Working as a lifeguard, he was able to save money for college.

d. Working as a lifeguard is an ideal summer job.

1. getting too much sun

a. _____

b. _____

c. _____

d. _____

2. working outside all day long

a. _____

b. _____

c. _____

d. _____

3. swimming every day

a. _____

b. _____

c. _____

d. _____

Now correct the fragments in the following exercises:

EXERCISE 1 Correcting Fragments

Rewrite each fragment so that it is a complete sentence.

1. the end of the day near my house

_____

2. light fading in the sky and streetlights coming on

_____

3. people home from work

_____

4. children on the streets, not willing to stop their play

_____

5. the smells of dinner coming through the open windows

_____

6. voices floating through the evening air

_____

7. no dogs or cats

_____

8. empty streets and doorways

_____

9. no voices heard in any house

_____

10. the final silence of sleep

_____

EXERCISE 2   Correcting Fragments

Each of the following groups of words is a phrase. First, name each phrase. Second, make each phrase into a complete sentence.

1. to create a work of art

   Name of phrase: _____

   Sentence: _____

2. to a different neighborhood

   Name of phrase: _____

   Sentence: _____

3. working hard

   Name of phrase: _____

   Sentence: _____

4. around the city

   Name of phrase: _____

   Sentence: _____

5. making plans

   Name of phrase: _____

   Sentence: _____

6. are now making

   Name of phrase: _____

   Sentence: _____

7. to remain seated

   Name of phrase: _____

   Sentence: _____

8. at the top of the pile

   Name of phrase: _____

   Sentence: _____

9. the Renoir oil painting

   Name of phrase: _____

   Sentence: _____

10. will be visiting

    Name of phrase: _____

    Sentence: _____

Mastery and editing tests

TEST 1   Recognizing and Correcting Fragments

The following description of people on a dance floor at the Peppermint Lounge appeared in the *New Yorker*. The description is made up entirely of fragments. Rewrite the description making each fragment into a sentence.

Place always jammed. Huge line outside. Portals closely guarded. Finally made it last night, after hour's wait. Exhilarating experience! Feel ten years younger. Hit Peppermint close to midnight, in blue mood. Inside, found pandemonium. Dance floor packed and popping. Was battered by wild swinging of hips and elbows. . . . Garb of twisters seems to run gamut. Some couples in evening dress, others in T shirts and blue jeans. Young. Old. Businessmen. Crew Cuts. Beatniks.

_____

_____

_____

_____

_____

_____

_____

_____

_____

_____

_____

TEST 2   Recognizing and Correcting Fragments

The following paragraph contains several fragments. Read the paragraph and underline each fragment. Then rewrite the paragraph, being careful to use only complete sentences.

Mrs. Taylor, the widow with whom I lived. On the edge of the campus. She was an example of old fashioned friendliness. A motherly woman with hair done up in a bun. Her husband had been the registrar at the college. She fixed up a cozy little room for me. At the top of the stairs. In the evenings after my classes, we sat in the living room. On the two rocking chairs. Chatting about the day's events. She always fixed me a snack in the afternoon. And again before bedtime. I have a wealth of enchanting memories. The smell of her cranberry nut bread. The smell of the fragrant coffee wafting up to my room every morning. The creaking porch swing. The sweet scent of lilacs in the spring.

_____

_____

_____

_____

_____

_____

_____

_____

_____

_____

_____

_____

_____

_____

_____

_____

TEST 3 Recognizing and Correcting Fragments

The following paragraph contains several fragments. Read the paragraph and underline each fragment. Then rewrite the paragraph, being careful to use only complete sentences.

Teddy Roosevelt was president at the turn of the century. Enjoyed the outdoors. And hunting. A 1902 trip to Mississippi and Louisiana for surveying and hunting. Each day passed. Didn't take a shot. On the last day, he finally saw a bear. Sitting in the forest eating honey. Raising his gun unable to shoot. He could not kill such a small sitting target. Newspapers picking up on the story. Reported in many national papers. In Brooklyn, New York, a candy store owner read about the hunt. His hobby of making children's toys, including stuffed animals. He decided to honor the president's little bear by making a toy bear. With buttons for eyes and a soft snout and mouth. He put the bear in his store window. The sign said, "Teddy Bear." The President loved it. Now a popular toy and a household name.

_____

_____

_____

_____

_____

_____

_____

_____

_____

_____

_____

_____

_____

_____

Combining Sentences Using the Three Methods of Coordination

1st Method: Use a comma plus a coordinating conjunction.

2nd Method: Use a semicolon, an adverbial conjunction, and a comma.

3rd Method: Use only a semicolon.

So far you have worked with the simple sentence. If you review some of these sentences (such as the practice sentences on page 00), you will see that writing only simple sentences results in a choppy style and also makes it difficult to express more complicated ideas. You will need to understand the possible ways of combining simple sentences. In this chapter, you will practice the skill of combining sentences using *coordination*.

What is coordination?

> *Coordination* is the combining of two simple sentences (which we will now refer to as *independent clauses*) that are related and contain ideas of equal importance. The result is a *compound sentence*.

Note: Don't be confused by the term *independent clause*. A *clause* is a group of words having a subject and a verb. An *independent clause* (IC) is a clause that could stand alone as a simple sentence. You may think of these terms in the following way:

simple sentence   = one independent clause

compound sentence = two independent clauses joined by coordination

First method: Use a comma plus a coordinating conjunction

> The most common way to form a compound sentence is to combine independent clauses using a comma plus a coordinating conjunction.

IC	, *coordinating conjunction*	IC
The budget was reduced	, and	several workers were let go.

Since there are only seven common coordinating conjunctions and three pairs of coordinating conjunctions, a little time invested in memorizing the list would be time well spent. By doing this now, you will avoid confusion later on when you must use a different set of conjunctions to combine clauses.

CONNECTORS: COORDINATING CONJUNCTIONS

and	*Used in Pairs*
but	either . . . or
or, nor	neither . . . nor
for (meaning *because*)	not only . . . but also
yet	
so	

PRACTICE

Each of the following compound sentences contains two independent clauses. Find the subject and verb in each clause and identify them by drawing a single line under the subject and a double line under the verb. Then draw a circle around the comma and coordinating conjunction that combines the two clauses. An example follows:

The actress walked to the front of the stage, and the audience became quiet.

1. The actress was nervous, for this was the night of her debut.

2. She had studied for years, and she had spent many summers on the road.

3. Now she had to win over her audience, or the critics would judge her harshly.

4. The other actors could not help her, nor could her old teacher advise her now.

5. The night was a success, but now she had to prove herself in new roles.

Did you find a subject and verb for both independent clauses in each sentence?

Now that you understand the structure of a compound sentence, you need to think about the meanings of the different coordinating conjunctions and how they can be used to show the relationship between two ideas, each idea being given equal importance.

MEANINGS OF COORDINATING CONJUNCTIONS

to add an idea:	and
to add an idea when the first clause is in the negative:	nor
to contrast two opposing ideas:	but, yet
to introduce a reason:	for
to show a choice:	or
to introduce a result:	so

EXERCISE 1   Combining Sentences Using Coordinating Conjunctions

Each of the following examples contains two simple sentences. These two sentences could be joined by a coordinating conjunction. First, decide the relationship between the two sentences. Then join the sentences by using the correct conjunction. An example follows:

Two simple sentences:

The two girls are sisters.
They share many childhood experiences.

Relationship of 2nd sentence to 1st: result
The conjunction that introduces this meaning: so
New compound sentence:

The two girls are sisters, so they share many childhood experiences.

1. Marcia is helpful to everyone.

   Her sister is cool and distant.

   _____

   _____

2. The retired couple worry.

   Their pension money may not be enough for them to live on.

   _____

   _____

3. The baby had cried all night.

   Everyone was tired the next day.

   _____

   _____

4. The recruit was eager to prove his abilities.

   He didn't volunteer to be the first one to jump.

   _____

   _____

5. Devon decided to help out in the cafeteria at lunch.

   She would make some money and meet a lot of the students.

   _____

   _____

6. Work was going well.

   Her social life was improving.

   _____

   _____

7. Being popular is important to many adolescents.

   Wearing the right clothes becomes a priority.

   _____

   _____

8. The dictionary entry was helpful.

   I still wasn't sure how to use the word correctly.

   _____

   _____

9. I couldn't take the train.

   I couldn't take the bus.

   _____

   _____

10. The original idea was good.

    Not everyone agreed.

    _____

    _____

EXERCISE 2   Combining Sentences Using Coordinating Conjunctions

For each example, add a second independent clause using the given coordinating conjunction. Be certain that your new sentence makes sense.

1. (and) Bowling is my favorite recreation _____

_____

2. (but) I have played at the Maple Avenue Lanes _____

_____

3. (or) Either I bowl on Friday nights _____

_____

4. (but) I would like to play in a championship tournament _____

_____

5. (and) Last Friday, we had a blizzard _____

_____

6. (so) We could not find anyone to do the driving _____

_____

7. (but also) Not only was the snow too deep _____

_____

8. (nor) We didn't go bowling _____

_____

9. (yet) I missed the night out _____

_____

10. (so) We are hoping for good weather next week _____

_____

EXERCISE 3   Composing Compound Sentences

Compose ten of your own compound sentences using the coordinating conjunctions indicated.

1. and _____

_____

2. but _____

_____

3. or _____

_____

4. for (meaning *because*) _____

_____

5. yet _____

_____

6. so _____

_____

7. nor _____

_____

8. neither/nor _____

_____

9. not only/but also _____

_____

10. either/or _____

_____

Second method: Use a semicolon, an adverbial conjunction, and a comma

A second way to form a compound sentence is to combine independent clauses by using a semicolon, an adverbial conjunction, and a comma.

IC	; *adverbial conjunction,*	IC
The budget was reduced	; therefore,	several workers were let go.

Another set of conjunctions are called **adverbial conjunctions** (or conjunctive adverbs). These conjunctions have meanings similar to the common coordinating conjunctions, but they sound slightly more formal than the shorter conjunctions such as *and* or *but*. These connecting words give a compound sentence more emphasis.

CONNECTORS: FREQUENTLY USED ADVERBIAL CONJUNCTIONS		
Addition (and)	**Alternative (or)**	**Result (so)**
In addition	instead	accordingly
also	otherwise	consequently
besides		hence
furthermore		therefore
likewise		thus
moreover		
Contrast (but)	**Emphasis**	**To Show Time**
however	indeed	meanwhile
nevertheless	in fact	
nonetheless		

PRACTICE

Each of the following compound sentences contains two independent clauses. Identify the subject and verb in each clause and draw a single line under the subject and a double line under the verb. Then draw a circle around the semicolon, adverbial conjunction and comma where they connect the two clauses. An example follows:

The hallway was newly painted; likewise, the lobby looked fresh and clean.

1. Plants had been placed on tables and counters; in addition, the windows had all been washed.

2. Comfortable new furniture had been purchased; consequently, the lobby was much more inviting.

3. The tenants were pleased; indeed, everyone felt a lift in spirits.

4. We asked the security guards about the changes; however, they did not seem to have much information.

5. My mother and I had been thinking of moving; instead, we now decided to stay.

EXERCISE 1   Combining Sentences Using Adverbial Conjunctions

Each pair of sentences below could be combined into a compound sentence. Join each pair by using a semicolon, an adverbial conjunction, and a comma. Be sure the conjunction you choose makes sense in the sentence. An example follows:

Two simple sentences: People laugh with ease.
They find it hard to laugh on command.

Compound sentence: People laugh with ease; however, they find it hard to laugh on command.

1. Most people laugh without thinking about it.

   Some scientists are studying laughter very seriously.

   _____

   _____

2. Research has tried to observe what makes people laugh.

   It has almost become a separate branch of science.

   _____

   _____

3. We do laugh at clever jokes.

   Most of what we laugh at is simply part of everyday social conversation.

   _____

   _____

4. Laughter is one way of communicating with others.

   It is one way for us to express the state of our mood.

   _____

   _____

5. Only rare individuals can laugh on command.

   They usually have some acting experience.

   _____

   _____

6. Social scientists are looking at laughter in other cultures.

   Language experts are trying to establish common patterns for people's laughter.

   _____

   _____

7. Laughter tends to be catching.

   A child's giggle is likely to make other children laugh too.

   _____

   _____

8. Many people laugh at very ordinary things.

   A great many people often laugh at their own statements.

   _____

   _____

9. Laughter works as a mood regulator for groups of people.

   Individuals also laugh by themselves.

   _____

   _____

10. We enjoy laughing at people in positions of authority.

    Be careful not to laugh at your supervisor or manager.

    _____

    _____

EXERCISE 2 Combining Sentences Using Adverbial Conjunctions

For each example, add the suggested adverbial conjunction and another independent clause that will make sense. Remember to punctuate correctly.

1. (instead) A growing number of people do not sit down to eat the traditional three meals a day.

   _____

   _____

2. (nevertheless) Liquid meals do not appeal to most people.

   _____

   _____

3. (however) Liquid breakfasts and dinners were first developed as supplements for the elderly or the sick.

   _____

   _____

4. (in fact) Many well known brands claim to have all the nutrients necessary for a good diet.

   _____

   _____

5. (consequently) Many liquid meals contain mostly water, oil, and sugar.

_____

_____

6. (therefore) Several brands of these supplements are high in fat.

_____

_____

7. (likewise) People over fifty often begin to think about supplements to keep themselves healthy.

_____

_____

8. (thus) Advertisements show professional athletes using these supplemental products.

_____

_____

9. (however) Advertisements suggest liquid supplements are better than anything else you could eat.

_____

_____

10. (furthermore) Why not eat apples or bananas?

_____

_____

Third method: Use a semicolon

The third and less commonly used way to form a compound sentence is to combine two independent clauses by using only a semicolon.

IC	;	IC
The budget was reduced	;	several workers were let go.

Two independent clauses: I saw *Master Class* at the theater last weekend. The play starred Zoe Caldwell.

Compound sentence: I saw *Master Class* at the theater last weekend; the play starred Zoe Caldwell.

The semicolon was used in this example to show that the content of both sentences is closely related and therefore could be combined in one sentence.

When sentences are combined using a semicolon, the grammatical structure of each sentence is often similar:

> Zoe Caldwell played the part of Maria Callas; Audra McDonald played the part of a young student singer.

EXERCISE 1 Combining Sentences Using a Semicolon

For each of the independent clauses below, add your own independent clause that has a similar grammatical structure or is a closely related idea.

1. The term paper was nearly finished.

   _____

   _____

2. The topics on some television talk shows have become unacceptable.

   _____

   _____

3. The driving test was scheduled for Tuesday afternoon.

   _____

   _____

4. The milk had gone sour.

   _____

   _____

5. Her mother was encouraging.

   _____

   _____

EXERCISE 2 Combining Sentences Using a Semicolon

For each of the independent clauses below, add your own independent clause that has a similar grammatical structure or is a closely related idea.

1. The movers arrived early.

   _____

   _____

2. The beach was crowded.

   _____

   _____

3. The room suddenly fell silent.

_____

_____

4. The book was missing from the shelves.

_____

_____

5. The dancers waited backstage.

_____

_____

Mastery and editing tests

TEST 1   Combining Sentences Using Coordination

Each pair of sentences below could be combined into a compound sentence. Join each pair by using a coordinating conjunction or an adverbial conjunction that will make sense for the intended meaning of the new sentence. Be sure your punctuation is correct.

1. Everyday memory blocks are embarrassing.

   They can be easily overcome.

_____

_____

2. People often forget someone's name.

   People can forget their own anniversaries.

_____

_____

3. No one can remember everything.

   No one can rely on others to constantly remind them.

_____

_____

4. Boosting your memory can stop your memory lapses.

   Your life will become more problem free.

_____

_____

5. Visualize an item in an exaggerated form before putting it down.

   This forces your mind to pay attention to the location of the item.

   _____

   _____

6. Post a calendar with important dates.

   You can see it there every day.

   _____

   _____

7. You can blank out on a person's name.

   You can associate a name with an object (like Michelle the sea shell).

   _____

   _____

8. Women tend to remember what they hear.

   Men are better at remembering things they see.

   _____

   _____

9. Visualize something unusual about an object like your keys.

   This image will force your mind to remember their location.

   _____

   _____

10. Forgetting things is frustrating.

    You can improve your memory.

    _____

    _____

TEST 2   Combining Sentences Using Coordination

The following paragraph contains opportunities to combine some of the ideas using coordination. Rewrite the paragraph, creating several compound sentences. Choose conjunctions that show the correct relationship between the two clauses of these new compound sentences. Use either coordinate or adverbial conjunctions. Be sure to punctuate the newly formed compound sentences correctly.

We can thank a man by the name of John Muir. He was instrumental in establishing Yosemite as a National Park. John Muir was raised and educated in Wisconsin. He moved to California in 1868. He had only planned to stay a few months. He was heading to South America to study botany. He desperately needed money. He took a job as a shepherd's assistant.

That brought him to Yosemite Valley. This move changed his life. He was so overwhelmed by the scenery and natural splendor. He stayed. He spent much of his time hiking, walking, and mountaineering. He yearned to encourage others to visit and experience the area. He created the Sierra Club. To this day, the Sierra Club is an active organization. It has thousands of members across the country. The Sierra Club is a leading voice in the conservation and preservation of this country's natural resources. The Club has a legal branch. It serves as counsel on environmental issues. The Sierra Club sponsors legislation. It lobbies for environmental laws. The Club is most known for its lectures and outings. It sponsors trips to such diverse places as the Galapagos Islands and Alaska. The Sierra Club has accomplished much in its one hundred years of existence. Most of its accomplishments can be attributed to the singular vision of its founder, John Muir.

TEST 3   Combining Sentences Using Coordination

The following paragraph contains opportunities to combine some of the ideas using coordination. Rewrite the paragraph, creating several compound sentences. Choose conjunctions that show the correct relationship between the two clauses of these new compound sentences. Use either coordinate or adverbial conjunctions. Be sure to punctuate the newly formed compound sentences correctly.

Patricia McDaniel is an antiques dealer. She has a very modern business. She supplies props for movies. Her name is never seen on the credits. She owns Old Storefront Antiques in Dublin, Indiana. She doesn't do enough business from local customers. She doesn't have many tourists coming through. This is one antique shop that depends on mail order business. Ms. McDaniel wanted to make some money on items in her shop. She could have read books and magazines about marketing. She had her own ideas. She sent out lists of her items to film companies. She would provide large numbers of old props. She would send them quickly. This made her successful. Her business became renting antique items to movie producers. These producers need props for different scenes in their films. Ms. McDaniel receives mail orders regularly from Hollywood. Her specialty is drug store items and grocery store items. Movie producers know and depend on her enormous stock and good service. She can often supply items that cannot be found anywhere else. Once she shipped out five hundred dollars worth of old Jello boxes. Once she rented out a hornet's nest.

_____

_____

_____

_____

_____

_____

_____

_____

_____

_____

_____

_____

_____

_____

Combining Sentences Using Subordination

Recognizing independent and dependent clauses

Using subordinating conjunctions

Using relative pronouns

In Chapter 14, when you used coordination, the idea in each clause in the compound sentence carried equal weight. However, a writer often wants to combine ideas that are not equally important. This chapter will focus on **subordination.** Here you will combine clauses that are not equally important. One idea will be dependent on the other.

What is subordination?

> *Subordination* is the combining of two clauses containing ideas that are not equally important. The more important idea is called the ***independent clause*** and the less important idea is called the ***dependent clause.*** The result is a ***complex sentence.***

In coordination, you used certain connecting words called coordinating conjunctions or adverbial conjunctions to combine ideas. In subordination, you use two different sets of connecting words: subordinating conjunctions or relative pronouns.

What is the difference between an independent and dependent clause?

An independent clause stands alone as a complete thought; it could be a simple sentence.

> *Independent clause:* She washed the car.

A dependent clause begins with a connecting word, and although the thought has a subject and a verb, it does not stand alone as a complete thought. The idea needs to be completed.

> *Dependent clause:* When she washed the car, ...

Before you write your own complex sentences, practice the following exercises being sure you understand the difference between an independent clause and a dependent clause.

EXERCISE 1   Recognizing Dependent and Independent Clauses

In the blank to the side of each group of words, write the letters IC if the group is an independent clause (a complete thought) or DC if the group of words is a dependent clause (not a complete thought, even though it contains a subject and a verb).

_____ 1. the train was seriously delayed
_____ 2. we stood under the awning
_____ 3. since it takes two days to get there
_____ 4. I chose the wrong day to travel
_____ 5. until I sat down and talked to them
_____ 6. even though you made a reservation
_____ 7. as the telephone rang in the office
_____ 8. the beauty of the countryside will refresh you
_____ 9. whenever the track is cleared of the debris
_____ 10. while the tickets are being prepared

EXERCISE 2   Recognizing Dependent and Independent Clauses

In the blank to the side of each group of words, write the letters IC if the group is an independent clause (a complete thought) or DC if the group of words is a dependent clause (not a complete thought, even though it contains a subject and a verb).

_____ 1. after the summer months had passed
_____ 2. when the reference librarian is available
_____ 3. unless you want to read all the articles
_____ 4. unfortunately the computer is down again
_____ 5. sometimes the room gets very cold
_____ 6. if Beverly returns
_____ 7. although he explained the procedure
_____ 8. in spite of the warning on the copy machine
_____ 9. everyone lost their money in the machine
_____ 10. tonight the library will close early

Using Subordinating Conjunctions

Study the list of subordinating conjunctions in the chart that follows. The use of one of these connecting words signals the beginning of a dependent clause. It is a good idea to memorize them just as you did the coordinating conjunctions and adverbial conjunctions in Chapter 14. Since each group has a different principle for punctuation, you need to memorize the words in these groups.

CONNECTORS: COMMON SUBORDINATING CONJUNCTIONS		
after	if, even if	unless
although	in order that	until
as, as if	provided that	when, whenever
as long as, as though	rather than	where, wherever
because	since	whether
before	so that	while
even though	though	

The next chart contains the subordinating conjunctions grouped according to their meanings. When you use these conjunctions, you need to be absolutely sure that the connection one of these conjunctions makes between the independent and dependent clause is the meaning you intend.

FUNCTION OF SUBORDINATING CONJUNCTIONS

To introduce a *condition:*   if, even if, as long as, provided that, unless (after a negative independent clause)

I will go *as long as* you go with me.

I won't go *unless* you go with me.

To introduce a *contrast:*   although, even though, though

I will go *even though* you won't go with me.

To introduce a *cause:*   because, since

I will go *because* the meeting is very important.

To show *time:*   after, before, when, whenever, while, until (independent clause is negative)

I will go *whenever* you say.

I won't go *until* you say it is time.

To show *place:*   where, wherever

I will go *wherever* you send me.

To show *purpose:*   in order that, so that

I will go *so that* I can hear the candidate for myself.

You have two choices of how to write a complex sentence. You can begin with the independent clause, or you can begin with the dependent clause.

First way:	*IC*	*DC*
Example:	The child cannot sleep	if the television is too loud.

Second way:	*DC*	,	*I*
Example:	If the television is too loud	,	the child cannot sleep.

Notice that only the second version uses a comma; this is because the second version begins with the dependent clause. When a sentence begins with the independent clause, no comma is used. Your ear may help you with this punctuation. Read a sentence that begins with a dependent clause. Do you notice that there is a tendency to pause at the end of that dependent clause? This is a natural place to put a comma.

PRACTICE

Use a subordinating conjunction to combine each of the following pairs of sentences. Remember, the independent clause will contain the more important idea in the sentence.

1. Use the subordinating conjunction *after*.

   Maria went to the party.

   She finished her work.

   a. Begin with the independent clause:

   _____

   b. Begin with the dependent clause:

   _____

2. Use the subordinating conjunction *when:*

   The dog scratched at the door.

   He wanted to go out.

   a. Begin with the independent clause:

   _____

   b. Begin with the dependent clause:

   _____

EXERCISE 1   Using Subordinating Conjunctions

Use each of the following subordinating conjunctions to compose a complex sentence. An example has been done for you.

Subordinating conjunction: after

Complex sentence: After the storm was over, the family walked to town.

Remember that a complex sentence has one independent clause and at least one dependent clause. Every clause must have a subject and a verb. Check your sentences by underlining the subject and verb in each clause.

Can you explain why the following sentence is not a complex sentence?

After the storm, the family walked to town.

After the storm is a prepositional phrase. *After,* in this case, is a preposition. It is not used as a subordinating conjunction to combine clauses.

1. as if

_____

_____

2. before

_____

_____

3. until

_____

_____

4. although

_____

_____

5. because (Begin with the independent clause. Traditional English grammar frowns on beginning a sentence with *because*. Ask your instructor for his or her opinion.)

_____

_____

EXERCISE 2 Combining Sentences Using Subordination

Combine each pair of sentences using subordination. Look back at the list of subordinating conjunctions if you need to. An example follows:

Two sentences: Come with me to the lecture series.
You will meet and hear Arthur Miller.

Combined by subordination: If you come with me to the lecture series,
you will meet and hear Arthur Miller.

1. They were sitting in class.

   News of the war was shouted from the hallways.

   _____

   _____

2. The mayor supported the judge.

   The people wanted the judge removed.

   _____

   _____

3. I will meet Joy Harjo tonight.

   She is reading her poetry at the college.

   _____

   _____

4. The teacher wanted to retire.

   He had three children to put through college.

   _____

   _____

5. The teacher wanted to teach the new summer module.

   He contacted his department chairperson.

   _____

   _____

Using a relative pronoun to create a complex sentence

Often sentences can be combined with a relative pronoun.

COMMON RELATIVE PRONOUNS	
who	
whose	refers to people
whom	
which	refers to things
that	refers to people and/or things

Combining sentences with a relative pronoun

Two simple sentences: The artist paints unusually fine portraits.
The artist sits beside me in sculpture class.

These sentences could sound short and choppy. To avoid this choppiness, a writer might want to join these two related ideas with a relative pronoun.

Incorrectly combined: The artist paints unusually fine portraits *who* sits beside me in sculpture class.

The relative pronoun *who* and its clause *who sits beside me in sculpture class* refers to *artist*. The clause must be placed directly after the word artist.

Correctly combined: The artist *who* sits beside me in sculpture class paints unusually fine portraits.

> Remember that the relative pronoun and its clause must immediately follow the word it relates to.

Now we could join a third idea:

Third idea: She plans to exhibit her portraits in the Coconut Grove Arts Festival in February.

Combining sentences using two relative pronouns:

The artist *who* sits beside me in sculpture class paints unusually fine portraits, *which* she plans to exhibit in the Coconut Grove Arts Festival in February.

PRACTICE 1

Combine the pairs of sentences into complex sentences by using relative pronouns. Use the relative pronoun *that*. These sentences will not require the use of commas. An example follows:

> **First sentence:**   The island is Hispaniola.
>
> **Second sentence:**   It lies east of Cuba.
>
> **Combined sentence:** The island that lies east of Cuba is Hispaniola.

1. The island is Hispaniola.

   The island is shared by Haiti and the Dominican Republic.

   Combined: _____

   _____

2. Trade winds blow to Haiti from the northeast.

   They bring rains to the island.

   Combined: _____

   _____

3. Haiti is largely protected from storms by high mountains.

   The mountains cover two thirds of the country.

   Combined: _____

   _____

How do you punctuate a clause with a relative pronoun?

Punctuating relative clauses can be tricky because there are two types of relative clauses:

1. Those clauses that are basic to the meaning of the sentence:

   > Try to buy paper *that has been recycled.*

   The basic meaning of the sentence is not *Try to buy paper* but *Try to buy paper that has been recycled.* The relative clause is necessary to restrict the meaning. This clause is called a **restrictive clause** and does not use commas to set off the clause. *Note:* The pronoun *that* is ordinarily used in these kinds of clauses.

2. Those clauses that are not basic to the meaning of the sentence:

   > The bakery's front window, *which was filled with fancy cakes,* was badly cracked.

   In this sentence, the relative clause *which was filled with fancy cakes* is not basic to the main idea. In fact, if the clause were omitted, the main idea would still be clear. This clause is called a **nonrestrictive clause.** Commas are required to indicate the information is nonessential to the main idea. *Note:* The pronoun *which* is ordinarily used in these kinds of clauses.

• PRACTICE 2

Choose whether or not to insert commas in the following sentences. Use the following examples as your models.

> The student *who is standing in the doorway* is my friend.

The student can only be identified by the fact that she is the one standing in the doorway. Therefore, the relative clause *who is standing in the doorway* is essential to the meaning. No commas are necessary.

> Jasmine, *who works as a DJ to earn money for college,* is my friend.

The main idea is that Jasmine is the friend. The fact that she works as a DJ is not essential to that main idea. Therefore, commas are needed to set off this nonessential information.

Insert commas as needed in each of the following sentences.

1. Colleges that take academic work very seriously have very strict policies about term papers and exams.

2. Princeton University which is one of our most traditional schools has a well known policy.

3. Every student at Princeton must write an essay that discusses the Princeton code.

4. Princeton students who may come from many different backgrounds have two responsibilities under the code.

5. All students who want to stay at Princeton must be honest in their own work and be willing to turn in fellow students who cheat.

Now you are ready to practice joining your own sentences with relative pronouns, being sure to punctuate whenever necessary. The following exercises ask you to insert a variety of relative clauses into simple sentences.

EXERCISE 1   Combining Sentences Using Relative Pronouns

Add a relative clause to each of the following ten sentences. Use each of the possibilities at least once: *who, whose, whom, which, that.* An example follows:

Simple sentence: The presidential election is one month away.

Complex sentence: The presidential election, which is still too close to call, is one month away.

1. The presidential candidates _____
   met in the television studio.

2. The leading candidate _____
smiled and greeted the others.

3. The broadcast _____
was to be seen throughout the country.

4. The moderator _____
had been chosen for her fairness.

5. The studio audience _____
filled the small space set aside for the evening.

6. Every campaign issue _____
was permitted for discussion.

7. Each candidate _____
shook hands with the others.

8. The debating rules _____
were explained once again.

9. All the people in the audience _____
gradually became quiet.

10. The debate _____
would be helpful to voters.

EXERCISE 2   Combining Sentences Using Relative Pronouns

Add a relative clause to each of the following ten sentences. Use each of the possibilities at least once: *who, whose, whom, which, that.* Be sure to use the correct punctuation. An example follows:

Simple sentence: The trip to Quito takes six hours.

Complex sentence: The trip to Quito, which is scheduled for August 16, will take six hours.

1. The young man _____
wanted to learn Spanish.

2. During his sophomore year _____
he began to plan for a semester abroad.

3. The problem _____
was finding the right program.

4. The International Studies Department _____
had an entire bulletin board devoted to study abroad.

5. He brought home four brochures _____

6. His Spanish teacher _____
was very encouraging.

7. His parents _____
were concerned about his financial arrangements as well as his health.

8. He finally selected Ecuador _____

9. In Ecuador he will live with a family _____

10. Quito _____
has some of the most outstanding examples of eighteenth-century architecture in the Americas.

Mastery and editing tests

TEST 1   Combining Sentences Using Coordination and Subordination

Below is a paragraph composed of mostly simple sentences. Rewrite the paragraph combining sentences wherever you think the combining would improve the meaning or style. Don't be afraid to change the wording slightly to accommodate the changes you want to make. Combine clauses using coordination or subordination.

Every decade seems to have its own sports fad. The fad of the 80s was snowboarding. The fad of the 90s is in-line skating. In-line skates are a cross between ice skates and roller skates. The wheels are in a single row down the middle of the skate. They usually have only one brake . The brake is on the heel of the right foot. This skate was developed to help hockey players practice off the ice. This practice has blossomed into a multi-million dollar industry, sport, and pastime. Look around you. You can probably see in-line skaters. There are stunt teams, racing teams, and skating clubs. "Blading" is its commonly known name. It is a popular form of recreation and exercise. You should be careful when attempting in-line skating. You must wear the proper protection. Protective pads should be worn over the elbows, wrists, and knees in order to cover all joints. The head is particularly vulnerable. A helmet should be worn at all times. You can achieve speeds of 5 to 25 miles per hour or more. Be prepared. You can have a lot of fun using in-line skates.

_____

_____

_____

_____

_____

_____

_____

_____

_____

_____

_____

_____

_____

_____

_____

_____

_____

_____

_____

_____

_____

_____

_____

TEST 2   Combining Sentences Using Coordination and Subordination

Below is a paragraph composed of mostly simple sentences. Rewrite the paragraph combining sentences wherever you think the combining would improve the meaning or style. Don't be afraid to change the wording slightly to accommodate the changes you want to make. Combine clauses using coordination or subordination.

In the fall of 1995, the people of Quebec, the Canadian province, voted. Should Quebec remain a part of Canada? The final count was taken. The vote was against secession. This separatist movement in Canada has been an ongoing battle. The people lost a 1980 independence referendum in 1980. The vote was 60-40 ratio against sucession. Quebec is a French-speaking province. Eighty percent of the people speak French. The vote was equally divided amongst the French-speaking population. The majority of English-speaking people of Quebec voted to remain a part of Canada. This is a difficult and emotionally charged issue. This vote will be sure to leave scars. The vote could have gone the other way. Then a significant number of Canadians would have been upset. Quebec represents one-fourth of Canada's population and one-sixth of its land. Losing Quebec would have devastated Canada's economy and identity. The separatist movement is bound to keep trying. This issue will resurface. Only time will tell. Will Quebec work out its problems with Canada? Will Quebec, in fact, become its own independent country?

_____

_____

_____

_____

_____
_____
_____
_____
_____
_____
_____
_____
_____
_____
_____
_____
_____
_____
_____
_____
_____
_____
_____
_____

TEST 3   Combining Sentences Using Coordination and Subordination

Below is a paragraph composed of mostly simple sentences. Rewrite the paragraph combining sentences wherever you think the combining would improve the meaning or style. Don't be afraid to change the wording slightly to accommodate the changes you want to make. Combine clauses using coordination and subordination.

Mary Anderson was the first great superstar in our theatrical history. She was born in Sacramento, California, in 1859. Her father was an officer in the Confederate Army. He was killed in Mobile, Alabama, early in the Civil War. Her mother struggled alone to raise her two young children. In Louisville, Kentucky, she met another Confederate officer. Dr. Griffin became her second husband. Young Mary was always very interested in acting. In 1875 she had the opportunity to play Juliet in Louisville. She was successful. Her talent was noticed. She made several tours throughout the country. Her debut in New York established her as an important Shakespearean actress. Her next challenge was to be accepted in London. She carefully prepared her role for English audiences. They were as enthusiastic as her New York audiences. Mary Anderson turned twenty-nine. Mary Anderson left acting forever. She married

Antonio de Navarro. She moved to a small town in England. It had the appropriate name of Broadway. She had a long retirement. It was for fifty years. She died in Broadway in 1940. She is not remembered by most people today. In her time, she was the most famous actress the United States had produced. For many people, she was a symbol of the healing between the North and the South in the period after the Civil War.

_____

_____

_____

_____

_____

_____

_____

_____

_____

_____

_____

_____

_____

_____

_____

_____

_____

_____

_____

_____

_____

_____

_____

THE SENTENCE

Chapter 16

Correcting the Run-On

In conversation, when we tell about an event involving a series of connected actions, we may string them together as if they were part of one long thought. However, this does not mean that we should write one long sentence; that would result in run-ons. When you put your spoken narrative into written form, there are many accepted ways to separate or combine the different parts into acceptable sentences. Turning ideas into sentences calls for a careful understanding of individual clauses and how we punctuate those clauses when we combine them. This chapter is about learning how to recognize and avoid run-on sentences in your own writing.

Below is a spoken narrative that became a single run-on sentence when the writer first put it into written form. Read the paragraph. Where are the places that need punctuation or some other change?

> Caitlin wanted to make a good impression on her first day of work but everything went wrong her alarm clock didn't go off and she had no time for breakfast or a shower so she hurriedly put on her work clothes and jumped into her old station wagon but the engine wouldn't start so she ran to her neighbor's house to ask for a ride but no one answered the door so Caitlin had to work on her car and the problem turned out to be a burnt fuse but luckily she had a replacement in her glove compartment but by now she only had fifteen minutes to get to work and she arrived a few minutes late and her manner was still frantic and she was preoccupied all day with the fact that she looked like she had just rolled out of bed.

What is a run-on?

Run-on sentences are independent clauses that have been combined incorrectly.

How many kinds of run-ons are there?

Run-on sentences occur when the writer is either unable to recognize where one complete idea has ended and another idea begins or is not sure of the standard ways of connecting the ideas. Certain punctuation signals where two clauses join. Other punctuation signifies the end of the thought. One of three mistakes are commonly made:

1. *The fused run-on:* Two or more independent clauses are run together without any punctuation.

   incorrect: She woke up late she made it to work on time.

2. *The comma splice:* Two or more independent clauses are run together with only a comma.

   incorrect: She woke up late, she made it to work on time.

3. *The "and" run-on:* Two or more independent clauses are connected with a co-ordinating conjunction, but there is no punctuation.

   incorrect: She woke up late but she made it to work on time.

How do you make a complete sentence from a run-on?

GUIDE FOR CORRECTING RUN-ONS

1. Make two sentences with end punctuation.

   correct: She woke up late. She made it to work on time.

2. Make a compound sentence using one of the three methods of coordination.

   correct: She woke up late, but she made it to work on time.
   She woke up late; however, she made it to work on time.
   She woke up late; she made it to work on time.

3. Make a complex sentence using subordination.

   correct: Although she woke up late, she made it to work on time.
   She made it to work on time although she woke up late.

EXERCISE 1   Revising Run-Ons

Each of the following examples is a run-on. Using the Guide for Correcting Run-ons, provide four possible ways to revise each run-on. An example is given.

Run-on:

Noel Coward's hideaway cottage on Jamaica is modest it is my favorite house on the island.

Two simple sentences:

Noel Coward's hideaway cottage on Jamaica is modest. It is my favorite house on the island.

Two kinds of compound sentences:

a. Noel Coward's hideaway cottage on Jamaica is modest, but it is my favorite house on the island.

b. Noel Coward's hideaway cottage on Jamaica is modest; however, it is my favorite house on the island.

Complex sentence:

Although Noel Coward's hideaway cottage on Jamaica is modest, it is my favorite house on the island.

1. Noel Coward, the great lyricist and playwright, died of a heart attack in his Jamaican cottage in 1973 his cottage was restored to look as it once did.

   Two simple sentences:

   _____

   _____

   _____

   Two kinds of compound sentences:

   a. _____

   _____

   b. _____

   _____

   Complex sentence:

   _____

   _____

2. The Queen came to lunch Noel Coward prepared a fine lobster mousse.

   Two simple sentences:

   _____

   _____

   _____

   Two kinds of compound sentences:

   a. _____

   _____

   b. _____

   _____

   Complex sentence:

   _____

   _____

3. The lobster mousse flopped he had to serve the Queen canned food.

Two simple sentences:

_____

_____

_____

Two kinds of compound sentences:

a. _____

_____

b. _____

_____

Complex sentence:

_____

_____

EXERCISE 2   Revising Run-Ons

Each of the following examples is a run-on. Using the guide on page 216, provide four possible ways to revise each run-on.

1. Jim wanted to travel he got a job working on a train in Alaska.

Two simple sentences:

_____

_____

_____

Two kinds of compound sentences:

a. _____

_____

b. _____

_____

Complex sentence:

_____

_____

2. He worked for minimum wage he saw some great sights.

   Two simple sentences:

   _____

   _____

   _____

   Two kinds of compound sentences:

   a. _____

   _____

   b. _____

   _____

   Complex sentence:

   _____

   _____

3. Jim fell in love with the state he might decide to stay.

   Two simple sentences:

   _____

   _____

   _____

   Two kinds of compound sentences:

   a. _____

   _____

   b. _____

   _____

   Complex sentence:

   _____

   _____

EXERCISE 1 Recognizing and Correcting Run-Ons

The following account was written as one sentence. Rewrite the account making sure to correct the run-on sentences. Put a period at the end of each complete thought. You may have to omit some of the words that loosely connect the ideas, or you may want to use coordination and subordination. Remember to make each new sentence begin with a capital letter.

Caitlin wanted to make a good impression on her first day of work but everything went wrong her alarm clock didn't go off and she had no time for breakfast or a shower so she hurriedly put on her work clothes and jumped into her old station wagon but the engine wouldn't start so she ran to her neighbor's house to ask for a ride but no one answered the door so Caitlin had to work on her car and the problem turned out to be a burnt fuse but luckily she had a replacement in her glove compartment but by now she only had fifteen minutes to get to work and she arrived a few minutes late and her manner was still frantic and she was preoccupied all day with the fact that she looked like she had just rolled out of bed.

_____

_____

_____

_____

_____

_____

_____

_____

_____

_____

_____

_____

_____

_____

_____

_____

EXERCISE 2 Recognizing and Correcting Run-Ons

The following account was written as one sentence. Rewrite the account making sure to correct the run-on sentences. Put a period at the end of each complete thought. You may have to omit some of the words that loosely connect the ideas, or you may want to use coordination and subordination. Remember to make each new sentence begin with a capital letter.

Mary Harris Jones came to America in 1841 from Ireland and she became an expert seamstress, she married George Jones and he was in the labor unions but during an epidemic of yellow fever and cholera George and their four children died so Mary then moved to Chicago and worked as a seamstress for wealthy families and during this time she saw the disparity between the comfort of the rich and the wretched conditions of the poor and she worked for more than fifty years organizing labor unions and she tried to get better pay for miners and textile workers and she was especially concerned about the plight of children in the factories so in 1903 Mother Jones led a group of children from a cotton mill in Alabama on a march through Philadelphia that eventually led to legal actions outlawing child labor so Mother Jones is celebrated today as a labor organizer, she devoted her life to the safety and quality of the lives of factory workers.

_____

_____

_____

_____

_____

_____

_____

_____

_____

_____

_____

_____

_____

_____

_____

_____

_____

_____

_____

Mastery and editing tests

TEST 1   Editing for Run-Ons

The following paragraph was written as a single run-on sentence. Rewrite the paragraph making all necessary changes.

Taxi drivers are very much like football players they have that aggressive determination of the player who is going to make a first down even if it means getting his shoulders dislocated and his jaw broken so as you jump into a cab you shout your destination above the noise of the radio and the blare of beeping horns and you are off, and as the driver barrels through crowded streets you crouch in the back seat looking nervously out the window or closing your eyes tightly hoping for the best, and the driver weaves from one lane to another while cutting in front of delivery vans or buses to gain some imagined small advantage and he swerves around startled pedestrians as he turns the corners while you are thrown onto the other side of the back seat you do not have enough courage to strike up any conversation but you should busy yourself with the calculation of the steadily climbing fare, this will divert your attention to an equally sobering situation, will you have enough money to pay for the sizable tip the cab driver will expect for risking the lives of countless people in order to get you to the dentist on time?

TEST 2   Editing for Run-Ons

Edit the following paragraph, correcting all run-on sentences.

When archaeologists began to dig in Egypt in the 19th century, they were looking for royal tombs filled with gold and other treasures so many of the other items that survived the centuries were ignored by them but as the years went by and the diggers realized there were items more valuable than gold, they had new respect for even the most humble pieces from the ancient world so when workers brought up lamps and common bowls and other everyday objects, they were studied with a new respect and people could look at a dish and realize that people of another time were able to bring beauty into daily life. These pieces are like time capsules because they are able to take us back to another culture and we can examine first-hand the reality of that culture. We are also able to judge our own lives and what we produce in our own culture when we put the past next to the present but on occasion just an accident will reveal a part of the past that we never realized was there. Over a hundred years ago, a British team was digging in Egypt but there had not been much success in finding royal tombs and the only items the workers had been able to uncover were a lot of crocodile mummies left there by the ancient Egyptians so when one worker had dug up yet another crocodile mummy, he was so angry that he took a mummified crocodile and smashed it against a rock. When the mummy broke, it was seen that it had been wrapped in papyrus, the paper that was used throughout the ancient world. Scientists had never realized that many important literary works had been preserved in mummies thousands of years old and this led to a whole new area of scientific study.

TEST 3   Editing for Run-Ons

Edit the following paragraph, correcting all run-on sentences.

One of our most popular snacks is Cracker Jack, a special combination of peanuts, molasses, and popcorn and it has been a favorite in the United States since 1882. From the time it was introduced in Chicago, this snack grew steadily in popularity but it was in 1893 at the Chicago World's Fair that it really became well known and was offered to over 21 million people who came to the Fair. After the Chicago Fair, the company had to double its production to satisfy the increased demand but a major problem had to be faced when the Cracker Jack was shipped in large wooden tubs and the mixture of candy and flavoring stuck together so the manufacturer invented a way to keep the sticky pieces separated and this method is still used today. The candy became even more well known when it became part of the song lyrics for "Take Me Out to the Ball Game" and even more fame was waiting for the product when the company included a prize in each box of Cracker Jack and everyone from children to adults searched in their boxes to find their surprises so they looked for them with genuine pleasure. It is amazing but true that since 1912, more than 17 billion Cracker Jack prizes have been put in boxes of this snack and people are still searching through their boxes and munching the sweet treats.

Making Sentence Parts Work Together

In Chapter 12, you focused on one major way that sentence parts must work together, namely, verbs must agree with their subjects. In this chapter, you will look at other elements in the sentence that must agree or be in balance. These include:

Pronouns and case

Pronoun-antecedent agreement

Parallel structure

Misplaced or dangling modifiers

With practice, you will learn to recognize these structures in your own writing.

Pronouns and case

Many personal pronouns change their form depending on how they are used in the sentence; that is, they can be used as subjects, objects, possessives, or reflexives.

You gave *her your* car keys *yourself.*

She gave *me her* car keys *herself.*

The following chart may be useful as a reference.

PRONOUNS AND CASE				
	Pronouns used as subjects	*Pronouns used as objects*	*Pronouns used as possessives*	*Pronouns used as reflexives*
Singular	I you he she it	me you him her it	my, mine you, yours his hers its	myself yourself himself herself itself
Plural	we you they	us you them	our, ours your, yours their, theirs	ourselves yourselves themselves
Singular or Plural	who	whom	whose	

- There are no such forms as *hisself* or *theirselves*.
- Do not confuse *whose* with *who's* or *its* with *it's*. (*Who's* means *who is* and *it's* means *it is*.)

In general, most of us use pronouns in the correct case without thinking. Three constructions, however, require some special attention: comparisons, compound constructions, and the use of *who/whom*.

1. Comparisons

In a comparison, choosing the correct pronoun is easier when you complete the comparison.

> His friend is a better sport than (he, him, his).
>
> His friend is a better sport than (he, him, his) is.

The second sentence shows that *he* is the correct form because the pronoun is used as the subject for the clause *he is*.

PRACTICE

1. The player did not regret the loss as much as (I, me).

   Hint: Try completing the comparison:
   The player did not regret the loss as much as (I, me) did.

2. The game was more exciting for me than (she, her).

   Hint: Try completing the comparison:
   The game was more exciting for me than it was for (she, her).

EXERCISE   Choosing the Correct Pronoun in Comparisons

Circle the correct pronoun in each of the sentences.

1. Joe and Chris arrived as late as (they, them).
2. People say the Germans are unbeatable, but we ski better than (they, them).
3. Without a doubt, you are as accomplished as (he, him).
4. That topic was not as popular as (us, ours, we).
5. Jane was happier with the outcome than (I, me).
6. The "purple" group finished it faster than (we, us).
7. In the end, the judges honored our meal over (them, they, theirs).

8. The award couldn't have meant more to (I, me) and (he, him).

9. Do those tickets belong to us, or are they (them, theirs)?

10. Maribel will stay at the hotel longer than (her, she).

2. Compound constructions

When you have a compound subject or a compound object, choosing the correct pronoun is easier if you read the sentence without one of the compound parts.

My father and (I, me) left early.

(I, me) left early.

• PRACTICE

1. The dentist and (she, her) studied the patient's chart.

> **Hint:** Try the sentence without *dentist*.
> (She, Her) studied the patient's chart.

2. They spoke to both the father and (I, me).

> **Hint:** Try the sentence without *father*.
> They spoke to (I, me).

EXERCISE   Choosing the Correct Pronoun in Compound Constructions

Circle the correct pronoun in each of the sentences.

1. The package came addressed to Mom and (I, me).

2. It was really meant for (her, she) and Jane, though.

3. Among Carol, Eileen and (I, me), Eileen is the tallest.

4. Not only did he surprise us with a party, he brought Nicole and (her, she) along as well.

5. Philip and (he, him) are definitely the best chess players.

6. However, (he, him) and (I, me) always beat Philip at backgammon.

7. (Who's, Whose) shoes are these?

8. We always tell you, if you aren't home on time you must call either (I, me) or (her, she).

9. Neither (he, him) nor (I, me) felt well after eating at that new fast-food restaurant.

10. Although Dad always talks to Fran and (him, he), he asks for Fran first.

3. Who/whom constructions

Choosing between these two pronouns is confusing, partly because in daily conversation many people do not use *whom*. When in doubt, you need to consider if the pronoun is used in a subject position (who) or in an object position (whom).

Subject position: *Who* is the conductor of the Chicago Symphony?

Object position: *Whom* did the conductor select for the solo?
To whom did the conductor give the solo?

If there is more than one clause in the sentence, it is helpful to cross out all other clauses so you can see how *who/whom* functions in its own clause.

• PRACTICE

1. He is the conductor (who, whom) I admired.

   look at: (who, whom) I admired

2. He is the conductor (who, whom) I knew would be available.

   look at: (who, whom) would be available

3. I am not sure (who, whom) will play the solo.

4. That is the musician (who, whom) I heard last month.

EXERCISE   Choosing the Correct Pronoun Using Who/Whom

Circle the correct pronoun in each of the sentences.

1. Do you know (who, whom) is appearing at Town Hall tonight?

2. My favorite dancer was the one (who's, whose) solo started Act II.

3. (Whoever, Whomever) broke that plate better be prepared to pay for it.

4. I'm not sure to (who, whom) I need to speak.

5. These extra blankets will go to (whoever, whomever) needs them the most.

6. (It's, Its) difficult to choose the winner.

7. (Who's, Whose) glasses fell behind the couch?

8. I'll only consider those (who, whom) accurately completed the application.

9. (Whoever, Whomever) was the last to arrive should close the door.

10. The baby crawled toward the child (who, whom) she knew.

In order to avoid confusion, remember you can always cross out other clauses in the sentence so you can concentrate on the clause in question.

~~You must choose~~ (who, whom) ~~you believe~~ will do the best job.
~~Is that the person~~ (who, whom) ~~you think~~ you should choose?

Use the following exercises to practice all three constructions that you have now studied.

EXERCISE 1   Choosing Correct Pronoun Forms

Circle the correct pronoun in each of the sentences.

1. Do you really believe that Shirley and (he, him) were born to be together?

2. Why don't you send it to Frank and (I, me)?

3. The book is a gift to (whoever, whomever) takes the class.

4. She always gets better grades than (he, him).

5. To (who, whom) should this dish be returned?

6. I will never be as tall as (she, her).

7. Their company is working at a much higher level than (us, our, ours).

8. Extra garlic is fine for me but not (he, him).

9. Mike prefers the teacher (who's, whose) classes are limited to eight people.

10. Ann Marie is not nearly as good at math as (I, me).

EXERCISE 2   Choosing Correct Pronoun Forms

Circle the correct pronouns in the following paragraph.

Auditioning for the play can be scary, so Carol and (I, me) decided to go together. When we arrived, we weren't sure to (who, whom) we should hand our pictures. A large group of men and women had already arrived and were waiting. Our names were closer to the top of the list than (them, theirs). That meant (her, she) and (I, me) would be called sooner. Carol's number was called, and she was paired with David. He's the one (who's, whose) voice always cracks. Although a few of the others actually laughed, Carol was nicer than (they, them). Furthermore, she sang her part so beautifully that (whoever, whomever) went next would have to be especially talented to be better than (her, she). As expected, Carol got the leading role. No one was jealous. She is a better singer than (us, we).

Pronoun-antecedent agreement

When we use a pronoun in our writing, that pronoun must refer to a word used previously in the text. This word is called the ***antecedent***.

An ***antecedent*** is a word (or words) that a pronoun replaces.

The dentist's office was shabby. *It* was not a place to spend a beautiful afternoon.

In this example, the pronoun *It* replaces the word *office. Office,* in this case, is referred to as the antecedent to the pronoun *it.*

Study the following three instances where the use of pronouns can cause trouble for writers.

1. **A pronoun must agree in number (singular or plural) with any other word to which it refers.** The following sentence contains a pronoun-antecedent disagreement in number:

   Lacks agreement: *Everybody* talked about *their* first day of school.

   The problem in this sentence is that *everyone* is a singular word, but *their* is a plural pronoun. You may have often heard people use the plural pronoun *their* to refer to a singular subject. In fact, the above sentence may sound correct, but it is considered a mistake in formal writing. Here are two approaches a writer might take to correct this sentence:

   Sexist: *Everybody* talked about *his* first day of school.

   Although you may often encounter this approach in current writing, it is unpopular because it is widely considered a sexist construction.

   Awkward: *Everybody* talked about *his or her* first day of school.

   This form is technically correct, but if it is used several times in the same paragraph it sounds awkward and repetitious.

   The best solution may be to revise such a construction so that the antecedent is plural:

   All of them talked about *their* first day of school.

   Another problem with pronoun-antecedent agreement in number occurs when a demonstrative pronoun *(this, that, these, those)* is used with a noun. That pronoun must agree with the noun it modifies:

   Singular: *this kind, that type*   Plural: *these kinds, those types*

   Incorrect: *Those type* of questions are difficult.

   Correct: *Those types* of questions are difficult.

   or

   That type of question is difficult.

● PRACTICE 1

Rewrite each of the following sentences so that the pronoun agrees with its antecedent in *number*.

1. Everyone should wear their uniforms to the picnic.

   _____

2. These kind of bathing suits will be popular this summer.

   _____

3. No one could believe what they just saw.

   _____

4. Those type of headphones can damage your hearing.

   _____

5. Each variety has their own distinguishing marks.

   _____

2. **Pronouns must also agree with their antecedents in *person*.** The following sentence contains a pronoun-antecedent disagreement in *person*.

   Incorrect: After sitting all day, *one* should do *your* basic stretching exercises.

   When you construct a piece of writing, you choose a "person" as the voice in that piece of writing. Some teachers ask students not to choose the first person *I* because they believe such writing sounds too personal. Other teachers warn students not to use *you* because it is too casual. Whatever guidelines your teacher gives you, the important point is to be consistent in person. Here are some of the possibilities for the sentence given above:

   After sitting all day, *one* should do *one's* stretching exercises.
   After sitting all day, *I* should do *my* stretching exercises.
   After sitting all day, *you* should do *your* stretching exercises.
   After sitting all day, *she* should do *her* stretching exercises.
   After sitting all day, *we* should do *our* stretching exercises.

● PRACTICE 2

Correct each of the following sentences so that the pronoun agrees with its antecedent in person.

1. I love reading books because as long as you have a good book you can never be bored.

   _____

   _____

2. You may read only mysteries, but even with this limitation, one can choose from thousands.

_____

_____

3. When we join a book club, you may save money on the books you buy during a year.

_____

_____

4. One might also buy a lot of books you never read.

_____

_____

5. When I return an overdue book to the library, one must pay a fine of twenty cents for every day overdue.

_____

_____

3. **The antecedent of a pronoun should not be *missing, ambiguous,* or *repetitious.***

a. **Missing antecedent:**

They made a discovery about the role of hemoglobin.

Possible revision:

Researchers at Duke University Medical Center made a discovery about the role of hemoglobin.

Explanation: In the first sentence, who is *they*? If the context has not told us that *they* refers to researchers, then the antecedent is missing. The sentence should be rewritten in order to avoid *they.*

b. **Ambiguous antecedent:**

Dr. Stamler told his assistant that *he* needed to revise one section of the report.

Possible revision:

Dr. Stamler said that his assistant needed to revise one section of the report.

Explanation: In the first version of the sentence, *he* could refer to either Dr. Stamler or the assistant. The sentence should be revised in a way that will avoid this ambiguity.

c. **Repetitious pronoun and antecedent:**

The journal Nature, *it* reported that this discovery has significant implications for the treatment of blood pressure.

Possible revision:

The journal <u>Nature</u> reported that this discovery has significant implications for the treatment of blood pressure.

Explanation: The subject for the verb *reported* could be the journal <u>Nature</u> or the pronoun *it,* but the subject could not be both the antecedent and the pronoun at the same time. Using both the antecedent and the pronoun results in needless repetition.

• PRACTICE 3

Rewrite the following sentences so that the antecedents are not *missing, ambiguous,* or *repetitious.*

1. Mrs. Kline she asked her neighbor to listen to the local news.

   _____

2. During the rehearsal, they said we wouldn't be ready for another two weeks.

   _____

3. Mom told me to give the baby her doll.

   _____

4. I refuse to contribute because they won't tell me how the money is used.

   _____

5. The plate fell off the shelf onto the counter, and it cracked.

   _____

EXERCISE 1   Making Pronouns and Antecedents Agree

The following sentences contain errors with pronouns. Revise each sentence so that pronouns agree with their antecedents, and the antecedents are not missing, ambiguous, or repetitious.

1. No one can take out materials without their library card.

   _____

2. If you want to take the tour, one must arrive early.

   _____

3. If we want help, you have to catch the waiter's eye.

   _____

4. Those type of books scare me.

   _____

5. Those secretaries are so good, she might get a raise.

   _____

6. If you hold onto it, they won't get lost.

   _____

7. These type of socks are easily snagged.

   _____

8. If you want to lose weight, one must control the urge to eat.

   _____

9. Everyone wore their cap and gown.

   _____

10. The firefighter let the boy wear his hat.

    _____

EXERCISE 2   Making Pronouns and Antecedents Agree

The following sentences contain errors with pronouns. Revise each sentence so that pronouns agree with their antecedents, and antecedents are not missing, ambiguous, or repetitious.

1. Nobody wants his taxes increased.

   _____

2. His friend sent him his favorite leather jacket.

   _____

3. The video cassette recorder ate the cassette, so it had to be replaced.

   _____

4. In the article, they said that some cancers might be genetic.

   _____

5. If one is interested in music, you should attend as many concerts as you can.

   _____

6. Mark generally passes these kind of tests.

   _____

7. The woman she must bring her coach to the next birthing class.

   _____

8. George gave Michael a copy of his photograph.

   _____

9. They really should do more about subway graffiti.

   _____

10. Nancy told Amy that the ship she was sailing on was completely booked.

   _____

Parallel structure: Making a series of words, phrases, or clauses balanced within the sentence

Which one of the following sentences achieves a better balanced structure?

> Her homework assignments include reading a chapter in psychology, writing up a lab report for biology, and an essay to compose for art history.

> or

> Her homework assignments include reading a chapter in psychology, writing up a lab report for biology, and composing an essay for art history.

If you selected the second sentence, you made the better choice. The second sentence uses parallel structure to balance the three phrases in the series: *reading, writing,* and *composing*. By matching each of the items in the series with the same *-ing* structure, the sentence becomes easier to understand and more pleasant to read. You can make words, phrases, and even sentences in a series parallel:

1. **Words in a series should be the same parts of speech.**

   Not parallel: The street was narrow, crowded, and the noise was terrible.
   (The series is composed of two adjectives and one clause.)

   Parallel: The street was narrow, crowded, and terribly noisy.
   (The series is composed of three adjectives: *narrow, crowded,* and *noisy.*)

2. **Phrases in a series should be the same parts of speech.**

   Not parallel: The street was at the outskirts of town, along the Allegheny River, and it wasn't far to walk to the major factory in town.
   (The series is composed of two prepositional phrases and one independent clause.)

   Parallel: The street was located at the outskirts of town, along the Allegheny River, and within walking distance of a lovely park.
   (The series is composed of three prepositional phrases.)

3. **Clauses in a series should be the same parts of speech.**

Not parallel: The street was narrow, the shops were charming, and crowds in the cafe.
(The series is composed of two clauses and one phrase.)

Parallel: The street was narrow, the shops were charming, and the cafe was crowded.
(The series is composed of three clauses.)

• PRACTICE

Each of the following sentences has an underlined word, phrase, or clause that is not parallel. Make the underlined section parallel.

1. The office is spacious, orderly, and <u>everything is clean.</u>

_____

_____

2. Her jobs include gathering the data, analyzing the data, and <u>she always prepares the annual report.</u>

_____

_____

3. This is the woman who designs stained glass windows, who creates beautiful glass jewelry, and <u>she is making Tiffany style shades for lamps.</u>

_____

_____

_____

EXERCISE 1   Revising Sentences for Parallel Structure

Each of the following sentences needs parallel structure. Underline the word, phrase, or clause that is not parallel and revise it so that its structure will balance with the other items in the pair or series.

1. Rick prefers to make dinner than going out.

_____

_____

2. My singing teacher told me to practice every day, breathe deeply, and with a full interpretation.

_____

_____

3. Content, good grammar, and to find a signature style are all elements of writing.

_____

_____

4. Our apartment is sunny, newly renovated, and has lots of space.

_____

_____

5. The subway is crowded, smelly, and the fare is too high.

_____

_____

6. However, it beats the bus, taking a cab, or walking.

_____

_____

7. At the gym, you can take a class, use the machines, or getting a massage.

_____

_____

8. Before you leave, go to the bathroom, wash your hands, and turning out the lights.

_____

_____

9. Rachel often goes to the park rather than to stay at home.

_____

_____

10. A parent must be loving, patient, and provide a stable environment.

_____

_____

EXERCISE 2   Revising Sentences for Parallel Structure

Each of the following sentences needs parallel structure. Underline the word, phrase, or clause that is not parallel and revise it so that its structure will balance with the other items in the pair or series.

1. I want to go to the beach, cruising to the islands, and to the mountains.

_____

_____

2. The books must be organized by size, title, and put them in alphabetical order.

_____

_____

3. He painted in oils, watercolors, and sometimes using leaves and flowers on the canvases themselves for a three-dimensional effect.

_____

_____

4. They would rather drink to your health than to toast that angry man.

_____

_____

5. My ancestors came from Ireland, Switzerland and some say there may be a bit of German.

_____

_____

6. Losing weight can be difficult, exhausting, and it can often be bad for your health.

_____

_____

7. Catherine may be the greatest actor in the group and can sing, too.

_____

_____

8. The garden has grubs and weeds, yet it produces the largest, firmest zucchini that taste the best.

_____

_____

9. You are my sister, my friend, and you inspire me.

_____

_____

10. Those diskettes need formatting, labelling, and then copy everything on the hard drive.

_____

_____

Misplaced and dangling modifiers

Notice how the meaning changes in each of the following sentences, depending on where the modifier *only* is placed:

Only Shirley talked to my sister last night.
Shirley *only* talked to my sister last night.
Shirley talked to *only* my sister last night.
Shirley talked to my *only* sister last night.
Shirley talked to my sister *only* last night.

> *Modifiers* are words or groups of words that function as adjectives or adverbs.
>
> **Examples:** my *only* sister
> the nurse *who is my sister*
> *only* last night
>
> A modifier must be placed close to the word, phrase, or clause that it modifies in order to be understood by the reader.

Misplaced modifiers

Be especially careful in your own writing when you use the words in the following list. They are often misplaced.

MODIFIERS OFTEN MISPLACED				
almost	exactly	just	nearly	scarcely
even	hardly	merely	only	simply

> A *misplaced modifier* is a modifier that has been placed in a wrong, awkward, or ambiguous position.

1. The modifier is in the wrong place.

Wrong: The teacher found the missing report of the student *that needed many corrections.*

           Who or what needed correction—the student or the report?

Revised: The teacher found the student's missing report *that needed many corrections.*

2. The modifier is positioned awkwardly, interrupting the flow of the sentence, as in the following split infinitive.

Awkward: Timothy intended *to only watch* the fight.

           The infinitive *to watch* should not be split.

Revised: Timothy *only* intended *to watch* the fight.

3. The modifier is in an ambiguous position; that is, it could describe the word or words on either side of it (sometimes called a *squinting modifier*).

Squinting: The artist having painted other portraits expertly painted the portrait of the well-known leader.

           Did she expertly paint other portraits or did she expertly paint the well-known leader? From the wording, the author's meaning is not clear.

Revised: Having expertly painted other portraits, the artist painted the well-known leader.

Dangling modifiers

A *dangling modifier* is a modifier without a word, phrase, or clause that the modifier can describe.

Dangling: Considering a romantic cruise, the brochure promised a memorable trip.

           Who is considering a romantic cruise? Is it the brochure or the couple?

Revised: Considering a romantic cruise, the couple read a brochure that promised a memorable trip.

EXERCISE 1   Revising Misplaced or Dangling Modifiers

Revise each sentence so there is no dangling modifier.

1. While writing his novel, the cat begged for food.

   _____

2. Taking a shower, the doorbell rang.

   _____

3. The baby sitter bathed the baby wearing rubber gloves.

   _____

4. Scurrying across the lawn, I noticed a group of rabbits.

   _____

5. After fetching the camera, the owl flew away.

   _____

6. At the age of five, my sister was born.

   _____

7. Bringing work home to finish the project, the teacher gave me extra credit.

   _____

8. Julian admired the ring in the case that cost $200.

   _____

9. I cleaned out the trunk wearing high heels.

   _____

10. She clutched the chair feeling dizzy.

    _____

EXERCISE 2   Revising Misplaced or Dangling Modifiers

Revise each sentence so there is no dangling modifier.

1. Walking down the street, the wind blew the umbrella inside out.

   _____

2. Kim strummed the guitar wandering through the restaurant.

   _____

3. Putting on a tuxedo, Mom said Dad looked very handsome.

   _____

4. While in the laboratory, the sign said "No Smoking."

_____

5. The butterflies were attracted to Nancy with the blue wings.

_____

6. Staring intently into the microscope, the microbes finally reproduced.

_____

7. We have the room with two closets that looks out on the beach.

_____

8. Sucking her bottle, Mother watched the baby take her first steps.

_____

9. Hiking in the Sierras, the air was crisp and clean.

_____

10. Lee consulted the dictionary searching for just the right word.

_____

Mastery and editing tests

TEST 1   Making Sentence Parts Work Together

Rewrite the following paragraph, correcting any errors you find in agreement, parallel structure, and misplaced or dangling modifiers.

Every living thing has their own unique circumstances: where they live, what they do, interacting with the environment, etc. Of course, no one types of organism live alone. A certain kind of scientist study these organisms and looking specifically at their habitats. They are called ecologists, and the science of studying habitats is called ecology. The word *ecology* comes from two Greek words meaning "study of the home or surroundings." Human beings and ants frequently share environments. We are much bigger than them. Scurrying around on the ground, we frequently step on them or their homes. Likewise, building our homes on 'their' ground, ants invade our kitchens as unwelcome guests. Obviously, whomever shares a habitat impacts all the other organisms in that environment. The ecologist's job is to carefully look at how all the other organisms and us interact. They attempt to ensure that none of the organisms who's habitats overlap are harming any others. Ecologists seek to learn the best way of mutual habitation.

_____

_____

_____

_____

_____

_____

_____

_____

_____

_____

_____

_____

_____

_____

_____

TEST 2　Making Sentence Parts Work Together

Rewrite the following paragraph, correcting any errors you find in agreement, parallel structure, and misplaced or dangling modifiers.

When one is sick, they usually are given antibiotics. These type of drug are chemicals that are used to kill microorganisms and helping your body fight disease. Made from tiny living things called microbes, scientists choose particular antibiotics for their ability to produce certain chemicals. These chemicals actually fights disease germs in the body because antibiotic chemicals are stronger than them. These chemicals are produced in large quantities in laboratories that are made into antibiotics and sold in drugstores. Many people now have learned that it is important not to take antibiotics every time you have a cold because microorganisms are growing immune to them. When we really need them, they will be useless to us.

_____

_____

_____

_____

_____

_____

_____

_____

_____

_____

_____

_____

_____

_____

_____

_____

_____

_____

_____

_____

_____

_____

_____

_____

_____

_____

_____

_____

_____

TEST 3   Making Sentence Parts Work Together

Rewrite the following sentences, correcting any errors you find in agreement, parallel structure, and misplaced or dangling modifiers.

1. They say you can't be spoiled or pampered if you're going to live on a working farm.

_____

_____

2. If you want to understand what rural life is like, one should try it out for a summer.

   _____

   _____

3. I had my own idealistic views about life in the country, but these sort of views turned out to be incorrect.

   _____

   _____

4. My husband and me lived three years on a farm in Iowa.

   _____

   _____

5. Our friends back in the city had much more leisure time than us.

   _____

   _____

6. We were getting up a five A.M. seven days a week, milking the cows even when we were sick, and we worked throughout the day until the sun set.

   _____

   _____

7. Putting hay into bales in 90 degree heat, the sun proved its power to us.

   _____

   _____

8. We worked among rows and rows of beans for several hours a day to exactly find out how much our backs could stand.

   _____

   _____

9. Everyone in the city should exchange places with those whom live in the country for at least one month.

   _____

   _____

10. Rural people they say farm life means working from sun up to sun down, but their lives are satisfying and full.

   _____

   _____

THE SENTENCE   *Chapter 18*

Practicing More with Verbs

So far in this book, you have already learned a great deal about verbs. In Chapter 11, you learned how to recognize the verb in a sentence. In Chapter 12, you learned that verbs must agree with their subjects. Chapter 13 discussed how to form participles, gerunds, and infinitives from the verb. This chapter will continue your study of verbs by focusing on:

- Principal parts of irregular verbs
- How to use the present perfect and past perfect tenses
- Sequence of tenses
- How to avoid unnecessary shifts in verb tense
- The difference between active or passive voice
- The subjunctive mode
- Correct use of *should* and *would*

What are the principal parts of the irregular verbs?

The English language has more than one hundred verbs that do not form the past tense or past participle with the usual *-ed* ending. Their forms are irregular. When you listen to children aged four or five, you often hear them utter expressions such as "Yesterday I *cutted* myself." Later on, they will hear that the verb "cut" is unusual, and they will change to the irregular form, "Yesterday I *cut* myself." The best way to learn these verbs is to listen to how they sound. You will find an extensive list of these verbs in the appendix of this book. Pronounce them out loud over and over until you have learned them. If you find that you don't know a particular verb's meaning, or you cannot pronounce a verb and its forms, ask your instructor for help. Most irregular verbs are very common words that you will be using often in your writing and speaking. You will want to know them well.

Practicing 50 irregular verbs

THE THREE PRINCIPAL PARTS OF IRREGULAR VERBS		
Simple Form	*Past Form*	*Past Participle*
(also called Infinitive Form)		(used with perfect tenses after, "has," "have," or "will have" or with passive voice after the verb "to be.")
ride	rode	ridden

EIGHT VERBS THAT DO NOT CHANGE THEIR FORMS (NOTICE THEY ALL END IN -T OR -D)		
Simple Form	*Past Form*	*Past Participle*
bet	bet	bet
cost	cost	cost
cut	cut	cut
fit	fit	fit
hit	hit	hit
hurt	hurt	hurt
quit	quit	quit
spread	spread	spread

TWO VERBS THAT HAVE THE SAME SIMPLE PRESENT FORM AND THE PART PARTICIPLE		
Simple Form	*Past Form*	*Past Participle*
come	came	come
become	became	become

PRACTICE 1

Fill in the correct form of the verb in the following sentences.

(become) 1. I _____ ecstatic last week to find out my sister is planning to be married in June.

(hurt) 2. She had been badly _____ in a car accident two years ago.

(come) 3. For more than eight months, her fiance _____ to the hospital every day.

(cost) 4. The medical fees _____ the family all of their savings.

(bet) 5. In spite of their troubles, I have _____ all my friends that this marriage will last.

TWENTY VERBS THAT HAVE THE SAME PAST FORM AND PAST PARTICIPLE		
Simple Form	*Past Form*	*Past Participle*
bend	bent	bent
lend	lent	lent
send	sent	sent
spend	spent	spent
creep	crept	crept
keep	kept	kept
sleep	slept	slept
sweep	swept	swept
weep	wept	wept
teach	taught	taught
catch	caught	caught
bleed	bled	bled
feed	fed	fed
lead	led	led
speed	sped	sped
bring	brought	brought
buy	bought	bought
fight	fought	fought
think	thought	thought
seek	sought	sought

In the following paragraph, five verbs are incorrect. Underline them first, and write the correct form on the lines provided.

Last year the fish farmer carefully feeded all of the stock in his tanks. After he catched them, he had a delivery problem. The fish had to be brung to market as quickly as possible. The farmer's trucks speeded to the city. He send his eldest son with the driver.

1. _____

2. _____

3. _____

4. _____

5. _____

TWENTY VERBS THAT HAVE ALL DIFFERENT FORMS		
Simple Form	*Past Form*	*Past Participle*
blow	blew	blown
fly	flew	flown
grow	grew	grown
know	knew	known
throw	threw	thrown
begin	began	begun
drink	drank	drunk
ring	rang	rung
shrink	shrank	shrunk
sink	sank	sunk
sing	sang	sung
spring	sprang	sprung
swim	swam	swum
bite	bit	bitten (or bit)
hide	hid	hidden (or hid)
drive	drove	driven
ride	rode	ridden
stride	strode	stridden
rise	rose	risen
write	wrote	written

PRACTICE 3

Fill in the correct form of the verb in the following sentences.

(fly)   1. As children, we _____ our kites in the fields around our house beginning every March.

(throw)   2. After school in the spring we _____ ourselves completely into the neighborhood baseball games.

(swim)   3. When summer rolled around, we _____ in the nearby creek.

(ride)   4. Sometimes we _____ our neighbor's horses.

(drink)   5. We played outside and _____ in the sun until mother called us in for dinner.

EXERCISE 1   Irregular Verbs

Supply the past form or the past participle for each verb in parentheses.

1. With an attitude of confidence, the salesperson _____ up the steps of
   (spring)

   the first office building on his new route.

2. He _____ the bell.
   (ring)

3. The job had _____ from a limited area of a few small towns to include
   (grow)

   a sizable city as well.

4. He had _____ for years, but in the city he could use public
   (drive)

   transportation.

5. He _____ all thoughts of past struggles from his mind.
   (sweep)

6. He _____ his case of samples with him on the bus.
   (bring)

7. He had _____ all of the previous evening planning his presentation.
   (spend)

8. Unfortunately he had _____ the company book, *Making a Sale* to a
   (lend)

   new employee in the company.

9. Luckily, he had _____ all the essential information written down
   (keep)

   in his notebook.

10. He _____ happily how he finally had the chance to show what he
    (think)

   could do.

EXERCISE 2   Irregular Verbs

Rewrite the paragraph below in the past tense.

Our town has a problem. Tax revenues keep declining. Officials spend a lot of time and effort worrying about the situation. Then it hits them. They do something very dramatic. They seek permission to open a large gambling casino complex. Other towns shrink their deficits when they open gambling casinos. The town council thinks this will sweep away all the town's financial problems. The news of the plan spreads quickly around the town. However, many people know that the gambling casino solution sends citizens a dangerous message. These citizens fight the proposal with great conviction. The council gradually finds other solutions to the financial troubles.

_____

_____

_____

_____

_____

_____

_____

_____

_____

_____

_____

_____

Appendix A at the back of this book gives an alphabetical listing of nearly every irregular verb. Use that list to supply the correct form for each verb in the following exercises.

EXERCISE 1   Practice with More Irregular Verbs

Supply the past form or the past participle for each verb in parentheses.

1. The storm _____ with surprising fury.
   (to strike)

2. Those who could _____ from their homes.
   (to flee)

3. Some were _____ and hid in closets or under mattresses.
   (to stick)

4. In the rush, some people ＿＿＿＿＿ their pets behind.
    (to leave)

5. In many cases, people ＿＿＿＿＿ the roofs of their houses.
    (to lose)

6. Luckily, most had ＿＿＿＿＿ for good insurance.
    (to pay)

7. This second disaster in the same area of the country ＿＿＿＿＿ the
    (to shake)

    citizens' sense of optimism about their future.

8. They ＿＿＿＿＿ discouraged about starting over again.
    (to feel)

9. Those who were in construction ＿＿＿＿＿ some comfort in the
    (to take)

    devastation.

10. This ＿＿＿＿＿ jobs for people rebuilding and replanting.
    (to mean)

EXERCISE 2   Practice with More Irregular Verbs

Rewrite the following paragraph in the past tense.

> He swings the metal detector back and forth. Suddenly he falls to the
> ground and digs for an object in the sand. Later he tells us about all the
> objects he has found. He meets with the owner of the town's resale shop.
> He slides a few gold objects out of his pocket and holds them out to the
> owner for consideration. Eventually he sells some of these to the owner.
> On a chain around his neck, he wears two of the rings he has found. We
> stand watching the transaction and think to ourselves that all of this is
> quite remarkable for a boy who is only seven years old.

＿＿＿＿＿＿＿＿＿＿＿＿＿＿＿＿＿＿＿＿＿＿＿＿＿＿＿＿＿＿＿

＿＿＿＿＿＿＿＿＿＿＿＿＿＿＿＿＿＿＿＿＿＿＿＿＿＿＿＿＿＿＿

＿＿＿＿＿＿＿＿＿＿＿＿＿＿＿＿＿＿＿＿＿＿＿＿＿＿＿＿＿＿＿

＿＿＿＿＿＿＿＿＿＿＿＿＿＿＿＿＿＿＿＿＿＿＿＿＿＿＿＿＿＿＿

＿＿＿＿＿＿＿＿＿＿＿＿＿＿＿＿＿＿＿＿＿＿＿＿＿＿＿＿＿＿＿

＿＿＿＿＿＿＿＿＿＿＿＿＿＿＿＿＿＿＿＿＿＿＿＿＿＿＿＿＿＿＿

＿＿＿＿＿＿＿＿＿＿＿＿＿＿＿＿＿＿＿＿＿＿＿＿＿＿＿＿＿＿＿

＿＿＿＿＿＿＿＿＿＿＿＿＿＿＿＿＿＿＿＿＿＿＿＿＿＿＿＿＿＿＿

＿＿＿＿＿＿＿＿＿＿＿＿＿＿＿＿＿＿＿＿＿＿＿＿＿＿＿＿＿＿＿

How many verb tenses are there in English?

Since the next sections of this chapter concern common problems with tense, a chart of the English Verb Tenses is given in case you want to refer to this list from time to time. Not all languages express time by using exactly the same verb tenses. Students for whom English is a second language know that one of their major tasks in learning English is to understand how to use each of these tenses. Along with the name of each verb tense, the chart gives a sentence using that particular tense.

ENGLISH VERB TENSES	
present	I talk
present continuous	I am talking
present perfect	I have talked
present perfect continuous	I have been talking
past	I talked
past continuous	I was talking
past perfect	I had talked
past perfect continuous	I had been talking
future	I will talk
future continuous	I will be talking
future perfect	I will have talked
future perfect continuous	I will have been talking

Note: The perfect tenses need special attention since they are generally not well understood or used consistently in the accepted way.

How do you use the present perfect and the past perfect tenses?

Forming the perfect tenses

Present perfect tense: *has* or *have* + past participle of the main verb
has studied
have studied

Past perfect tense: *had* + past participle of the main verb
had studied

What do these tenses mean?

The *present perfect tense* describes an action that started in the past and continues to the present time.

Jay *has studied* at the university for four years.

This sentence indicates that Jay began to study at the university four years ago and is still studying there now.

Examine the following time line. What does it tell you about the present perfect tense?

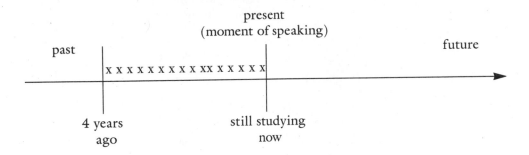

Other example sentences of the present perfect tense:

She *has lived* in this apartment since 1980.

I *have* always *walked* this way to work.

> The ***present perfect tense*** can also describe an action that has just taken place, or an action where the exact time in the past is indefinite.

Has Jay *received* his diploma yet?

Jay *has* (just) *received* his diploma.

Have you ever *been* to the university's art gallery?

No, I *have* never *been* there.

If the time were definite, you would use the simple past:

Jay *received* his diploma last week.

Yes, I *was* there last Tuesday.

> The ***past perfect tense*** describes an action that occurred in the past before another activity or another point of time in the past.

Jay *had studied* at the university for four years *before* he *received* his diploma.

In this sentence, there are two past actions: Jay *studied,* and Jay *received.* The action that took place first is in the past perfect (*had studied*). The action that took place later, and was also completed in the past, is in the simple past (*received*).

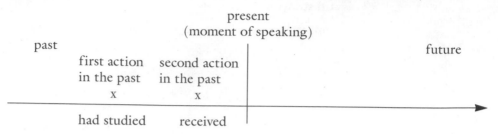

Other example sentences using the past perfect tense:

> I *had* just *finished* dinner when the phone *rang.*

> She *claimed* that Rafael *had discovered* a hidden bank account.

> He *had given* the account over to the examiner *long before* last week's meeting.

PRACTICE

Complete each of the following sentences by filling in each blank with either the present perfect tense or past perfect tense of the verb given.

1. The orchestra conductor _____ at the college for only three years.
   (teach)

2. He _____ conducting at Eastman School of Music in Rochester, New
   (study)
   York, before he took this position.

3. _____ you ever _____ to Rochester?
   (be)

4. No, I _____ never _____ there.
   (visit)

5. The rehearsal _____ when Peter arrived.
   (begin)

What is the sequence of tenses?

> The term *sequence of tenses* refers to the proper use of verb tenses in complex sentences (sentences that have an independent clause and a dependent clause).

The following guide shows the relationship between the verb in the independent clause (IC) and the verb in the dependent clause (DC).

SEQUENCE OF TENSES

Independent Clause	Dependent Clause	Time of the DC in Relation to the IC

If the tense of the independent clause is in the present (He *knows*), here are the possibilities for the dependent clause.

He knows	that she *is* right.	same time
	that she *was* right.	earlier
	that she *will be* right.	later

If the tense of the independent clause is in the past (He *knew*), here are the possibilities for the dependent clause.

He knew	that she *was* right.	same time
	that she *had been* right.	earlier
	that she *would be* right.	later

If the independent clause is in the future (He *will tell*), here are the possibilities for the dependent clause.

He will tell us	if she *goes*.	same time
	if she *has gone*.	earlier
	if she *will go*.	later

EXERCISE   Sequence of Tenses

In each of the following sentences, choose the correct verb tense for the verb in the dependent clause. Use the guide above if you need help.

1. If the artists <u>will donate</u> more of their work, the funding for the arts program _____ .
   (continue)

2. Educators <u>believe</u> that computers _____ placed in every school in the country.
   (to be + soon)

3. Thirty years ago, fans of the Beatles <u>did not realize</u> that one day the group _____ for a new generation of music lovers.
   (return)

4. The judge <u>did not know</u> that the witness _____ the truth at yesterday's news conference.
   (tell)

5. The mother <u>knew</u> from experience that her child _____ to go swimming right after lunch.
   (want)

6. The supervisor <u>realizes</u> the employee _____ his job in a few weeks.
   (lose)

7. Some state legislatures <u>want</u> divorce to be more difficult; this _____
   (encourage)
   more couples to stay together.

8. He <u>found out</u> yesterday that the landlady _____ his rent while he was
   (raise)
   on vacation.

9. The movie director <u>thinks</u> that he _____ a mistake in hiring that actress
   (make)
   last autumn.

10. The parent <u>suspected</u> that the child _____ the gum from her purse.
    (take)

Avoid unnecessary shift in verb tense

Do not shift verb tenses as you write unless you intend to change the time of the action.

Shifted tense: The student *requested* (past tense) the research material again, but the librarian *informs* (present tense) him that the materials *are* (present tense) not yet available.

Revised: The student requested (past tense) the research material again, but the librarian *informed* (past tense) him that the materials *were* (past tense) not yet available.

NOTE: An exception to this occurs when the subject is a creative work such as a book, play, poem, or piece of music. In this case the present tense is always used to indicate the work is still in existence today.

All My Sons remains (present tense) a frequently performed play. It <u>was</u> written by Arthur Miller.

I Know Why the Caged Bird Sings is (present tense) a widely read autobiography. It <u>was</u> written by Maya Angelou.

EXERCISE 1 Correcting Unnecessary Shifts in Verb Tense

Each sentence has an unnecessary shift in verb tense. Revise each sentence so that the tense remains consistent.

1. While driving in heavy traffic, the bus driver was blinded by the sun and strikes a parked car.

_____

_____

2. At the start of the examination, I was nervous and unsure of myself; by the end, I am smiling and feeling pretty good.

   _____

   _____

3. The flutist performs perfectly as always and enchanted the audience.

   _____

   _____

4. After we make the change on your application, we placed a copy into your file.

   _____

   _____

5. The editorial criticized the politician, but in my opinion, it doesn't go far enough.

   _____

   _____

6. She was feeling healthy until she suddenly comes down with the chicken pox.

   _____

   _____

7. The officer demanded that the recruits be up by 5 A.M. and that they will be ready to leave by 5:15.

   _____

   _____

8. He walks up to his partner and gave him the good news.

   _____

   _____

9. In the documentary, several people talk about meeting Martin Luther King; they recalled his charismatic personality.

   _____

   _____

10. Her research was going fine when she goes and quits the course.

   _____

   _____

EXERCISE 2 Correcting Unnecessary Shift in Verb Tense

The following paragraph contains unnecessary shifts in verb tense. Change each incorrect verb to its proper form.

Charles Kuralt began his journalistic career as a radio writer for CBS News in 1957. Then he becomes a correspondent, hosting the TV series *Primetime*. He worked as a correspondent both in Latin America and on the West Coast. In between these two assignments, he visits Vietnam several times. He is perhaps the first American correspondent to be shot at there. His book *A Life on the Road* details some of these experiences.

In 1967, he began a project that was supposed to last three months. He goes on the road in a motor home taking with a camera crew. Nobody ever told him to stop. He travels for more than twenty years looking for little known places with interesting stories. He will tell us about watching the cranes in New Mexico in November or tasting the Ketchikan shrimp in Southeast Alaska. He wrote about the lives of rural people who are unchanged by modern trends. He loves to learn about the small pieces of their history and customs.

Charles Kuralt found that some things hadn't changed: He hears banjos and storytellers in the mountains of North Carolina and he sees that people still "hang out" in Key West.

_____

_____

_____

_____

_____

_____

_____

_____

_____

_____

_____

_____

_____

_____

_____

_____

_____

What is the difference between passive and active voice?

> ### PASSIVE AND ACTIVE VOICE
>
> In the *active voice*, the subject does the acting:
>
> > The board prepared the budget.
>
> **Choose the active voice generally in order to achieve direct, economical and forceful writing. Most writing, therefore, should be in the active voice.**
>
> In the *passive voice*, the subject is acted upon:
>
> > The budget was prepared by the board.
> > > or
> > The budget was prepared.
>
> Notice in these passive sentences, the actor is not only deemphasized by moving out of the subject place but may be omitted entirely from the sentence.
>
> **Choose the passive voice to deemphasize the actor or to avoid naming the actor altogether.**

Discuss the following sentences with your classmates and instructor. All three sentences state the fact of the assassination of President James Garfield. What makes each sentence different from the other two? By choosing a particular sentence, what would the writer be emphasizing?

1. Charles Guiteau, a mentally disturbed office seeker, shot and killed President James Garfield in 1881.

2. President James Garfield was shot and killed by Charles Guiteau in 1881.

3. President James Garfield was shot and killed in 1881.

How do you form the passive voice?

Subject Acted Upon	+ Verb "To Be"	+ Past Participle	+ "by" Phrase (Optional)
The award	was	presented	(by the mayor)
The dress	had been	designed	(by Oscar de la Renta)
The money	is	collected	(by volunteers)

EXERCISE 1   Active and Passive Voice

Fill in the following chart by showing how the sentences in the active voice could be put into passive voice and how the sentences in the passive voice could be put into the active voice. Then discuss with your classmates and instructor the circumstances under which you would choose active or passive voice to express these ideas.

Active Voice

1. The jury announced the verdict after five hours of deliberation.

2. _____

   _____

3. The sleet turned the old municipal building into an ice castle.

4. _____

   _____

   _____

5. _____

   _____

   _____

   _____

   _____

   _____

Passive Voice

1. _____

   _____

   _____

2. Modern pop music was created by Elvis Presley.

3. _____

   _____

   _____

4. The priceless vase was smuggled by someone out of the country.

5. More attention and concern were shown by television viewers over the Super Bowl than over the outbreak of a conflict in which the United States was involved.

EXERCISE 2   Active and Passive Voice

Fill in the following chart by showing how the sentences in the active voice could be put into passive voice and how the sentences in the passive voice could be put into the active voice. Then discuss with your classmates and instructor the circumstances under which you would choose active or passive voice to express these ideas.

Active Voice

1. _____

   _____

   _____

2. _____

   _____

   _____

Passive Voice

1. The plans for peace were announced by the three world leaders.

2. From the 8th to the 11th century, Spain was dominated by the Moors.

Active Voice

3. The sun melted the ice, which fell in huge chunks off the bridge.

4. _____
_____

5. Milagros borrowed a pickup truck to move her furniture to the new apartment.

Passive Voice

3. _____
_____
_____

4. The poem was written by Carl Sandburg in 1936.

5. _____
_____
_____

What is the subjunctive?

> The *subjunctive* is an as yet unrealized situation.

Recognize the three instances that call for the subjunctive and note the form of the verb that is used in each case.

1. Unreal conditions using *if* or *wish,* use *were:*

    If John were my brother, I would give him my advice.

    I *wish* he were my brother.

2. Clauses starting with *that* after verbs such as *ask, request, demand, suggest, order, insist,* or *command,* use the infinitive form of the verb:

    I *requested* that John bring his report.

    The family *demanded* that every document be exhibited.

3. Clauses starting with *that* after adjectives expressing urgency, as in *it is necessary, it is imperative, it is urgent, it is important,* and *it is essential,* use the infinitive form of the verb:

    It is important he be on time.

    It is imperative that he answer every question truthfully.

In each of these three instances, notice that the verb following the italicized word or phrase does not agree with its subject.

PRACTICE

In the following sentences, circle the word or phrase that calls for using the subjunctive. Then choose the correct form of the verb. An example follows:

The college insisted that the rules be followed.

1. Mika wishes she (was, were) ready for the exam.

2. Her teacher suggested that she (waits, wait) until next semester to take it.

3. The college requires that everybody (takes, take) a writing proficiency test.

4. It is necessary she (passes, pass) this test in order to graduate in May.

5. If she (was, were) wise, she would devote herself to the preparation for this test.

Confusions with *should* and *would*

Do not use more than one modal auxiliary *(can, may, might, must, should, ought)* with the main verb.

Incorrect: Magdalene *shouldn't ought* to borrow more money.
Correct: Magdalene *shouldn't* borrow more money.
or
Magdalene *ought* not borrow more money.

Do not use *should of, would of,* or *could of* to mean *should have, would have,* or *could have.*

Incorrect: The caller *would of* told you if he had known the answer.
Correct: The caller *would have* told you if he had known the answer.

Mastery and editing tests

TEST 1   Solving Problems with Verbs

Revise each of the following sentences to avoid problems with verbs.

1. If he was my son, I would insist on a complete physical examination.

2. He has broke his arm more than once playing sports.

3. When he first begun to play football, his mom had worried.

4. They could of won the game if they had concentrated more.

5. The coach said that the teachers were attending the game tonight.

6. We hadn't ought to judge others.

7. The guest requested that the room is ready.

8. The sun bleached the uniform. (Change to passive.)

9. I drunk the entire quart of lemonade before the game.

10. One team member weeped when they lost the championship.

TEST 2   Solving Problems with Verbs

Revise each of the following sentences to avoid problems with verbs.

1. Her family organized every detail of the wedding. (Change to passive voice.)

2. It was necessary that the mother makes the wedding gown.

3. The occasion requires that each detail is just right.

4. By the time the bride arrived, the guests are seated.

5. Most of the food was brung by the family to the reception hall.

6. If it was baked carefully, the cake would be delicious.

7. The wedding gifts were hid under a table covered with a long tablecloth.

8. She throwed the bouquet to her sister.

9. Her brothers sweeped up the hall after the reception.

10. They should of taken more pictures on their honeymoon.

TEST 3   Solving Problems with Verbs

Edit the following paragraph to correct all errors with verbs. Use all that you have learned about verbs in this chapter.

I have avoided the dentist long enough. The day comes when I picked up the phone and made an appointment. The secretary should of been surprised to hear my voice, but if she was, she soon has recovered and tells me I had to wait a week for their first opening. I insisted that she gives me an appointment early in the morning. Every night after that I fall asleep and dreamed I see the dentist leaning over me and talking about "the first opening." By the time the day arrived, I feel scared. Arriving at the office, I see the white uniforms and all the gleaming equipment. My heart sinks. The receptionist smiles and takes me to one of the small rooms, but I did not feel comfortable. The large dentist's chair fills the room. As I sit there, the room becomes more and more like a cell. The venetian blinds looked like bars against the grey sky. I have sat there in solitary confinement for what seemed like years. Then the dentist came in. She is so charming that nearly all my fears have vanished.

Using Correct Capitalization and Punctuation

Ten basic rules for capitalization

Many people are often confused or careless about the use of capital letters. Sometimes writers capitalize words without thinking, or they capitalize "important" words without really understanding what makes them important enough to deserve a capital letter. The question of when to capitalize words becomes easier to answer when you study the following rules and carefully apply them to your own writing.

1. Capitalize the first word of every sentence.

2. Capitalize the names of specific things and places.

   Specific buildings:

   > The singer performed in Constitution Hall.
   > *but*
   > The singer performed in the concert hall.

   Specific streets, cities, states, countries:

   > He lives on Colonial Road.
   > *but*
   > He lives on a road near our farm.

   Specific organizations:

   > Martha donates clothes to the Red Cross.
   > *but*
   > Martha contributes to several charities.

   Specific institutions:

   > Ellen borrowed money from the University Credit Union.
   > *but*
   > Dominic went to a credit union for his car loan.

Specific bodies of water:

> My cousins spend every vacation at Lake George.
> *but*
> My cousins spend every vacation at the lake.

3. Capitalize days of the week, months of the year, and holidays. Do not capitalize the names of seasons.

> The first Monday in September is Labor Day.
> *but*
> My favorite season is autumn.

4. Capitalize the names of all languages, nationalities, races, religions, deities, and sacred terms.

> Veronique who is Haitian speaks Creole.
>
> The Dead Sea Scrolls tell us much about ancient Judaism.

5. Capitalize the first word and every important word in a title. Do not capitalize articles, prepositions, or short connecting words in the title.

> *Shadows on the Rock* is a novel written by Willa Cather.
>
> Her favorite short story is "A Trip for Mrs. Taylor."

6. Capitalize the first word of a direct quotation.

> The minister said, "You are my official representative."
> *but*
> "You are," the minister said, "my official representative."

> **Note:** *my* is not capitalized because it is not the beginning of the sentence in quotation marks.

7. Capitalize historical events, periods, and documents.

> The French and Indian War
>
> The Roaring Twenties
>
> The Code of Hammurabi

8. Capitalize the words north, south, east, and west when they are used as places rather than as directions.

> She was born in the South.
> *but*
> Their house is two miles south of the state line.

9. Capitalize people's names.

Proper names:

Elaine James

Professional titles when they are used with the person's proper name:

| Governor Paul Patton | *but* | the governor |
| Councilwoman Jane Watson | *but* | the councilwoman |

Term for a relative (like mother, sister, nephew, uncle) when it is used in the place of the proper name:

I invited Mother to attend.

Note: terms for relatives are not capitalized if a pronoun, article, or adjective is used with the name.

I invited my mother to attend.

10. Capitalize brand names.

| Peter Pan Peanut Butter | *but* | peanut butter |
| Philadelphia Cream Cheese | *but* | cream cheese |

EXERCISE 1   Capitalization

Read the paragraph and insert capitalization wherever necessary.

The boys' choir meets to rehearse mondays through fridays. Everyone grows silent when conductor timothy archer enters the music room. The boys' choir is preparing for their concert tour of the west. They will sing in several high schools and colleges from tacoma to san diego. In hollywood, they will sing at the hollywood bowl. One of the songs on their program is in latin, and another is in french. The boys' favorite song is an african-american spiritual entitled "my lord! what a morning." Their printed program explains, "these boys spend many hours each day in musical training in addition to keeping up a strenuous academic program." These boys aspire to the excellence of the vienna boys' choir or the harlem boys' choir. Much of their financial support has come from the national endowment for the arts.

EXERCISE 2　Capitalization

Read the paragraph and insert capitalization wherever necessary.

> In 1977, the clean air act amendments set standards for people's right to see a clear sky in the daytime. However, no such standards protect the night sky. After world war II, the growing population and development in the countryside meant more light everywhere. The night sky around a typical suburb like rutherford, new jersey, is more than ten times as bright as the natural night sky. The light over cities like Detroit or Miami is nearly fifty times as bright as the natural light. the problem for astronomers is obvious. The mount wilson observatory in southern california is for all practical purposes useless for deep space work even though it is a major observatory with a 100-inch reflecting telescope. The growth of los angeles has brought too much light to the area. Believe it or not, even a larger observatory like the one on hawaii's mauna kea, which is 14,000 feet above sea level and considered one of the most perfect sites for an observatory, is feeling the adverse effects of light pollution. Perhaps in the future, students will have to go to australia if they hope to find a dark enough place to see the universe through a telescope.

Eight basic uses of the comma

You may feel uncertain about when to use the comma. The starting point is to concentrate on a few basic rules. These rules will cover most of your needs.

The tendency now in English is to use fewer commas than in the past. There is no one perfect complete set of rules on which everyone agrees. However, if you learn these basic eight, your common sense will help you figure out what to do in other cases. Remember that a comma usually signifies a pause in a sentence. As you read a sentence out loud, listen to where you pause within the sentence. Where you pause is often your clue that a comma is needed. Notice that in each of the examples for the following eight uses, you can pause where the comma is placed.

1. Use a comma to separate items in a series (more than two items).

   My friend is calm, helpful, and patient.

   She never loses her temper, never refuses to lend a hand, and never judges people harshly.

   - Some writers omit the comma before the *and* that introduces the last item.

     My friend is calm, helpful and patient.

   - When an address or date occurs in a sentence, each part is treated like an item in a series. A comma is put after each item, including the last:

     They moved to 615 Delaware Avenue, San Francisco, California, last month.

     The twins were born October 13, 1993, in a taxicab.

- A group of adjectives may not be regarded as a series if some of the words "go together." You can test this by putting *and* between each item. If you can put *and* between two adjectives, use a comma.

The balloon rose in the cloudless, deep blue sky.

The words *deep blue* go together. You would not say *a deep and blue sky* because *deep* is meant to qualify the color blue. Therefore, you cannot separate the two adjectives with a comma. However, you could say *a cloudless and deep blue sky*. The lack of clouds is a separate issue from the color of the sky. Therefore, a comma should separate *cloudless* from *deep blue*.

PRACTICE 1

In each of the following sentences, insert commas wherever they are needed.

1. People who get enough sleep are more rested alert and focused than those who have stayed up late the night before.

2. The need for sleep varies according to age: ten to twelve hours for children nine hours for teenagers seven and a half hours for adults up to age sixty and about six and a half hours for those over sixty.

3. Our muscles relax during light sleep relax even more in deeper sleep and stop activity completely in what is called "dream sleep."

4. Have you ever seen the telltale dark blue circles under the eyes of people who regularly go without sufficient sleep?

5. Call the Sleep Disorder Center Columbia Presbyterian Medical Center New York for the number of a center near your home if you feel you are sleep deprived.

2. Use a comma along with a coordinating conjunction to combine two simple sentences (also called independent clauses) into a single compound sentence. (See Chapter 14 on coordination.)

The survey was brief, but the questions were carefully phrased.

Be careful that you use the comma with the conjunction only when you are combining sentences. If you are combining only words or phrases, no comma is used:

The survey was brief but carefully phrased.

The weather and sports followed the news.

She was either on the telephone or in the shower.

PRACTICE 2

In each of the following sentences, insert commas wherever they are needed.

1. Olive oil is a very common ingredient for cooking but people do not realize the range of differences among the many kinds of olive oil.

2. You may choose an inexpensive olive oil from your supermarket or you might buy a bottle for as much as $35 at a fancy-food shop.

3. Most good olive oils are from Italy yet there are fine oils from other countries.

4. Betty Pustarfi is devoted to the virtues of olive oil and she can be found conducting free tastings of as many as twenty oils from many countries every Saturday morning at the Bountiful Basket in Carmel, California.

5. At her tastings, Ms. Pustarfi provides detailed sheets to explain the properties of olive oil and the characteristics of each oil in the tasting.

3. Use a comma to follow introductory words, expressions, phrases, or clauses.

   A. Introductory words (such as *yes, no, oh, well*)

      Yes, I'll be there.

   B. Introductory expressions (transitions such as *as a matter of fact, finally, secondly, furthermore, consequently*)

      As a matter of fact, I plan to arrive early.

   C. Introductory phrases

Long prepositional phrase:	For the psychology of his characters, the writer draws on his own experience.
Participial phrase:	Working without an outline, she needs to make many revisions.
Infinitive phrase:	To be sure, a writer needs imagination.

   D. Introductory dependent clauses beginning with a subordinating conjunction (See Chapter 15.)

      When the food arrived, we all grabbed for it.

      When the first draft is written, it is far from perfect.

PRACTICE 3

In each of the following sentences, insert commas wherever they are needed.

1. For many companies in the nineties a revised dress code for employees is an idea whose time has come.

2. Taking a hint from large corporations companies of every size are relaxing the rules of dress.

3. To keep in step with the times employers want to appear flexible and up to date.

4. If an employee wants to "dress down" on a certain day the new rules allow this freedom of choice.

5. Yes the more casual atmosphere of the workplace is a welcome change for many people.

4. Use commas surrounding a word, phrase, or clause when the word (or group of words) interrupts the main idea.

A. Interrupting word

> Jeff has, therefore, changed his plans.

B. Interrupting phrase

> Jeff has, in this case, changed his plans.
>
> Jeff, my uncle's stepson, has changed his plans.

C. Interrupting clause

> Jeff has, I am told, changed his plans.
>
> Jeff, who is my cousin, has changed his plans.

Note: Sometimes the same word, phrase, or clause can be used in more than one way. Often this changes the rule for punctuation.

Example: The word *therefore*

Use commas if the word interrupts in the middle of a clause:

> Jeff has, therefore, changed his plans.

Use a semicolon and a comma if the word connects two independent clauses:

> Jeff has won the scholarship; therefore, he has changed his plans.

> **Example:** The relative clause beginning with *who*

Use commas if the clause interrupts and is not essential to the main idea:

> Jeff, who is my cousin, has changed his plans.

Do not use commas if the clause is part of the identity, necessary to the main idea:

> The student who has won the scholarship is my cousin.

The clause *who has won the scholarship* is necessary for identifying which student is the cousin.

PRACTICE 4

In each of the following sentences, insert commas wherever they are needed.

1. Politics and public relations it must be admitted have become harder to separate.
2. Political commercials on television for example depend heavily on the use of images.
3. Washington, D.C. usually a political center becomes a center for advertising campaigns during every presidential campaign.
4. Political debate which used to appeal to people's thinking now must use dramatic images.
5. Every voter however must make up his or her own mind how to vote.

5. Use a comma around nouns in direct address. (A noun in direct address is the name or title used in speaking to someone.)

> I tell you this, Rebecca, in strictest confidence.

PRACTICE 5

In each of the following sentences, insert commas wherever they are needed.

1. Doctor the lab results came today.
2. I hope dear that you know what you're doing.
3. Sir the taxi is waiting.
4. You don't mother understand my point.
5. Theresa are you ready?

6. Use a comma in numbers of one thousand or larger.

2,555

2,555,555

PRACTICE 6

In each of the following numbers, insert commas wherever they are needed.

1. 10000000
2. 504321
3. 684977509
4. 20561
5. 9999999999

7. Use a comma to set off exact words spoken in dialogue.

"I've always depended," Blanche said, "on the kindness of strangers."

- The comma as well as the period is always placed inside the quotation marks.

PRACTICE 7

In each of the following sentences, insert commas wherever they are necessary.

1. "Joan didn't" they explained "do an adequate job."
2. She declared "I did exactly what I was told to do."
3. "The truth of the matter is" the publisher admitted "we can't use her work."
4. "Shall the company" we ask "be forced to pay for poor quality work?"
5. The judge said "The contract must be upheld."

8. Use a comma where it is necessary to prevent a misunderstanding.

Meaning is unclear: Before slicing the cooks must wash their hands.
In this case, the reader at first thinks the cooks are being sliced up.

Meaning is clear: Before slicing, the cooks must wash their hands.

PRACTICE 8

In each of the following sentences, insert commas wherever they are needed.

1. Striking the workers picketed the factory.

2. For Grace Suzanne Britt is her favorite essay writer.

3. Honking the driver alerted the biker.

4. The procedure does not hurt the child says.

5. Whatever that was was certainly strange.

EXERCISE 1   Using the Comma Correctly

Edit the following paragraph by inserting commas wherever needed.

After the stock market crash of 1929 Americans felt a tremendous sense of insecurity and experienced a loss of faith in their government. Herbert Hoover the United States president during the 1929 crash did not inspire the confidence needed for national recovery. Hoover projected such pessimism in fact that Secretary of State Henry Stimson noted "It was like sitting in a bath of ink to sit in his room." When Franklin D. Roosevelt took office in 1932 the American public felt hopeful that economic change was on the horizon. Roosevelt's very persona seemed to inspire confidence: a warm mellow voice an infectious smile and an obvious ease with crowds. The country needed more however than just a positive attitude. By November of 1932 more than fifteen million workers had lost their jobs. Roosevelt wished to tackle the problems of unemployment and financial insecurity so he expanded the powers of the federal government. The President put the banks under federal regulation put the unemployed to work building roads and dams and employed artists and writers in government-run projects. The real secret of the Roosevelt administration however was the trust and confidence the President instilled in the American spirit.

EXERCISE 2   Using the Comma Correctly

Edit the following paragraph by inserting commas wherever needed.

Spinning weaving and sewing have always been considered among the most basic of women's domestic tasks. Spinning was an important household task and spinners were considered essential members of every family. The term "spinster" which today often has a negative connotation was originally a term used for those who performed this indispensable work. This work was so important in fact that the Massachusetts legislature decreed in the mid 1600s that each household must contain at least one spinner. Before machinery took over the task the process of spinning consisted of raising crops of flax and cotton spinning the fibers into thread weaving the thread into cloth and then sewing the cloth into clothing and blankets. Because of the technological advancements over the past 150 years spinning is no longer done by hand. Spinning was one of the earliest crafts to be industrialized yet cottage weavers could still be found doing the work at home in the 1930s. A domestic task spinning provided a creative outlet for women who stayed in the home. When the textile factories began their operations factory owners looked to women as potential workers because of their history in cloth-making. The Lowell Mill a factory opened in Massachusetts in 1823 used as their workforce the daughters of rural New England farmers.

Three uses for the apostrophe

1. To form the possessive:

   A. Add *'s* to singular nouns:

   > the pen of the teacher   = the teacher*'s* pen
   >
   > the strategy of the boss = the boss*'s* strategy
   >
   > the work of the week   = the week*'s* work

   Watch out that you choose the right noun to make possessive. Always ask yourself *who* or *what* possesses something. In the sentences above, the teacher possesses the pen, the boss possesses the strategy, and the week possesses the work.

   Note these unusual possessives:

Hyphenated words:	father-in-law*'s* business
Joint possession:	Ronald and Nancy*'s* children
Individual possession:	Marcia's and Christopher*'s* opinions

   B. Add *'s* to irregular plural nouns that do not end in *-s*.

   > the games of the children = the children*'s* games
   >
   > the court for the people   = the people's court

   C. Add *'s* to indefinite pronouns:

   > anybody's guess
   >
   > someone's mistake

INDEFINITE PRONOUNS			
anyone	everyone	no one	someone
anybody	everybody	nobody	somebody
anything	everything	nothing	something

Possessive pronouns in English (his, hers, its, ours, yours, theirs, whose) do *not* use an apostrophe.

Whose jacket is this?

The jacket is *hers*.

The jackets are *theirs*.

D. Add an apostrophe only to regular plural nouns ending in -*s*.

the mothers of the babies = the babies' mothers

the company of the brothers = the brothers' company

• A few singular nouns ending in the *s* or *z* sound are awkward-sounding if another *s* sound is added. You may drop the final *s*. Let your ear help you make the decision.

Jesus' robe *not* Jesus's robe

Moses' law *not* Moses's law

2. To form certain plurals in order to prevent confusion, use 's.

A. Numbers: 100's

B. Letters: *a*'s and *b*'s

C. Years: 1800's or 1800s

D. Abbreviations: Ph.D.'s

E. Words referred to in a text: He uses too many *and's* in his writing.

• Be sure *not* to use the apostrophe to form a plural in any case other than these.

3. To show where letters have been omitted in contractions, use an apostrophe.

cannot   = can't

should not = shouldn't

will not   = won't (the only contraction that changes its spelling)

I am   = I'm

she will   = she'll

EXERCISE 1   **Using the Apostrophe**

Fill in each of the blanks below, using the rules you have just studied for uses of the apostrophe.

1. the armor of the knight   the _____ armor

2. the stride of the runner   the _____ stride

3. the choir of the children   the _____ choir

4. the work of the girls   the _____ work

5. the plans of the architects   the _____ plans

6. the footprints of a bear   the _____ footprints

7. the home of John and Marlene   _____ home

8. I will not answer you.   I _____ answer you.

9. You have not told me yet.   You _____ told me yet.

10. the opinions of the mother-in-law   the _____ opinions.

EXERCISE 2   **Using the Apostrophe**

Rewrite each of the following sentences using an apostrophe to make a contraction or to show possession. An example follows:

> The title of the book is *Reviving Ophelia*.
>
> The book's title is *Reviving Ophelia*.

1. What is happening to the lives of our girls when they enter puberty?

   _____

   _____

2. It does not work to use the experience of any previous generation of women; girls today live in a different world.

   _____

   _____

3. Reports from therapists detail a tremendous increase of serious and even life-threatening problems among junior high girls.

   _____

   _____

4. The author and therapist Mary Pipher believes the girls of today are being poisoned by our media-saturated culture.

   _____

   _____

5. She claims that America today limits <u>development of our teenagers</u>.

    _____

    _____

6. At puberty, girls crash into <u>the junk culture of our society</u>.

    _____

    _____

7. Girls know something is wrong but they do not think of blaming it on <u>the cultural problems of society</u>; they tend to blame themselves or their own families.

    _____

    _____

8. <u>The lives of our adolescent girls</u> are filled with pressures to be beautiful and sophisticated; this translates into junior high girls becoming involved with chemicals and being sexual.

    _____

    _____

9. <u>The advice from several national leaders</u> is unmistakably clear.

    _____

    _____

10. <u>The environment of our culture</u> must be more nurturing and less violent and sexualized.

    _____

    _____

Other marks of punctuation

Four uses for quotation marks

1. For a direct quotation:

   "Certainly," he answered, "you may wait in the lobby."

   Not for an indirect quotation:

   He said that she could wait in the lobby.

2. For material copied word for word from a source:

   In *Natural History* magazine, the scientist noted, "The danger from asteroids crashing into earth is very remote."

3. For titles of shorter works such as short stories, one-act plays, poems, articles in magazines and newspapers, songs, essays, and chapters of books:

"Once More to the Lake," an essay by E.B. White, is an American masterpiece.

"A Good Long Sidewalk" is one of my favorite short stories.

4. For words used in a special way:

"Lift" is the word used in England for an "elevator."

Underlining

> Underlining is used in handwriting or typing to indicate a title of a long work such as a book, full-length play, magazine, or newspaper. (In print, such titles are put in italics.)

In type or handwriting: Many interviews with writers appear in Poets and Writers.

In print: Many interviews with writers appear in *Poets and Writers.*

• PRACTICE 1

In each of the following sentences, insert quotation marks or underlining wherever needed.

1. Edgar Allan Poe's The Raven was first published in the Evening Mirror in 1845.
2. In one of his plays, Shakespeare asks, What's in a name?
3. The nurse said that the patient would have to return in a week.
4. A groupie is a person who follows popular musicians from place to place.
5. Max Beerbohm's essay Going Out for a Walk appeared in the book The Magic of Walking.

Three uses for the semicolon

1. To join two independent clauses whose ideas and sentence structure are related:

He did not vote in the primary; he did vote in the general election.

2. To combine two sentences using an adverbial conjunction:

He did not vote in the primary; however, he did vote in the general election.

3. To separate items in a series when the items themselves contain commas:

> The mayor met with Frank Burns, Chief of Police; Shelia MacKaye, Press Officer; and James Wheatley, District Attorney.

If the writer had used only commas to separate items in the last example, the reader might think six people had met with the mayor.

PRACTICE 2

In each of the following sentences, insert a semicolon wherever needed.

1. Walking in the city can be stimulating relaxing in a park can be refreshing.

2. The car needs a new alternator now otherwise you could break down at any time.

3. The children spent the entire day watching *All Dogs Go to Heaven* a comedy *The Little Mermaid* an animated Disney movie and *Heidi* a classic starring Shirley Temple.

4. The town made an effort to attract tourists as a result its financial situation has improved.

5. The teacher was very patient however the paper was due last week.

Four uses for the colon

1. After a completed independent clause (often using the expressions *the following* or *as follows*) when the material that follows is a list, an illustration, or an explanation:

   A. A list:

   > Please bring the following items: binoculars, camera, and film.

   Notice colons are not used in the middle of clauses in which such expressions as *consists of, including, like,* or *such as* introduce a list.

   > Please bring items such as binoculars, camera, and film.

   B. An explanation or illustration:

   > He came up the hard way: he started in the mail room.

2. For the salutation of a business letter:

   > To whom it may concern:
   >
   > Dear Personnel Director:

3. In telling time:

The plane departs 10:55 A.M.

4. Between the title and subtitle of a book:

Bearing Witness: Selections from African-American Autobiography in the Twentieth Century.

PRACTICE 3

In each of the following sentences, insert colons as needed.

1. Three inventions have changed our lives in this century electricity, the airplane, and television.
2. The sport's fan had only one problem how to get the player's autograph.
3. She looked for a copy of *Song of the Hills Memories of a Country Childhood.*
4. She promised she would be on the 1018 from Pittsburgh.
5. I need several items such as paper clips, tape, and a stapler.

The dash and parentheses

The comma, dash, and parentheses can all be used to show an interruption of the main idea. The particular form you choose depends on the degree of interruption.

> Use the dash for a less formal and more emphatic interruption of the main idea.

He wrote—I discovered—in code.

The president spoke—and I recall this clearly—without any notes.

> Use the parentheses to insert extra information that some of your readers might want to know but that is not at all essential for the main idea. Such information is not emphasized.

Christa McAuliffe (1948–1986) was scheduled to be America's first teacher in space.

The contract clearly shows (see the last clause) that our position is valid.

PRACTICE 4

Insert dashes or parentheses wherever needed.

1. He was or so she believed a spy from another company.

2. He will bring us at once and this is really crucial his passport and other documents of identification.

3. The study see the charts on file was completed in 1989.

4. George Burns his real name was Nathan Birnbaum lived to be a hundred.

5. All public figures and I mean actors, politicians, writers, and sports figures must be sensitive to the feelings of every group of people.

EXERCISE 1 Using Other Marks of Punctuation Correctly

In each of the following sentences, insert apostrophes, quotation marks, underlining, semicolons, colons, the dash, or parentheses wherever they are needed.

1. Sweet Lorraine is the essay James Baldwin wrote as a tribute to Lorraine Hansberry.

2. To help your children plan their summer, you must do the following keep their interests in mind, keep an eye on their friends, and keep your budget in view.

3. Writing that letter gave him a lasting emotion satisfaction.

4. The Fall of the Roman Empire 476 A.D. was a critical point in human history.

5. She wanted to rent a car he wanted to go by train.

6. Everything she predicted came true my watch stopped, my car broke down, and it rained that night.

7. Elvis Presley also known as the King of Rock and Roll changed the direction of popular music in America.

8. Do you know how to say muchas gracias in any other languages?

9. Andrew Jackson also known as Old Hickory was one of our most colorful presidents.

10. She gave me her word I remember this clearly that she would call back today.

EXERCISE 2 Using Other Marks of Punctuation Correctly

In each of the following sentences, insert apostrophes, quotation marks, underlining, semicolons, colons, the dash, or parentheses wherever they are needed.

1. She borrowed the book entitled Howard Hughes the Untold Story.

2. The road leading to success in business depends on two factors a lot of hard work and a little luck.

3. I cannot help you he answered but I will try to be supportive.

4. Her best jewelry the pieces she keeps in the bank came from her grandmother.

5. John Updike's A & P is a short story that has led to a lot of interpretations.

6. Movies in fact all parts of the entertainment industry depend on a system of superstars.

7. We refer to that long period after World War II as the Cold War.

8. Einsteins theory of relativity E=mc^2 still confuses many people.

9. The band was made up of some find musicians including Tom Fox, guitar Betty Ahern, bass and Joyce Blake, flute.

10. The bands director called for extra rehearsals.

Mastery and editing tests

TEST 1 Editing for Correct Capitalization and Punctuation

Read the following paragraph and insert the correct marks of punctuation and capitalization wherever they are needed.

The los angeles lakers basketball team had an exciting day at the great western forum. The team had enjoyed a satisfactory season but something was missing. Then a familiar face made everyone suddenly sit up and pay attention. The crowd became excited and some people even yelled out a loud yes when the player was seen on the court. Here was a man who had been away for five years but now he was back. Earvin Johnson or magic Johnson as he is best known is the most famous hiv patient in the world. Many people were stunned by the announcement of his condition others wondered if his medical condition would lead to full blown aids and still others expressed fear that other players would be in danger just by playing with him. However number 32 feels confident and upbeat as he prepares to reconquer the national basketball association.

TEST 2 Editing for Correct Capitalization and Punctuation

Read the following paragraph and insert the correct marks of punctuation and capitalization wherever they are needed.

The mother of a young student at the walker upper elementary school in charlottesville virginia teaches an unusual subject penmanship. The son almost never uses script to write anything. He does sign a card to his mother on three occasions her birthday on valentines day and on mothers day. Like many other people in the united states this student is either printing everything letter by letter or using a computer to write. Penmanship today pretty much stops at the printing level says rose matousek of the american association of handwriting analysts. The post office reports that only fifteen percent of all handwritten envelopes are written in script another fifteen percent are hand printed. A related problem reported in Newsweek magazine march 18 1996 is the legibility of what people write. 10000000 pieces of mail end up in the dead letter office of the post office because no one is able to read the handwriting. One researcher reports that 58 percent of all information on hospital charts is also difficult or impossible to read. This is an important fact because a patient who needs seldane but who gets feldene will have a very different reaction. Dont you think handwriting is important when your life depends on it?

TEST 3   Editing for Correct Capitalization and Punctuation

Read the following paragraph and insert the correct marks of punctuation and capitalization wherever they are needed.

Perhaps the most famous comet in the world is halleys comet which visits our part of the universe very rarely. However an even more brilliant visitor to our skies is comet hyakutake which has made usually calm scientists very excited. Steven Ostro of nasas jet propulsion laboratory in Pasadena california observed that Hyakutake may be remembered as the most outstanding comet of our century. On a monday in march 1996 it made its closest approach to earth at about 2 A.M. it was as bright as the stars of the big dipper and as large as a full moon. Throughout the entire northern hemisphere even where there were bright lights from big cities this comet was clearly visible. People all across the united states were having what they called viewing parties and one astronomy club in lincoln nebraska stated publicly that it would make its telescope available until everyone was tired of looking. comets like the current one come from an area known as the oort cloud where 100 billion comets are held each one waiting for a pull of gravity from the sun. It is believed that Hyakutake last came to our neighborhood 18000 years ago but let us hope we will not have to wait that long for another spectacular comet.

Chapter 20

Step 3 Review: Using All You Have Learned

Revising more complicated fragments and run-ons

By now, you have learned to recognize the basic fragment or run-on error in your writing. You have worked with revising fairly uncomplicated sentences so that they are correct.

This chapter presents sentences that are more complicated. Even though a sentence may have more than one dependent clause and several phrases, you must always remember that the sentence must have an independent clause with a subject and verb. For example:

> After the investigator examined every part of the engine, which had failed during the airplane's recent Atlantic flight, he suspected that metal fatigue would be the conclusion of the government experts.

Cross out all dependent clauses and phrases. Can you find the independent clause? What is the subject? What is the verb? *He suspected* is the independent clause. All other parts of the sentence are dependent clauses that include many prepositional phrases.

The following exercises require mastery of all the skills you have learned in this unit on the sentence. See if you can now revise these more complicated sentences to rid them of fragments and run-ons.

EXERCISE 1   **Correcting Fragments and Run-Ons**

Read each of the following examples and mark each one as a fragment (F), a run-on (R), or a complete sentence (C). If an example is a fragment or a run-on, revise it so that it is correct. Use methods you have learned for coordination and subordination.

———   1. As a child, Gebrselassie, the great long distance runner, shared a pair of running shoes with his older brother, Tekeye, and a younger sister, Yeshi, the family could not afford to buy each one a pair of running shoes.

_____

_____

_____

———   2. Gebrselassie and his brothers who tended the crops with oxen and wooden plows and they walked up to four miles to haul drinking water from wells.

_____

_____

_____

———   3. Their father wanting them to be doctors, teachers, clerks, anything but runners and discouraging the sport, believing it had no practical use.

_____

_____

_____

———   4. When Gebrselassie was ten his mother died during childbirth so his older sister raised the children.

_____

_____

_____

———   5. Following sports through a battery-powered transistor radio and learning of Ethiopia's Yifter winning a double victory at the 1980 Moscow Olympic Games.

_____

_____

_____

———   6. Gebrselassie walked or ran six miles to school, and to this day, he has a slight hitch in his form which developed from carrying his books to one side.

_____

_____

_____

_____ 7. Even though Gebrselassie could afford to live in style after he became world famous, he lives in a modest house and routinely goes to bed by 9 P.M. awakening by 5:30 A.M. and goes without a personal coach or a private car because he believes that he should live as his people live.

_____

_____

_____ 8. With five world records and expected to win the gold in the 5,000 and 10,000 meters at the Atlanta Olympics.

_____

_____

_____ 9. Everyone knows Ethiopia is poor but when Gebrselassie breaks a world record he hopes that people of the world see that Ethiopians do what they can with what they have.

_____

_____

_____

_____ 10. He runs with effortless grace his head is totally still some say he looks like he's out there for a fun run.

_____

_____

_____

EXERCISE 2   Correcting Fragments and Run-Ons

Read each of the following examples and mark each one as a fragment (F), a run-on (R), or a complete sentence (C). If an example is a fragment or a run-on, revise it so that it is correct. Use methods you have learned for coordination and subordination.

_____ 1. The banjo as we know it today with its long history.

_____

_____ 2. The five-string banjo has been on the move.

_____

———— 3. Such as originating in Africa, coming across the ocean on slave ships, becoming popular in theaters in the 1800s and reaching the hands of Jerry Garcia of the Grateful Dead.

_____

_____

———— 4. The well-known banjo player Tony Trischka owns more than a dozen banjos that reflect the history of the instrument.

_____

_____

———— 5. For example, a banza made from a gourd, a classical banjo made in Boston a century ago, and a bluegrass instrument from the 1930s.

_____

_____

———— 6. Joel Walker Sweeney was one of the nineteenth century's great banjo players, showing what the banjo could do, he performed in minstrel shows throughout the country.

_____

_____

———— 7. As a child, Sweeney so intent on playing a banjo that he killed the family cat in order to make himself his first banjo.

_____

_____

———— 8. Bluegrass is at the heart of most Banjo music today, the banjo was the instrument that souped up bluegrass music.

_____

_____

———— 9. Tony Trischka's recordings show a wide range of music he appreciates both African music and classical, both hard-driving bluegrass and banjo rock.

_____

_____

———— 10. The Kingston Trio used the banjo in a song called "MTA" and when Tony heard the song at the age of thirteen, he knew this was the instrument for him.

_____

_____

Mastery and editing tests

TEST 1   Editing for Errors

Edit the following paragraph. Hint: you will find an opportunity to correct each of the following:

Punctuation for a compound sentence using coordination

Punctuation for a complex sentence using subordination

Comma after an introductory phrase or clause

Apostrophe for possessive

Apostrophe for contraction

Punctuation for a full length work of art

Punctuation for an appositive

Punctuation for city and state

Irregular Verb Form

A run-on

At the age of thirty-seven Arthur Miller wrote The Crucible a play that is considered one of the greatest of all American plays. Its taught in most high schools across the country. The setting is Salem Massachusetts at the time of the Salem witch trials its theme is what happens when a society becomes paranoid. Now at the age of eighty, Miller has wrote the screenplay for a movie of this play. Writing the screenplay for the movie was different from writing the original play because he had to proceed with images rather than words. After Miller viewed some shots for the movie he was overwhelmed with the power of the visual. He was pleased with the results. Arthur Miller sees the theme of hatred and paranoia as a universal theme and he points to todays American politics as especially filled with hatred and paranoia.

TEST 2   Editing for Errors

Edit the following paragraph. Hint: you will find an opportunity to correct each of the following:

A run-on

Incorrect use of the apostrophe

Fragment

Punctuation for a compound sentence using coordination

Punctuation for a word or phrase that interrups

Punctuation for a complex sentence using subordination

Capitalization

Punctuation for a series

Subject-verb agreement

Need for parentheses

Many centuries ago, the Chinese pounded together a mixture of rags tree bark and old fish nets. Then they placed the mixture in a vat filled with water soon tiny fibers from the mixture were hanging suspended in the water. If a person dipped a mold into the water and lifted it out the mixture would dry and become a piece of paper. Today, paper production depends on machinery and modern technology but the basic process is the same as the one originally used by the ancient Chinese. Fine writing papers still contains a large percentage of rags although most paper made today contains a great deal of wood. The method of converting wood pulp into paper discovered only a little more than a century ago. Although the Chinese developed paper making and sold paper to merchants who traveled through China, they kept the secret of how to make paper for a long time. After a few hundred years however the Japanese learned how to produce it, and not long after that around the year 700 the Arabs learned the secret. After that, Arabs introduced paper wherever they traded, and by the year 1200 europeans were making their own paper. By the 1700s, people in Europe were consuming so much paper that they were running out of rags to use in the process. They also found a wider variety of uses for paper. They built chairs and bookcases out of paper, and in 1793 in Norway, a paper church that could hold 800 people was built. It served it's congregation for nearly 40 years.

TEST 3   Editing for Errors

Edit the following paragraph. Hint: you will find an opportunity to correct each of the following:

Inconsistency in verb tense

Capitalization

An apostrophe for possessive

Irregular verb form

Wrong pronoun form

Dangling modifier

Punctuation for compound sentence using coordination

Punctuation for a series

Subject-verb agreement

Fragment

The famous painter Paul Gauguin with an adventurous life and a troubled career. He was born in France in 1848. Three years later, the family traveled to Lima, Peru but on the way his father died. Young Paul and his mother lived for four years with relatives in the capital of Peru. After the family returns to France, Paul finished school and went to work in a business office. His marriage to a young danish woman seemed to give him a traditional lifestyle, but Gauguin now begun to turn his attention more and more to art. He bought paintings for hisself became friends with artists of the day and soon had a studio of his own in Paris. By 1883, he was so interested in art that, over his wifes objections, he quit his job and painted full time. Moving his large family from Paris to save money, his savings soon ran out. When he died several years later, Gauguin's belongings had to be sold to pay off his debts. One person paid $1.50 for the last painting he ever did. Today, any one of his hundreds of paintings are worth millions.

Step 4

UNDERSTANDING THE POWER OF WORDS

CONTENTS

Choosing Words That Work

Using words rich in meaning

Writing is a constant search to find the right word to express thoughts and feelings as accurately as possible. When a writer wants to be precise, or wants to give a flavor to a piece of writing, the possibilities are almost endless for word choice and sentence construction. The creative writer looks for words that have rich and appropriate meanings and associations.

For instance, if you were describing older people, you might choose one of these words or phrases:

> retirees
>
> pensioners
>
> senior citizens
>
> old fogeys
>
> the elderly
>
> golden agers

Some words have no associations beyond the strict dictionary meaning. These words are said to be neutral. Which word in the above list is strictly neutral, with no positive or negative emotional associations? (The answer is *the elderly*.) The person who is writing a brochure for a community center for older people would probably choose the phrase *senior citizens* because these words respectfully identify the age of the group involved. A person who is addressing a group of people who have questions about their social security benefits might use the term *retirees*. In some cases, companies would refer to their workers who are receiving pensions as *pensioners*. A person who is trying to interest people in investing in a retirement community might use the term *golden agers* to give a glowing impression of life during retirement. Which slang phrase might an impatient person use to describe a couple of elderly people who are not up to date or aware of current thinking and events? (The answer is *old fogeys*.)

EXERCISE 1   Using Words Rich in Meaning

The following five words all have the same basic meaning: a method or program for doing something. For each word, however, an additional meaning makes the word richer and more specific. Match each word in Column A with the letter of the definition from Column B that best fits the meaning of the word.

Column A

_____ 1. blueprint

_____ 2. design

_____ 3. scheme

_____ 4. strategy

_____ 5. outline

Column B

a. a preliminary draft or plan for a piece of writing using Roman numerals and/or Arabic numerals to enumerate the points

b. a well thought out plan to achieve a goal, like a company's plan to market a product or a team's plan to win a game

c. a plan that is usually in an artistic or graphic form

d. technical drawings rendered as white lines on a blue background often associated with architectural plans

e. a systematic plan of action, often secretive or devious

The following five words all have the basic meaning: to exchange opinions on important issues. Match each word in Column A with the letter of the definition from Column B that best fits the meaning of the word.

Column A

_____ 1. argue

_____ 2. debate

_____ 3. discuss

_____ 4. contend

_____ 5. dispute

Column B

a. to sharply oppose another person's ideas

b. to examine a subject by exchanging opinions

c. to support a position against others using facts and opinions

d. to argue formally usually in public

e. to strive in debate or controversy

EXERCISE 2   Using Words Rich in Meaning

Listed under each word or phrase are four words that share the general meaning. Each word, however, has a more precise meaning as well. In each case, give the word's more precise definition.

to be funny

1. droll   _____

2. amusing   _____

3. comical   _____

4. hilarious   _____

to be polite

1. civil   _____
2. genteel   _____
3. mannerly   _____
4. courteous   _____

a special way of speaking

1. lingo   _____
2. gibberish   _____
3. dialect   _____
4. jargon   _____

to be frightened

1. terrorized   _____
2. startled   _____
3. alarmed   _____
4. frantic   _____

Understanding loaded words: Denotation/connotation

The careful writer must consider more than the dictionary meaning of a word. Some words have different meanings for different people.

> The *denotation* of a word is its strict dictionary meaning.
>
> The *connotation* of a word is the meaning (apart from the dictionary meaning) that a person attaches to a word because of the person's personal experience with the word.
>
> | | |
> |---|---|
> | *word:* | liberal |
> | *denotation:* | to favor nonrevolutionary progress or reform |
> | *possible connotations:* | socially active, free thinking, too generous, far left, favoring many costly government programs |

Politicians are usually experts in understanding the connotations of a word. They know, for instance, that if they want to get votes in a conservative area, they should not refer to their views as liberal. The strict dictionary meaning of *liberal* is "to favor nonrevolutionary progress or reform," certainly an idea that most people would support. However, when most people hear the words *liberal* or *conservative*, they bring to the words many political biases and experiences from their past: their parents' attitudes, the political and social history of the area in which they live, and many other factors that may correctly or incorrectly color their understanding of a word.

Choosing words that are not neutral but that have more exact or appropriate meanings is a powerful skill for your writing, one that will help your reader better understand the ideas you want to communicate. As your vocabulary grows, your writing will become richer and deeper. Your work will reflect your understanding of all the shades of meanings that words can have.

EXERCISE 1   Denotation/Connotation

In this exercise you have the opportunity to think of words that are richer in associations than the neutral words that are underlined in the sentences below. Write your own word choice in the space to the right of each sentence. Discuss with others in your class the associations you make with the words you have chosen.

1. Tony works on his car nearly every night. _____

2. Last week he asked some people he knows to help. _____

3. They worked on the project for three or four hours one evening. _____

4. I could hear the sounds all the way down the street. _____

5. The radio played their favorite music. _____

6. After several hours, the workers went downtown to pick up some refreshments. _____

7. Later, we saw their vehicles return. _____

8. We thought we saw the addition of several more people. _____

9. Their voices became more audible. _____

10. The work had ended, and now they were having a good time. _____

EXERCISE 2   Denotation/Connotation

Below are several sentences that contain words that may have positive or negative associations for the reader. Read the sentences and study the underlined words that often carry "emotional" meanings not contained in the dictionary meaning. Below each sentence, write the emotional meaning you associate with the underlined word. Discuss your answers with your classmates.

1. The young woman gazed at the photograph of her father.

_____

2. He appeared to be wearing some kind of uniform.

_____

3. At least two airplanes could be seen in the background.

_____

4. Her mother always kept the photograph next to the <u>religious statue</u> on the nightstand.

   _____

5. The <u>ocean</u> had separated them from each other.

   _____

Wordiness: In writing, less can be more!

In *The Elements of Style,* essayist E.B. White quotes his old teacher William Strunk, Jr. who said that a sentence "should contain no unnecessary words" and a paragraph "no unnecessary sentences." Strunk's philosophy of writing included the commandment he gave many times in his class at Cornell University, "Omit needless words!" It was a lesson that E.B. White took to heart, with wonderful results that we see in his own writing. Often, less is more.

A summary follows of the most important ways you should cut the actual number of words in order to strengthen the power of your ideas. As you read each example of wordiness, notice how the revision has cut out unnecessary words.

Wordy Expressions	Revision

1. Avoid redundancy.

exact same	same
large jumbo size	jumbo
round in shape	round

2. Avoid wordy phrases.

due to the fact that	because
for the stated reason that	because
in this day and age	today
at this point in time	now

3. Avoid overuse of the verb *to be*.

That chair is in need of a new slipcover.	That chair needs a new slipcover.

4. Avoid repeating the same word too many times.

Dogs make great pets. Dogs provide companionship.	Dogs make great pets by providing companionship.

5. Avoid beginning a sentence with *there is* or *it is* whenever possible.

It is wonderful to travel.	Travel is wonderful.

6. Avoid flowery or pretentious language.

I am completely overwhelmed when I consider that the theatrical event that I have just witnessed will linger long in my memory.	I'll never forget this play.

	Wordy Expressions	**Revision**

7. **Avoid apologetic, tentative expressions.**

in my opinion

| In my opinion, the grading policy for this course should be changed. | The grading policy for this course should be changed. |

it seems to me

| Right now, it seems to me that finding a job in my field is very difficult. | Right now, finding a job in my field is very difficult. |

I will try to explain

| In this paper, I will try to explain my views on censorship of the campus newspaper. | Censoring the campus newspaper is a mistake. |

if I may say so

| If I may say so, the shoes you want to buy do not fit. | The shoes you want to buy do not fit. |

EXERCISE 1   **Revising Wordy Sentences**

For each of the following sentences, underline the part that is unnecessarily wordy, and on the line below the sentence provide the revision.

1. Tuesday we will first begin the study of violence in the news media.

     _____

2. The violence in the news is making many people in the public to be very paranoid.

     _____

3. There is hardly a news program today without the graphic description of murders and other violent assaults.

     _____

4. Many children have the fear that they should not go outside their homes.

     _____

5. We are all in a need of feeling safer in our neighborhoods.

     _____

6. As far as mothers are concerned, their children are not safe.

     _____

7. We are in the process of evaluating the quality of our lives.

     _____

8. Due to the fact of the violence, children's freedom has become limited.

   _____

9. In our opinion, it would seem to us that the need for more supervised activities for children is essential.

   _____

10. It is not good that children come home to empty apartments and houses.

    _____

EXERCISE 2   Revising Wordy Sentences

For each of the following sentences, underline the part that is unnecessarily wordy, and on the line below the sentence provide the revision.

1. In these difficult times we must make decisions based on solid information.

   _____

2. Her graduation dress is red in color.

   _____

3. In terms of artistic expression, Mildred's playing is superb.

   _____

4. It would appear that we have a flat tire.

   _____

5. I will try to provide all the reasons for the decline of the Roman Empire.

   _____

6. There are several objections to the president's plans for congressional action.

   _____

7. It thrills and excites every member of the class to talk about details of the upcoming square dance, to be followed by a full chicken dinner.

   _____

8. The war was supposed to be the last war, but many wars since then have proved this not to be true.

   _____

9. The piece of property is in the shape of a square.

   _____

10. She is desirous to be helpful.

    _____

Recognizing appropriate language for formal writing

In speaking or writing to our family and friends, an informal style is always appropriate because it is relaxed and conversational. On the other hand, writing and speaking in school or at work requires a more formal style, one that is less personal and more detached in tone. In formal writing situations, slang is not appropriate and any use of language that is seen as sexist or disrespectful to any individual or groups of individuals is not at all acceptable.

> *Slang* is a term that refers to a special word or expression that a particular group of people use, often with the intention of keeping the meaning to themselves. A characteristic of a slang word or expression is that it is often used for a limited period of time and then is forgotten. For example:
>
> The party was *grand*. (1940s)
>
> The party was *awesome*. (1990s)

Slang or Informal Words	Acceptable
bucks	dollars
kids	children
cops	police
a bummer	a bad experience
off the wall	crazy
yummy	delicious

Clipped Language	
doc	doctor
pro	professional
t.v.	television

Sexist Language	
mailman	mail carrier
common man	average person
The teacher is an important man. He can influence the lives of many children in the community.	Teachers are important people. They can influence the lives of many children in a community.

Notice that in the last example, one way to revise sentences that contain the male references *he, him,* or *his,* is to put each singular reference into the plural. Therefore, *man* becomes *people,* and *he* becomes *they.*

EXERCISE 1   Recognizing Inappropriate Language for Formal Writing

The following sentences contain words that are informal, slang, or sexist. Circle the word in each sentence that is inappropriate for formal writing, and on the line to the right of each sentence, provide a more formal word or expression to replace the informal word.

1. The leader of that group is a screwball.   _____

2. He's always wired over something.   _____

3. Is it guts or just ego that makes him argue about every little thing?   _____

4. Listening to him yakking even makes his followers tired sometimes.   _____

5. No one can accuse him of being a slacker.   _____

6. However, his opponents accuse him of being tacky.   _____

7. Also, he does his own thing and never listens to anybody else.   _____

8. The chairman of our committee has just published a very critical letter about his professional conduct.   _____

9. Several t.v. clips have raised some questions.   _____

10. His shenanigans are going to get him into trouble.   _____

EXERCISE 2   Recognizing Inappropriate Language for Formal Writing

The following sentences contain words that are informal, slang, or sexist. Circle the word in each sentence that is inappropriate for formal writing, and on the line to the right of each sentence, provide a more formal word or expression to replace the informal word.

1. He's hyper tonight.   _____

2. The entire team is pumped up for the game.   _____

3. They intend to skunk the other team.   _____

4. Here come his pals Jeremy and Gia; They're an item these days.   _____

5. What's the crummy weather going to be tonight?   _____

6. The weathermen predict the continuation of this wind and rain.   _____

7. My bro' won't go with us if the weather is bad.   _____

8. He's the most up-tight person you can imagine.   _____

9. Why don't you fib and tell him the rain will stop by nine?   _____

10. He'd never be a sucker for that story.   _____

Mastery and editing tests

TEST 1   Editing for Wordiness and Inappropriate Language

The following paragraph contains examples of wordiness as well as inappropriate language (slang, clipped words and sexist terms). Underline the problems as you come to them and then revise the paragraph. (Hint: Find and revise at least 10 words or phrases.)

One of the most outstanding scientists in the U.S. today came from China in 1936. She is Chien-Hsiung Wu, and her story is the story of the development of physics in our century. When Miss Wu came to America in 1936, she intended to do grad work and hightail it back to China. However, World War II broke out and she remained instead to teach at Smith College, where she enjoyed working with the Smithies. Very soon after that, she was employed by Princeton U. At that time, she was the only girl physicist hired by a top research university. Later, she became an important worker on Columbia University's Manhattan Project, the project that developed the A bomb. She hunkered down at Columbia for more than thirty years, her many scientific discoveries bringing her world recognition. In 1990, Wu became the first living scientist to have an asteroid named in her honor. This celestial object whirling in the darkest corners of outer space is now carrying her name.

TEST 2   Editing for Wordiness and Inappropriate Language

The following paragraph contains examples of wordiness as well as inappropriate language (slang, clipped words and sexist terms). Underline the problems as you come to them and then revise the paragraph. (Hint: Find and revise at least 10 words or phrases.)

In terms of social manners, people are becoming more and more concerned. I mean like what has happened to consideration for others? Cars do not even stop for old geezers trying to cross the street, and very few people will help a gal who is trying to carry several heavy bags of groceries in the rain. There is more and more talk about this as people talk about what we can do to encourage people to be more polite. When it comes to pregnant women riding trains or buses, the situation is even more serious. All the docs say that a woman who is expecting should not be on her feet when she is all wiped out. She should be given a seat on a train or bus, especially when there are guys just sitting there, reading the paper in their snazzy business suits. One pregnant woman was really ticked off when she broke her arm in her seventh month of pregnancy. There she was, on her feet in a subway car, and not one man would get up for her.

TEST 3   Editing for Wordiness and Inappropriate Language

The following paragraph contains examples of wordiness as well as inappropriate language (slang, clipped words and sexist terms). Underline the problems as you come to them and then revise the paragraph. (Hint: Find and revise at least 10 words or phrases.)

Parents and kids often butt heads when it comes to homework, but this does not have to be the case. A number of basic points should be kept in mind when a parent helps her offspring with an assignment. First, find the right spot for the homework to be done. This usually is the kitchen table. You can even place a sign, such as "Buzz off!" in the area so that everyone in the family will respect the attempts being made by the little scholar to accomplish all the necessary tasks. Also important is the need for a regular schedule: plan a time in the P.M. when homework gets done. Also, do not do your son's homework for him; this only creates dependence and gives the teach the wrong impression. It is necessary that parents keep riding their offspring if academic things are to get done.

Paying Attention to Look-Alikes and Sound-Alikes

Many words are confusing because they either sound alike or look alike, but they are spelled differently and have different meanings. Master the words in each group before proceeding to the next group. The first column gives the word. The second column gives the definition, and the third column gives a sentence using the word correctly.

Group I: Words that sound alike

1. it's/its

it's	contraction of *it is*	It's raining.
its	possessive pronoun	Its wheel is missing.

2. they're/their/there

they're	contraction of *they are*	They're busy.
their	possessive pronoun	Their job is done.
there	at that place	The report is there.

3. we're/were/where

we're	contraction of *we are*	We're delayed.
were	past tense of *are*	We were delayed.
where	at or in what place	Where is the train?

4. who's/whose

who's	contraction of *who is*	Who's responsible?
whose	possessive pronoun	Whose job is this?

5. you're/your

you're	contraction of *you are*	You're the winner.
your	possessive pronoun	Your trophy is here.

6. aural/oral

aural	related to hearing	After the aural exam, he received a hearing aid.
oral	related to the mouth	Good oral hygiene saves your teeth.

7. buy/by

buy (verb)	to purchase	She only buys items on sale.
by (prep.)	near	He is waiting by the train.
	past	The actress walked by her fans.
	not later than	I will see you by midnight.

8. capital/capitol

capital (adj.)	major	He had a capital idea.
	fatal	Opponents of capital punishment are many.
	leading city	The capital of California is Sacramento.
	money	The businessman ran out of capital.
capitol (noun)	a legislative building	They light the capitol building every night.

9. close/clothes

close	to shut	*Close* the window.
clothes	garments	His *clothes* are worn.

Note: *cloth* is a piece of fabric, not to be confused with the word *clothes,* which is always plural.

10. coarse/course

coarse (adj.)	rough	It was a *coarse* comedy.
	common or of inferior quality	The dress was made of a *coarse* fabric.
course (noun)	direction	The ship went off *course.*
	part of a meal	The main *course* was fish.
	a unit of study	She took all her required *courses.*

11. complement/compliment

complement (noun)	something that completes	The *complement* of the angle is 45 degrees.
(verb)	to complete	The hat *complements* her dress.

compliment			
	(noun)	an expression of praise	She happily accepted the *compliment*.
	(verb)	to praise	All her friends *complimented* her.

12. forward/foreword

forward	to send on to another address	She *forwarded* my mail.
	moving toward the front or the future	Please go *forward*.
	bold	He is a very *forward* child.
foreword	introduction to a book	The *foreword* was better than the book.

13. passed/past

passed (verb)	moved ahead	She *passed* every exam.
past (noun)	time before the present	He lives in the *past*.
(prep.)	beyond	She drove *past* the diner.
(adj.)	no longer current	The *past* semester was difficult.

14. plain/plane

plain (adj.)	ordinary	The children prefer *plain* vanilla ice cream.
	clear	Her *plain* dress was attractive.
(noun)	flat land without trees	The African *plains* are beautiful.
plane	an aircraft	The *plane's* arrival was delayed.
	a flat, level surface	The *plane* of the diamond gleamed.
	a carpenter's tool for leveling wood	The carpenter's *plane* broke.
	a level of development	She thinks on a different *plane*.

15. presence/presents

presence	the state of being present	Your *presence* is required.
	a person's manner	The queen's *presence* was unforgettable.
presents	gifts	They received many wedding *presents*.

16. principal/principle

principal (adj.)	most important		The *principal* singer was replaced.
(noun)	main		The *principal* task has been done.
	the head of a school		The *principal* announced the exam.
	a sum of money		He paid the interest but not the *principal*.
principle	a rule or standard		She would not violate her *principles*.

17. rain/reign/rein

rain	water falling to earth in drops	The *rain* turned to sleet.
reign	a period of rule for a king or queen	King Tut's *reign* was brief.
rein	a strap attached to a bridle, used to control a horse	The *rein* was useless to the jockey.

18. sight/site/cite

sight	the ability to see a view	He kept the wolf in *sight*.
site	the plot of land where something is located; the place for an event	They chose a new *site* for the gym.
cite	to quote as an authority or example	Please *cite* the correct law.

19. stationary/stationery

stationary (adj.)	standing still	The truck was *stationary* in the mud.
stationery (noun)	writing paper and envelopes	The printed *stationery* was expensive.

20. to/too/two

to (prep.)	in a direction toward	Bill came *to* the party.
too (adv.)	also	Sally came *too*.
	very	It was *too* crowded.
two	number	The *two* of them went home.

21. vain/vane/vein

vain	conceited	The film star was very *vain*.
	unsuccessful	They tried in *vain* to save the dog.

vane	an ornament which turns in the wind (often in the shape of a rooster, seen on tops of barns)	The weather *vane* rusted on the barn.
vein	a blood vessel	The surgeon repaired the *vein*.
	the branching framework of a leaf	We could see the *veins* on the leaf.
	an area in the earth where a mineral like gold or silver is found	The *vein* of gold was visible in the rock.
	a passing attitude	He talked in a comic *vein*.

22. waist/waste

waist	the middle portion of a body or garment	The tailor measured his *waist*.
waste (verb)	to use carelessly	He *wasted* his money.
(noun)	discarded objects	The factory dumped its *waste* in the river.

23. weather/whether

weather (noun)	atmospheric conditions	The *weather* was cold and rainy.
whether (conj.)	if it is the case that	Things happen *whether* or not you are ready.

24. whole/hole

whole	complete	The *whole* pie was eaten.
hole	an opening	Moths made a *hole* in the dress.

25. write/right/rite

write	to form letters and words; to compose	*Write* a post card to Fred.
right	correct	Tell me the *right* approach.
	to conform to justice, law, or morality	He has a *right* to a trial.
	toward a conservative point of view	His political thinking is to the *right*.
rite	a traditional, often religious ceremony	Most societies have *rites* for newborn babies.

EXERCISE 1 **Group I: Words that Sound Alike**

In the following paragraph, ten words that are often confused are underlined. In the spaces provided, write C if the word is correct. If the word is incorrect, write the correct word.

In order to discover our cultural <u>passed</u>, <u>aural</u> history is not enough; we must also recover our written heritage. Part of that heritage is the work of William Wells Brown, a 19th century African-American writer <u>who's</u> writings are being studied today. Brown was born a slave in Kentucky around 1815, but soon was moved to Missouri where he suffered under a <u>coarse</u> master. When he was put to work in St. Louis in 1827, he suffered under another cruel owner. However, he had a better experience when he worked at the *St. Louis Times,* <u>were</u> he obtained his first education. After escaping in Cincinnati in 1834, Brown taught himself to read and <u>rite</u>, and by the time he moved to Buffalo in 1840, he was able to organize a stop on the famous Underground Railroad. His literary career went <u>foreword</u> when be began to lecture, but he really became well known when his books, including novels and essays, began to be published in 1847. His <u>principle</u> book, *The Rising Son,* was one of the very first books to trace the roots of African-American people. <u>Its</u> rediscovery has thrown new light on this writer from an earlier time. The ideas contained in his writings <u>compliment</u> the work of some African-American authors of today.

1. _____   6. _____
2. _____   7. _____
3. _____   8. _____
4. _____   9. _____
5. _____   10. _____

EXERCISE 2 **Group I: Words that Sound Alike**

In the following paragraph, ten words that are often confused are underlined. In the spaces provided, write C if the word is correct. If the word is incorrect, write the correct word.

<u>Its</u> a surprise to many people, but in the earliest days of television, there were no taped shows—every program was live. This made it difficult for actors to quickly change <u>cloths</u> for the next scene. In addition, if something went wrong, all the TV viewers saw and heard it. Producers always stayed in the studio; they never took their cameras to an outside <u>cite</u>. One of the first TV stars <u>whose</u> popularity was nationwide was Milton Berle, a comedian with an unforgettable <u>presents</u>. Berle was never <u>stationery</u> before the cameras. The <u>principle</u> idea on all his shows was to keep moving and to keep the audience laughing. Once when he was doing an underwater routine, something went wrong and he nearly drowned. Viewers watched the scene live as it was happening. As Berle's popularity

soared, so to did the sales of TV sets. Berle's <u>rein</u> as the king of television lasted for years, and those who remember him think we look in <u>vane</u> to find a better comedian today. Unfortunately, since most of these shows were never taped, <u>your</u> not likely to see any reruns.

1. _____
2. _____
3. _____
4. _____
5. _____

6. _____
7. _____
8. _____
9. _____
10. _____

Group II: Words that sound or look almost alike

1. accept/except

accept (verb)	to receive	I *accept* the invitation.
	to admit	I *accept* the blame.
	to regard as true or right	I *accept* the judge's decision.
except (prep.)	other than, but	Everyone *except* me went to the party.

2. advice/advise

advice (noun)	opinion as to what should be done about a problem	I listened to the lawyer's *advice*.
advise (verb)	to suggest; to counsel	The counselor *advised* me to choose a different major.

3. affect/effect

affect (verb)	to influence; to change	The election *affected* the president's thinking.
effect (noun)	result	The *effect* of the defeat was a change in government.
(verb)	to bring about (with a result)	The election *effected* a deep change in the country.

4. breath/breathe

breath (noun)	air that is inhaled or exhaled	He took a deep *breath*.
breathe (verb)	to inhale or exhale	*Breathe* in when the doctor tells you.

5. choose/chose

choose (present tense)	select	Please *choose* a number.
chose (past tense)	selected	Last weekend we *chose* to stay home.

6. conscience/conscious/conscientious

conscience	recognition of right and wrong	In Pinocchio, a cricket is the puppet's *conscience*.
conscious	awake; aware of one's own existence	Is the sick child *conscious*?
conscientious	careful; thorough	The mother was very *conscientious* about the care of her children.

7. costume/custom

costume	a special style of dress for a particular occasion	He rented a *costume* for the play.
custom	a common tradition	Trick or Treating is a national *custom*.

8. council/counsel/consul

council (noun)	a group that governs	The village *council* met last evening.
counsel (verb)	to give advice	He *counseled* troubled youth.
(noun)	advice; a lawyer	The judge appointed a *counsel*.
consul	a government official in the foreign service	The *consul* met the other diplomats.

9. desert/dessert

desert (verb)	to abandon	No soldier should *desert* an army.
(noun)	barren land	The *desert* was full of surprising plants.
dessert	last part of a meal, often sweet	The dinner ended with a fancy *dessert*.

10. diner/dinner

diner	a person eating dinner	The *diner* ate alone.
	a restaurant with a long counter and booths	I like coffee and donuts at the *diner*.
dinner	main meal of the day	*Dinner* will be served at eight.

11. emigrate/immigrate/emigrant/immigrant

emigrate	to leave a country	The family *emigrated* from Russia.
immigrate	to come into a country	A century ago, many Europeans *immigrated* to the United States.
emigrant	a person who leaves one country to settle in another	Many *emigrants* from Europe left poverty and war behind.

| immigrant | a person who comes into a country to settle | Many *immigrants* to the United States had valuable skills. |

12. farther/further

| farther | greater distance (physically) | I cannot walk any *farther*. |
| further | greater distance (mentally); to help advance a person or a cause | She gave *further* evidence at the trial. |

13. loose/lose

loose	not tightly fitted	Her *loose* jacket felt comfortable.
lose	unable to keep or find	Don't *lose* the ticket.
	to fail to win	Our team cannot *lose*.

14. personal/personnel

| personal | relating to an individual; private | Her *personal* life is a mystery. |
| personnel | people employed by an organization | The director asked all *personnel* to report Monday morning. |

15. quiet/quit/quite

quiet	free from noise; calm	The *quiet* library was a retreat.
quit	to give up; to stop	She *quit* her job last week.
quite	completely	It is *quite* all right to ask for help.

16. receipt/recipe

| receipt | a bill marked paid | You need a *receipt* to get a refund. |
| recipe | a formula to prepare a mixture, especially in cooking | The chefs exchanged *recipes* for their desserts. |

17. special/especially

| special (adj.) | not ordinary | He gave the dog a *special* treat. |
| especially (adv.) | particularly | Those cakes are *especially* delicious. |

18. than/then

| than | used to make a comparison | I would rather walk *than* ride. |
| then | at that time; in that case | I went to the bakery and *then* came home. |

19. thorough/though/thought/through/threw

| thorough (adj.) | finished, fully done | He made a *thorough* inspection of the house. |

though (adv. conj.)	however, despite the fact	They bought the house even *though* it was old.
thought (verb)	past tense of *to think*	She *thought* about restoring the house to its original beauty.
through (prep.)	to enter one side and exit from the other side	They looked *through* dozens of decorating books.

Note: *thru* is not considered standard spelling.

threw	past tense of *to throw*	She *threw* her heart into the project.

20. use/used to

use	to bring or put into service, to make use of	I *used* the telephone a lot last year.
used to	indicates an activity that is no longer done in the present	I *used to* make too many long distance calls.
	accustomed to or familiar with	I am *used to* calling my family whenever I feel lonely.

EXERCISE 1   Group II: Words that Sound Almost Alike

In the following paragraph, ten words that are often confused are underlined. In the spaces provided, write C if the word is correct. If the word is incorrect, write the correct word.

Except for a very few people, most of us like to gossip. "Don't breath a word!" some people will say, and than they will tell you a deep secret they heard from someone else. This can be dangerous, especially if the gossip gets back to the person who has been discussed. Many friendships have been ruined because of these personnel misunderstandings, and in families, the affects of gossip can be disastrous. A farther point in all of this is the intentions that people have when they gossip. It is one thing to want to be helpful when talking about other people; it is quiet another thing to chose to gossip for its own sake. That is often a receipt for disaster.

1. _____   6. _____

2. _____   7. _____

3. _____   8. _____

4. _____   9. _____

5. _____   10. _____

EXERCISE 2   Group II: Words that Sound Almost Alike

In the following paragraph, ten words that are often confused are underlined. In the spaces provided, write C if the word is correct. If the word is incorrect, write the correct word.

Feeling disorganized is no fun. Some heads of families sit down, have a family <u>counsel</u> and make a <u>through</u> review of everything they do in order to organize their daily lives. First, they discuss what they <u>use to</u> do, and promise each other they will mend their ways. Next, they give each other <u>advise</u> on the most important changes that should be made. If it is the <u>custom</u> in the house to hope everyone gets up on time in the morning, then an alarm clock should be purchased because a <u>lose</u> morning schedule always results in chaos. The end of the day is just as important, with <u>diner</u> being an important time for family cooperation. If everyone works in a <u>conscience</u> way to help make a good meal, there could even be time for <u>dessert</u>. One <u>effect</u> of all this will be that everyone will know what is expected every day. Routine is important if a family is to run smoothly.

1. _____   6. _____

2. _____   7. _____

3. _____   8. _____

4. _____   9. _____

5. _____   10. _____

Group III: Lie/lay; rise/raise; sit/set

These six verbs are perhaps the most troublesome verbs in the English language. First, one must learn the principal parts because they are irregular and easily confused with each other. Secondly, one set is reflexive and cannot take an object while the other set always takes a direct object.

THE PRINCIPAL PARTS OF THE REFLEXIVE VERBS LIE—RISE—SIT				
Verb Meaning	**Present**	**Present Participle**	**Past**	**Past Participle**
to recline	lie	lying	lay	has or have lain
to stand up or move upward	rise	rising	rose	has or have risen
to take a sitting position	sit	sitting	sat	has or have sat

Reflexive verbs never take an object.

> *I lie* down.
>
> *The cat is lying* on the rug.
>
> *I rise* up.
>
> *The sun rose* in the East.
>
> *She sits* down.
>
> *The woman has sat* on her hat.

Remember: When reflexive verbs are used, the subject is doing the action without any help. No other person or object is needed to accomplish the action.

THE PRINCIPAL PARTS OF THE VERBS LAY—RAISE—SET				
Verb Meaning	**Present**	**Present Participle**	**Past**	**Past Participle**
to put something	lay	laying	laid	has or have laid
to move raised something up	raise	raising	raised	has or have
to place something	set	setting	set	has or have set

These verbs always take a direct object.

> I *lay the book* down.
>
> I *raise the flag*.
>
> I *set the table*. (Exception: The sun sets)

EXERCISE 1   Group III: Lie, Lay; Rise, Raise; Sit, Set

In the following paragraph, ten words that are often confused are underlined. In the spaces provided, write C if the word is correct. If the word is incorrect, write the correct word.

   The United States is <u>setting</u> on an enormous amount of information about our oceans. This information <u>has laid</u> in government files for years and only now is it being revealed. It was forty years ago that our country was in a cold war with Russia. Scientists became concerned with tracking Russian submarines and in the process, their systematic surveys of the world's oceans <u>lay</u> the foundation for present day environmental studies. Some of this knowledge has military importance, but most of it <u>raises</u> issues that are of great use to science. For example, weather forecasting, pollution control, and commercial fishing are areas where this new information <u>has raised</u> the possibility of real improvement and control. Naval submarines sometimes <u>laying</u> in the depths of the ocean have taken measurements that tell us much about volcanoes under the sea. Other government vessels have set on ocean bottoms to investigate how sound waves bounce off the ocean floor, information that will be valuable for mining under the sea. Even satellite construction has been helped by careful observation of how light raises in the water. As a submarine rises, the changing perception of the light has been recorded. Scientists are very happy to have all of this important information. They feel it is better to have the material for their use rather than have it setting in some sealed government file.

1. _____   6. _____

2. _____   7. _____

3. _____   8. _____

4. _____   9. _____

5. _____   10. _____

EXERCISE 2   Group III: Lie, Lay; Rise, Raise; Sit, Set

In the following paragraph, ten words that are often confused are underlined. In the spaces provided, write C if the word is correct. If the word is incorrect, write the correct word.

The new Boeing 777 jet is described as the plane for the 21st century. Although setting on the runway it may look like the 767 and the 757, only bigger, it represents a huge change in the way aircraft is built. Its reputation has been rising because it is the first Boeing plane to be designed entirely by a computerized system that the company calls "digital product design." 5000 engineers lay down all the details about the 4 million parts for this airplane and entered the data into the computerized system. The computer could look at every part in three dimensions and match piece to piece before trying to put the parts together. This method rose the hopes of aircraft engineers everywhere. Before this, parts never matched up on the first attempt to put the parts together. Now the parts went together—snap, snap, snap! Engineers raised many other issues, one of them pointing out how each additional coat of paint that is applied rises the cost due to additional fuel needed to fly the plane. Think and test, think and test is the rule laid down by plane makers. Planning and construction costs have, of course, raised in recent years, and so the new airplane is a very expensive project. It seems impossible to sit a limit on the cost. However, engineers have been very excited about the construction of this aircraft. They want to see this process set the example for airplane construction in the next century.

1. _____   6. _____

2. _____   7. _____

3. _____   8. _____

4. _____   9. _____

5. _____   10. _____

Mastery and editing tests

TEST 1   Words Commonly Confused

In the following paragraph, ten words have been used incorrectly. Circle the words and write them correctly below the paragraph.

Years ago, many people past their vacations by traveling by trailer. They use to travel with gleaming aluminum trailers hitched to their cars. These people, known as tin-can tourists, probably saw more sites then most travelers do today. They camped in mountains, valleys, and desserts. They enjoyed cooking diner in their trailers. If you visit Shady Dell Campground in Bisbee, Arizona, you can have quiet an experience by staying in one of these original trailers from the 1930s. Its a nostalgic experience to lay in your bunk in the trailer and listen to music from the 30s on the radios. When you stay at the Shady Dell, you can loose yourself in a way of life that is now gone.

1. _____
2. _____
3. _____
4. _____
5. _____

6. _____
7. _____
8. _____
9. _____
10. _____

TEST 2   Words Commonly Confused

In the following paragraph, ten words have been used incorrectly. Circle the words and write them correctly below the paragraph.

Its a booming electronic age, and the emerging connections among telephone, television, and internet services suggest what a new age it will be. The new telecom bill, just passed in Washington, is a capitol idea that will effect everyone's life. The idea behind the bill is simple: Were all going to benefit. Future cable services, for example, will be complimented by the use of phone lines to bring more video choices into our homes. The new bill also brings the so-called V-chip into our homes. This will allow parents to except or reject violent programs for the children in a family. However, the television industry does not intend to take all of this laying down. It intends to fight the government's plan in this area. One prediction is that prices for cable services will raise before they fall. If we are waiting for lower phone rates, we may wait in vein for a real bargain. Everyone is very conscience that a new world is indeed almost here.

1. _____   6. _____

2. _____   7. _____

3. _____   8. _____

4. _____   9. _____

5. _____   10. _____

TEST 3 Words Commonly Confused

In the following paragraph, ten words have been used incorrectly. Circle the words and write them correctly below the paragraph.

Explorers are celebrated for there influence on the course of history. One of the most important figures to change the history of South America was Hernando De Soto. He went further than any other European of his time, reaching the Inca Empire in 1536. His famous conquest of Peru was a personnel triumph, but De Soto could not remain stationery. He was given the rite to explore Florida, a privilege that was granted to the explorer in the rein of the Emperor Charles V. Florida was supposed to be the cite of the Fountain of Youth and fabulous treasures, including gold. Of course, this expedition for gold was a waist of time, but as De Soto went westward from Florida, into what is now Louisiana, he was no wiser then Ponce de Leon had been in 1513, when he followed the council of others and looked for a paradise in the same region.

1. _____   6. _____

2. _____   7. _____

3. _____   8. _____

4. _____   9. _____

5. _____   10. _____

APPENDICES

CONTENTS

IRREGULAR VERBS

Alphabetical listing of principal parts of irregular verbs

Simple Form	Past Form	Past Participle
arise	arose	arisen
bear	bore	borne
beat	beat	beat or beaten
become	became	become
begin	began	begun
bend	bent	bent
bet	bet	bet
bind	bound	bound
bite	bit	bitten, bit
bleed	bled	bled
blow	blew	blown
break	broke	broken
breed	bred	bred
bring	brought	brought
build	built	built
burst	burst	burst
buy	bought	bought
cast	cast	cast
catch	caught	caught
choose	chose	chosen
cling	clung	clung
come	came	come
cost	cost	cost
creep	crept	crept
cut	cut	cut
deal	dealt	dealt
dig	dug	dug
dive	dived, dove	dived
do	did	done
draw	drew	drawn
drink	drank	drunk

Simple Form	Past Form	Past Participle
drive	drove	driven
eat	ate	eaten
fall	fell	fallen
feed	fed	fed
feel	felt	felt
fight	fought	fought
find	found	found
fit	fit	fit
flee	fled	fled
fling	flung	flung
fly	flew	flown
forbid	forbade, forbad	forbidden
forget	forgot	forgotten
forgive	forgave	forgiven
freeze	froze	frozen
get	got	gotten
give	gave	given
go	went	gone
grind	ground	ground
grow	grew	grown
hang	hung, hanged	hung, hanged
have	had	had
hear	heard	heard
hide	hid	hidden
hit	hit	hit
hold	held	held
hurt	hurt	hurt
keep	kept	kept
kneel	knelt	knelt
know	knew	known
lay (to put)	laid	laid
lead	led	led
leave	left	left
lend	lent	lent
let	let	let
lie (to recline)	lay	lain
lose	lost	lost
make	made	made

Simple Form	Past Form	Past Participle
mean	meant	meant
meet	met	met
mistake	mistook	mistaken
pay	paid	paid
prove	proved	proved, proven
put	put	put
quit	quit	quit
read	*read	*read
ride	rode	ridden
ring	rang	rung
rise	rose	risen
run	ran	run
say	said	said
see	saw	seen
seek	sought	sought
sell	sold	sold
send	sent	sent
set	set	set
sew	sewed	sewn, sewed
shake	shook	shaken
shave	shaved	shaved, shaven
shed	shed	shed
shine	shone	shone
shoot	shot	shot
show	showed	shown, showed
shrink	shrank, shrunk	shrunk, shrunken
shut	shut	shut
sing	sang	sung
sink	sank	sunk
sit	sat	sat
slay	slew	slain
sleep	slept	slept
slide	slid	slid
sling	slung	slung
slink	slunk	slunk
slit	slit	slit

---

* Pronunciation changes in past and past participle forms.

Simple Form	Past Form	Past Participle
sow	sowed	sown, sowed
speak	spoke	spoken
speed	sped, speeded	sped, speeded
spend	spent	spent
spin	spun	spun
spit	spat	spat
split	split	split
spread	spread	spread
spring	sprang	sprung
stand	stood	stood
steal	stole	stolen
stick	stuck	stuck
sting	stung	stung
stink	stank, stunk	stunk
stride	strode	stridden
strike	struck	struck
string	strung	strung
swear	swore	sworn
sweep	swept	swept
swim	swam	swum
swing	swung	swung
take	took	taken
teach	taught	taught
tear	tore	torn
tell	told	told
think	thought	thought
throw	threw	thrown
wake	woke, waked	woken, waked
wear	wore	worn
weep	wept	wept
weave	wove	woven
wet	wet	wet
win	won	won
wind	wound	wound
wring	wrung	wrung
write	wrote	written

PARTS OF SPEECH

Words can be divided into categories called *parts of speech.* Understanding these categories will help you work with language more easily, especially when it comes to revising your own writing.

Nouns

A *noun* is a word that names persons, places, or things.

Common Nouns	Proper Nouns
officer	Michael Johnson
station	Grand Central Station
magazine	*Newsweek*

Nouns are said to be *concrete* if you can see or touch them.

window

paper

river

Nouns are said to be *abstract* if you cannot see or touch them. These words can be concepts, ideas, or qualities.

meditation

honesty

carelessness

To test for a noun, it may help to ask these questions.

- Can I make the word plural? (Most nouns have a plural form.)
- Can I put the article *the* in front of the word?
- Is the word used as the subject or object of the sentence?

Pronouns

A *pronoun* is a word used to take the place of a noun. Just like a noun, it is used as the subject or object of a sentence.

Pronouns can be divided into several classes. Here are some of them:

PRONOUNS

Note: Personal pronouns have three forms depending on how they are used in a sentence: as a subject, object, or possessive.

Personal Pronouns

	Subjective		*Objective*		*Possessive*	
	Singular	**Plural**	**Singular**	**Plural**	**Singular**	**Plural**
1st person	I	we	me	us	my (mine)	our (ours)
2nd person	you	you	you	you	your (yours)	your (yours)
3rd person	he	they	him	them	his (his)	their (theirs)
	she		her		her (hers)	
	it		it		its (its)	

Relative Pronouns	*Demonstrative Pronouns*
who, whom, whose	this
which	that
that	these
what	those
whoever, whichever	

Indefinite Pronouns

Singular

everyone	someone	anyone	no one
everybody	somebody	anybody	nobody
everything	something	anything	nothing
each	another	either	neither

Singular or **Plural** (depending on meaning)

all	more	none
any	most	some

Plural

both	few	many	several
			others

Adjectives

> An *adjective* is a word that modifies a noun or pronoun. Adjectives usually come before the nouns they modify, but they can also come in the predicate.

The adjective comes directly in front of the noun it modifies:

> The *unusual* package was placed on my desk.

The adjective occurs in the predicate but refers back to the noun it modifies:

> The package felt *cold*.

Verbs

> A *verb* is a word that tells what a subject is doing as well as the time (past, present, or future) of that action.

Verbs can be divided into three classes:

1. *Action Verbs*

> *Action verbs* tell us what the subject is doing and when the subject does the action.

The action takes place in the present:

> The athlete *runs* five miles every morning.

The action takes place in the past:

> The crowd *cheered* for the oldest runner.

2. *Linking Verbs*

> A *linking verb* joins the subject of a sentence to one or more words that describe or identify the subject.

The linking verb *was* identifies *He* with the noun *dancer:*

> He *was* a dancer in his twenties.

The linking verb *seemed* describes *She* as *disappointed:*

She *seemed* disappointed with her job.

COMMON LINKING VERBS	
be (am, is, are, was, were, have been)	
act	grow
appear	look
become	seem
feel	taste

3. *Helping Verbs* (also called "auxiliaries")

> A *helping verb* is any verb used before the main verb.

The helping verb could show the **tense** of the verb:

It *will* rain tomorrow.

The helping verb could show the **passive voice:**

The new civic center *has been* finished.

The helping verb could give a **special meaning** to the verb:

Annie Lennox *may be* singing here tonight.

COMMON HELPING VERBS
can, could
may, might, must
shall, should
will, would
forms of the irregular verbs *be, have,* and *do*

Adverbs

> An *adverb* is a word that modifies a verb, an adjective, or another adverb. It often ends in -ly, but a better test is to ask yourself if the word answers one of the questions *how, when,* or *where.*

The adverb could modify a *verb*:

> The student walked *happily* into the classroom.

The adverb could modify an *adjective*:

> It will be *very* cold tomorrow.

The adverb could modify another *adverb*:

> Winter has come *too* early.

Here are some adverbs to look out for:

COMMON ADVERBS	
Adverbs of Frequency	*Adverbs of Degree*
often	even
never	extremely
sometimes	just
seldom	more
always	much
ever	only
	quite
	surely
	too
	very

Prepositions

> A *preposition* is a word used to relate a noun or pronoun to some other word in the sentence. The preposition with its noun or pronoun is called a *prepositional phrase.*

> The letter is *from* my father.
>
> The envelope is addressed *to* my sister.

Read through the following list of prepositions several times so that you will be able to recognize them. Your instructor may ask you to memorize them.

COMMON PREPOSITIONS

about	below	in	since
above	beneath	inside	through
across	beside	into	to
after	between	like	toward
against	beyond	near	under
along	by	of	until
among	down	off	up
around	during	on	upon
at	except	outside	with
before	for	over	within
behind	from	past	without

Conjunctions

A *conjunction* is a word that joins or connects other words, phrases, or clauses.

A conjunction connecting *two words:*

> Sooner *or* later, you will have to pay.

A conjunction connecting *two phrases:*

> The story was on the radio *and* in the newspaper.

A conjunction connecting *two clauses:*

> Dinner was late *because* I had to work overtime at the office.

CONJUNCTIONS

Coordinating Conjunctions	*Subordinating Conjunctions*
and	after
but	although
or	as, as if, as though
nor	because
for (meaning "because")	before
yet	how
so	if, even if
	provided that
	since
	unless
	until
	when, whenever
	where, wherever
	while

Correlative Conjunctions

either . . . or
neither . . . nor
both . . . and
not only . . . but also

Adverbial Conjunctions (also known as "conjunctive adverbs")

To add an idea:	furthermore
	moreover
	likewise
To contrast:	however
	nevertheless
To show results:	consequently
	therefore
To show an alternative:	otherwise

Interjections

An *interjection* is a word that expresses a strong feeling and is not connected grammatically to any other part of the sentence.

Oh, I forgot my keys.

Well, that means I'll have to sit here all day.

Study the Context

Since one word can function differently or have different forms or meanings, you must often study the context in which the word is found to be sure of its part of speech.

for functioning as a preposition:

The parent makes sacrifices *for* the good of the children.

for functioning as a conjunction meaning *because:*

The parent worked two jobs, *for* her child needed a good education.

READINGS

CONTENTS

A Valentine Lost at 3, Kept in Mind for 51 Years

JOHN LANG

Everyone has a first infatuation from childhood, a recollection of a special person that never fades. In the following autobiographical sketch, John Lang shows his own memory of a first love. Appropriately, his essay was published on February 14, 1996.

1 The memories of first love are warped and yellowed like the old photographs. Mine show us sitting side by side on her front steps, our dark heads close, looking at each other and smiling with immense satisfaction. In another picture we are standing in her front yard, hugging and grinning proudly.

2 If it weren't for the snapshots, I might not have remembered, for they fix the moment. Yet, every time I come across the cracked and faded images, I can almost hear her. She has just said, "I love you," or, "You're my boyfriend," and I am astonished and thrilled by the sudden understanding that a girl who is not my mother may care for me.

3 The only other memory from that afternoon in Memphis is of the rival. He came from a house several doors up from hers, and he was mean and nasty. Somehow I think of him as needing a bath. He tried to kiss her, or he said something taunting, and we didn't like it. I pushed him down, and he ran away, or she did the shoving. I really don't remember. And it doesn't matter much who protected whom when you are 3 years old.

taunting: mocking

4 The moment is glorious because, united, we won. Anyone can tell from the photos how happy we were. That is all I have of her. Two small pictures taken from too far by someone we hardly noticed. I don't know if we kissed, then or ever. I can only suppose that we must have held hands. I'm not even sure how to spell her name now, because I couldn't spell it then.

5 One day, and it couldn't have been long after the photos were taken, I went to visit my grandmother and asked to be led across the street to see her.

6 "She's moved away," I was told.

7 I haven't forgotten those awful and frightening words. People move away? They pack up and leave their home? How can they do that? Why? Where to? Why wasn't I told?

8 I think I had a tantrum. I know I cried. It wasn't fair—my first intimation that life often wouldn't be—and I was inconsolable. They told me she had to move, her father had got another job far away, in Cincinnati, maybe it was. I didn't care about his job; it was stupid.

9 Finally I asked, "Will she come back?" "Maybe, sometime," they said, most likely doubting it. That gave me some hope, but she never did, although I kept a watch on her vacant house for the longest time.

10 I imagine that behind the hugs and kisses my family smiled at my tears. Puppy love, they must have thought—and what could that mean to such a little boy?

11 Just this. It was 51 years ago, and I have not forgotten her.

12 Whenever I am back in my hometown I drive past my grandparents' old home at the intersection of Galloway and Willett, now a house of strangers, and I slow

down to look at it, and sometimes I glance across the street to the steps where I sat with the first girl to love and leave me.

13   There is no anguish now, no hurt for half a century. Others have come, and others have gone. One bore my children, and some broke my heart, and sometimes I broke theirs. Other faces and other voices, greater promises and worse betrayals, are clearer in remembrance.

14   I'm sure she, too, has known bigger disappointments and larger loves. No doubt she is as worn by time and gravity as I am, and would look equally ridiculous these days in those sunsuits we wore with naked knees and straps over our bare shoulders.

15   If I saw her today, it's certain I would walk right by and never know. It's possible I have already done so. Still, I will always wonder . . .

16   Oh where are you, Elizabeth Rude?

Questions for Critical Thinking

1. People tend to smile at "puppy love," and not take it too seriously. When is this not a good idea?

2. Take a survey of your classmates. How many students in the class had to move away from a childhood home? What were some of the effects of having to leave friends and familiar places?

3. In some ways, this is a very painful story. Do you think the writer's message is that life is basically unfair, or that often in our lives events are not within our control?

4. What are the different kinds of loss that people suffer throughout their lives? What gives people strength to go on with a positive outlook?

Writing in Response

1. Very few of us can remember anything that happened to us before the age of five. What memory are you able to recall from your childhood only because you have a photo or other keepsake of the event, or because someone has told you about it?

2. In the past, people tended to remain in the towns and neighborhoods where they were born. Now many children lose their first childhood friends because so many of them move away for one reason or another. Write an essay that recalls your friends from childhood. What happened to all these friendships? What was important about each of these friendships? Are you still in contact with any of these people?

3. Sooner or later all of us experience the loss of friends and loved ones. Individuals move away, grow apart, or die. Tell the story of your relationship with someone who was once important in your life. How did the relationship end?

4. This piece was published on Valentine's Day because it had something to say about young love. Everyone remembers their first love. Tell a story about your own first love.

5. Imagine that Elizabeth Rude came across this essay in the newspaper and got in touch with John Lang. What do you think their first meeting in fifty years would be like? Write an essay in which you imagine that reunion.

6. This essay was published on Valentine's Day because its subject was young love. Write an essay that involves a holiday setting such as a family reunion on Thanksgiving Day or a camping trip over the Fourth of July. In the telling of the events, remember the story should have some point. What was the meaning or importance of the events in your life or in the lives of others?

Sea Island Daughter
TINA McELROY ANSA

Sometimes we feel instantly at home in a place we come to for the first time. This was the experience novelist Tina McElroy Ansa had when she first came to St. Simons Island, one of the Sea Islands off the coast of Georgia. In the following essay, the writer, who has made her home on St. Simons for the past ten years, examines her feelings as a recent inhabitant of an area with a deep cultural history. She also explores the different levels of acceptance people can experience, even in places they call "home."

1 On the day after I got married 17 years ago, I discovered "home" on a two-lane causeway that connected a small Sea Island to the Georgia coast. I wasn't even looking for it.

2 On that first trip to St. Simons Island, I had come as a landlocked Georgia girl on her honeymoon. Until then, home to me was a dry, dusty town in the middle of the state. The salty air of the Atlantic was still foreign to my nose. Since birth, I had breathed the fishy smell of the muddy, slow-moving Ocmulgee River, which ran by my hometown of Macon. I was used to the heavy red clay of middle Georgia, not the soft, pearlized sand of the Georgia shore. The trees I played under as a child were tall, familiar pines and thick, annoying mulberries, not the strange squat palms and ghostly moss-draped live oaks I have come to love on the Georgia coast.

miasmic: thick, and filled with fumes and vapors

3 But all these differences drifted to nothing as soon as I was close enough to sniff the miasmic scent of life in the saltwater marshes that weave through the island. This place—seen and heard in Julie Dash's haunting film *Daughters of the Dust* and in Gloria Naylor's perfectly pitched novel *Mama Day*—called to me. It *called* to me.

4 As our car neared the shores of St. Simons Island that first time, I heard a voice say clearly: *This is where you belong.* I remember looking around the car for the source of that voice, but no one other than my new husband, Jonee, was there. And Jonee had heard it, too.

5 It took us six years of moving around the country to grow brave enough to listen to that voice. But at last Jonee, a videographer, and I, a writer, answered the call and moved to the island. It is a decision that I celebrate and give thanks for every day, because here in the Sea Islands, the cradle of African culture in this country, I have found the peace and acceptance of home.

6   It is not merely the physical beauty of the place that draws my soul. It is also that voice whispering to me. The voice should have been no surprise, considering that the spirits of our ancestors—Black folks who lived and worked as slaves on the region's plantations—seem to hang in the very air. But the voice was just the beginning. In my ten years here, everything on St. Simons Island has told me the same thing: *This place is yours.*

7   I go to the post office, and elderly Black women scoot their grandkids over to meet me. Some mornings I wake to find that our neighbor, Mr. Buck, has left on our doorstep something from his garden or latest fishing expedition. I look at the island's famous lighthouse and recall the Black labor and expertise that went into its construction but got none of the recognition in local history.

8   On this island, history is personal. Slavery is personal. Here I have learned that the surviving nineteenth-century structure around the corner from where I live is not merely a "slave cabin." It is also where, at the turn of the century, an African-American family by the name of White resided. Mrs. Palmer, who lives down the street, used to play there with her best little girlfriend. I can never go past that cabin (now an elegant gift shop) without thinking of Mrs. Palmer (now a grandmother) as a little girl skipping about the sandy yard, laughing with Mr. White's granddaughter.

9   Of course, I am not deceived into thinking that because I belong here, I am *from here*. Islanders take pride in reminding me that although I am welcomed here, am loved here, I am not *from here*. Rather, I am a *come-here*. And if I die here, I, like all other *come-heres,* will be buried in the Strangers' Cemetery.

10   It is not a pleasant thing to be called a stranger. The implication is that you are an interloper, an intruder. But for Sea Islanders, whose ancestral roots are sunk into the sandy loam of these islands, being *from here* goes deep. It implies a shared bond of bloodlines, experience, song, isolation and a transcendence of pain that strangers can appreciate but never fully know. I am not offended. Instead, I am warmed by neighborly assurances that this stranger is welcome to lay her body down here. A pity all strangers are not treated as lovingly as I have been on this island. I am in good company. I am home.

loam: soil that is made up of moist clay and sand

Questions for Critical Thinking

1. The first paragraph of this essay tells us that one of the writer's concerns is what *home* means to her. What does *home* mean to you? How do you define *home* and what is your concept of an ideal place to live?

2. Compare the writer's description of her Macon home (in paragraph 2) with her current Sea Island home.

3. On her island, Tina McElroy Ansa discovered not only personal fulfillment but also a deep sense of her cultural roots. Find the passages where the writer describes this. How important is it to understand one's cultural identity? How can each one of us discover something of our own cultural identity and history, even if we cannot live in a place as filled with historical reminders as St. Simons Island?

4. Tina McElroy Ansa is fortunate to be able to live in the place she loves the most. What are the factors that have made it possible for her to do this?

Writing in Response

1. Write an essay that takes a look at a home where you have once lived. What are the distinguishing characteristics of the place that make it special to you? What lessons of life did you learn in this home?

2. How important is *place* in a person's life? What, for instance, is the role of climate, or the role of an urban or rural setting? Write an essay which discusses the importance of several factors about a place and the impact these factors have on a person's quality of life.

3. In her final paragraph, the writer notes that it is "not a pleasant thing to be called a stranger." Write an essay discussing the problems people have when they are looked upon as strangers where they live. What can people do to remove the label of "stranger"?

There Goes the Neighborhood

JIM SHAHIN

Although all neighborhoods may change over time, some aspects of living in a community remain the same. In the following essay, Jim Shahin's fond memories of his old neighborhood lead him to realize that while his life has progressed far beyond the little world of his childhood, some truths about living with others in a community will always remain.

1   There is an order to my neighborhood, a rhythm to its life. It is an order and a rhythm I've come to know during the eight years I've lived in my house. But the order has been disrupted and the rhythm set off its beat. The reason is the house next door.

2   The house next door has been empty since before Thanksgiving, maybe Halloween, I don't remember exactly. I only know it's been a while and the suspense is killing me: What's happening with the house? When is somebody going to move in? Who is it going to be?

3   I keep hoping the new occupant will be a family with a kid my son's age and parents we like. But it'll probably be me of twenty years ago—some guy with a loud stereo and weird friends.

4   Please, God, not that. Please, not all-night parties with people hanging out on the front porch drinking keg beer until dawn. Please, no hard rock blasting through the walls causing visitations from the police. And please, please, please, no colored plastic owls with little light bulbs in them illuminating the backyard with its furniture of metal folding chairs and telephone-cable-spool tables.

5   As I look back on those days, I recall the mother's curse: May you have a child just like yourself. A worse fate is to have neighbors in their twenties who are just like you when you were that age.

resilient: able to come back to its shape *indelible:* impossible to erase

6   A neighborhood is a delicate thing, but a resilient thing. There are deaths and births and graduations, and tuna casseroles at all of them. Neighborhoods are also indelible. You remember everything about where you grew up—the way the misty light from the street lamp shone on the snow, the person who lived next

door, the smell in the bluish evening air of roasting meats at dinner time, the closest kid your age, the mounds of raked leaves piled every year at the same place by the curb. These, anyway, are among the things I remember.

7   There are nice people, like the woman who tipped me a dime every week when I went to collect for my paper route. There are mean people, like the guy across the street who would make a face, shake his fist, and keep our ball if it rolled into his yard. (We started tormenting him by smacking crab apples onto his lawn with a tennis racket.) And there are the just plain weird people, like the guy who went a little nuts one night and, when asked by his neighbor to turn off his porch light because it was shining into their side of the duplex, responded by grabbing a shotgun and marching down the middle of the street blasting it into the air and yelling admonitions, while his wife trailed behind him in her bathrobe hollering, "You tell him, hon!"

admonitions: warnings

8   I remember playing handball, stickball, and football in the street. I remember the enormous sixty-foot blue spruce on the corner of our yard and climbing to the very top and swaying back and forth in the wind and being afraid. I remember beating up a kid who was a year older than me because I caught him beating up my younger brother. I remember my friends with their unlikely names, Itchy and Rusty, and going to their houses and wondering at Rusty's why my family couldn't have hoagies for dinner like this family did and at Itchy's discovering the transcendent delight of peanut butter and butter on toast.

9   I remember the blond girl about five or six years older than me, who I thought was absolutely gorgeous and who baby-sat me. I forgave her because I adored her. She was sitting on my porch baby-sitting one summer evening when suddenly I was overcome with an uncontrollable urge to kiss her. I did. Rather than make me feel like the foolish little kid that I was, she said simply, "I could use a root beer. Let's go inside." And she rose from the lawn chair, all poise and dignity, rolled up the teen magazine she had been reading, and went into the house. I stayed on the porch, frozen with mortification at what I had done. Then I ran off into the neighborhood, hoping it hadn't seen, and looking to it for comfort.

mortification: shame

10   As a kid growing up, your neighborhood is the world and it takes a long time before you realize that the world is not your neighborhood. These days, the world of the neighborhood belongs more to Sam, my six-year-old son, than to me. The impressions he is forming of his place will stay with him forever, shaping in some important ways his sense of the world, and I often wonder what those impressions are.

11   We live in an older neighborhood of gently rolling hills, big houses, and large old pecan and live oak trees. Geographically it is small and, depending on your viewpoint, either within walking distance of restaurants, grocery stores, doctors offices, record stores, a nightclub, a liquor store, some fast-food joints, a coffee bar, a vintage-clothes place, a comic-book shop, and assorted other retail outlets, or it is in the ever-tightening vice grip of commercial development.

vice grip: a very strong hold

12   An in-town neighborhood a few blocks from the university, its social mix is diverse. There are retirees, twentysomethings, families, professors, graduate students, state government employees, fast-food workers, rock-and-rollers, and a few people whose lives I think it's probably best I didn't know much about. It is a quiet neighborhood. Few kids live in it. And although it is close to campus, it does not attract the bare-chested, Jeep-riding, beer-swilling crowd.

13   What will Sam remember of all this? Maybe the little girl down the street with whom he sometimes plays. Probably the ice-cream parlor a few blocks away. Undoubtedly the burger joint down the hill.

clomping: walking heavily and noisily

14   My wife says he'll most likely recall the sound of clomping feet. Built in 1911, our house is two stories, but, like many of the houses in the neighborhood, it was carved into a triplex years ago. We live on the first floor and rent out the two units above us. The floors are hardwood throughout. Great aesthetically. Not so hot acoustically.

aesthetically: relating to beauty

15   Maybe, though, it won't be the clomping that Sam remembers. Maybe it'll be the cooing of the doves that one of the tenants keeps. Or maybe it will be the neighborhood itself, its shadings and scents and sounds, or maybe the people who comprise it, such as the large elderly man across the street who, I'm told, is a professor of English at the university and who we usually see doing something industrious like chopping wood, or the guy who walks his dogs so much it seems like it's his job.

16   Or maybe his memories will be of the house next door. Lately, there has been some activity in and around the house. We've seen a beige collie in the backyard on occasion. And we've heard music coming from the house while power drills are running. But no one lives there yet.

17   I haven't seen the guy, only glimpsed his dog and heard his music. He likes his music loud. We can hear it from our porch. It's rock. Hard rock. Hard, loud, depresso, scream, rage rock. The kind of stuff I fear I would be listening to if I was in my twenties.

18   I contemplate the possibilities. Maybe he's a carpenter doing some renovation work for the people who are moving in and he likes to bring his dog to the job site. Or maybe he's the new neighbor, getting the place ready before setting up residence.

19   And I remember my mother's words. And I figure I could do worse. The neighborhood's resilient. So am I.

20   Maybe I'll take him a tuna casserole.

Questions for Critical Thinking

1. The author's title gives the reader one impression of what the essay will be about, but it is not until paragraph five that we learn who is being referred to in that title. Why does the writer give us the title he does, and why does he keep us waiting before he reveals his true subject?

2. What are the sources of humor in this essay? Why are we amused at so many of the writer's details?

3. How does the conclusion bring the point of the essay into focus? What is the significance of the tuna casserole at the very end? What exactly is the author's thesis?

4. In paragraphs 6 through 9, Jim Shahin describes the neighborhood of his youth. Make a list of the kinds of memories he has. In paragraphs 10 through 18, he describes the neighborhood he now lives in. Does he cover the same topics that he discussed about his childhood neighborhood? What would be the list of memories you would make of your childhood neighborhood?

5. If a new neighbor were to move in to the apartment or house next door to you tomorrow, what kind of person would you want that neighbor to be? Take a survey in your class. Is there any agreement about what the ideal neighbor should be like?

Writing in Response

1. Write an essay in which you classify the kinds of neighbors that have moved in and out of your neighborhood.

2. Write an essay classifying the neighborhoods you have moved in and out of during your life.

3. Describe the best or the worst neighbor you have ever encountered.

4. Define your neighborhood for someone who has never seen it. Study Jim Shahin's descriptions to get ideas for the kinds of details you can include.

5. Argue about the benefits of living in a culturally diverse neighborhood as opposed to living in a neighborhood with only one ethnic group.

6. Argue about the benefits of living in a neighborhood with all age groups as opposed to only young families or only retired couples, or all college students.

7. Define what makes a good neighbor.

Woes of a Part-Time Parent

NICK CHILES

Many Americans in the nineties have had to adapt to difficult family situations that make being a good parent an even harder task. The following observations by Nick Chiles not only show his objectivity as a reporter (he writes for the Newark Star Ledger), but also reveal his personal dilemma as a parent who cannot be present at all the important moments in his child's life.

1   I often feel something is missing. A living, vital part of me that sprouted under my eyes for two years is now a part-time visitor in my life. For about ten hours during the week and every waking hour every other weekend, my son, Mazi, and I tinker with our developing relationship. We laugh a lot, and sometimes he cries a lot—often in a span of ten minutes. During those few hours I can feel my heart hum along at a peaceful clip, uncluttered, dancing atop a divine Sarah Vaughan contralto.

2   But then he is gone. He's off to brighten another corner of the world with his 3-year-old's unleavened energy and infectious glee. He's out of my sight, out of my realm of knowing, until the next time.

3   What I regret most about the dissolution of my marriage is the absence of a partner conversant in Mazi, fluent in Mazispeak. Sure, I can talk with his grandparents or my friends about his latest leap in reasoning or physical advance. But their interest doesn't compare with the undying fascination of a parent. I miss

tinker: repair by experimenting

contralto: low female voice

unleavened: not mixed with anything else

realm: area or sphere

dissolution: ending

conversant: familiar

having a companion with whom I can exchange reports about Mazi's day or Mazi's behavior—or misbehavior—in day care. I miss the daily conversation about his life.

4   Being a part-time parent means being cut off from a huge portion of your child's life. It means not having any idea what he does with much of his time when you're not around. His life with Mommy is now in another place. Does that also make him another child?

5   My notions of fatherhood were formed as much by television and the mass media as my life with my own dad. For me, being a father means being the stolid protector, the rock-solid shoulder to lean on when the child gives up a homer in the last inning. It means being Mr. Brady on *The Brady Bunch.* How can you be these things when half the time you aren't there? How can you avoid missing some of the important moments when your child needs you?

6   As Mazi is carried off into the night, I can't help but wonder where he's going and if he'll be okay. If he's not, am I to blame? He seems so happy to see Mommy. Have I done something wrong? My guilt is strong. It's the gnawing ache I feel when I must go days without seeing him. The second he is in my arms, the ache disappears. The second he disappears, it resumes its burdensome place.

7   I don't foresee that ache ever leaving me. I fear it only mutates to fit new circumstances. I'm beginning to learn to live with it, however, accepting it as a cloying companion, dressing it up as parental concern, paternal responsibility, love. Perhaps one day I'll come to respect the guilt, acknowledging its power to feed my fatherly instincts and impel me to make the extra effort on behalf of my son. But for the time being the guilt just throws me into a deep funk.

8   One day I spent time in the house Mazi shares with his mother, doing some repairs in preparation for its sale. As I stumbled upon his toys and the evidence of his life there, I was shocked by how strangely unfamiliar and distant it all seemed to me. He could now walk up and down the stairs with ease. Did he have free run of all four floors? There were new toys I had never seen him play with. Did he still use the combo climber? Had he become bored with the large number mats? What did he do here? I couldn't really get the answers to these questions, even if his mother provided daily dissertations. You have to be there.

9   Things probably won't get better as Mazi's world begins to widen and his outside interests broaden. Our visits will be even more infrequent when his mother relocates to a new job out of state. I still won't know what happens during much of his waking hours. Then when he goes to school and begins to immerse himself in the awesome possibilities beyond his home, I will merely join legions of parents the world over who agonize over the same basic question every day: I wonder what he's doing now?

stolid: showing little emotion

mutates: changes

cloying: too overwhelming
impel: urge
funk: state of depression

dissertations: formal discussions

immerse: to be completely involved in
legions: a large number, a multitude

Questions for Critical Thinking

1. Which one of the writer's sentences best states the thesis of the essay?

2. The essay reveals much about the author's involvement in his child's life. What examples does Nick Chiles give that tell us what kind of parent he is?

3. In paragraph 3, the author makes the point that the language, "Mazispeak," he speaks with his son, is a special way of communicating with the child. What

are some other examples of "a special language" that two people (or a group of people) use to communicate?

4. Make a list of the part-time parent's special problems, as the writer presents them. (Do not forget to add the problems mentioned in the last paragraph.) Are there any additional problems the author has not included?

5. The father in this essay regrets the limited time he has with his son. How important is the amount of time a parent spends with a child? Do you believe it is not the *quantity* of time but the *quality* of that time that matters when it comes to taking care of a child?

6. In paragraph 5, the writer tells us that his ideas of fatherhood "were formed as much by television and the mass media as my life with my own dad." To what extent have your own ideas and beliefs about being a parent been shaped by what you have seen on television or in the movies, by your own parents, and by personal influences outside your own immediate family?

Writing in Response

1. Write a story that focuses on the struggle of a person who is trying to be a good parent.

2. Write an essay of definition and analysis that presents the essential qualities of a good parent.

3. Write an essay that classifies the types of parents you have observed.

4. Write an essay in which you give advice to parents who are separated from their children. What can they do to maintain a close relationship?

5. Write an essay about the effects on a child of growing up in a single parent household.

6. Argue for or against the following statement: Children always need to grow up in a home that has two parents if these children are to feel safe and psychologically healthy.

Salvation

LANGSTON HUGHES

When a person shares a private experience that took place in a larger community setting, it can often result in a very dramatic revelation. In the following selection, from *The Big Sea*, first published in 1940, Langston Hughes describes just such a situation and makes a dramatic revelation about a memorable evening from his childhood.

1 I was saved from sin when I was going on thirteen. But not really saved. It happened like this. There was a big revival at my Auntie Reed's church. Every night for weeks there had been much preaching, singing, praying, and shouting, and

some very hardened sinners had been brought to Christ, and the membership of the church had grown by leaps and bounds. Then just before the revival ended, they held a special meeting for children, "to bring the young lambs to the fold." My aunt spoke of it for days ahead. That night I was escorted to the front row and placed on the mourners' bench with all the other young sinners, who had not yet been brought to Jesus.

2   My aunt told me that when you were saved you saw a light, and something happened to you inside! And Jesus came into your life! And God was with you from then on! She said you could see and hear and feel Jesus in your soul. I believed her. I had heard a great many old people say the same thing and it seemed to me they ought to know. So I sat there calmly in the hot crowded church, waiting for Jesus to come to me.

dire: dreadful

3   The preacher preached a wonderful rhythmical sermon, all moans and shouts and lonely cries and dire pictures of hell, and then he sang a song about the ninety and nine safe in the fold, but one little lamb was left in the cold. Then he said, "Won't you come? Won't you come to Jesus? Young lambs, won't you come?" And he held out his arms to all us young sinners there on the mourners' bench. And the little girls cried. And some of them jumped up and went to Jesus right away. But most of us just sat there.

4   A great many old people came and knelt around us and prayed, old women with jet-black faces and braided hair, old men with work-gnarled hands. And the church sang a song about the lower lights are burning, some poor sinners to be saved. And the whole building rocked with prayer and song.

5   Still I kept waiting to see Jesus.

a rounder: a drinker

6   Finally all the young people had gone to the altar and were saved, but one boy and me. He was a rounder's son named Westley. Westley and I were surrounded by sisters and deacons praying. It was very hot in the church, and getting late now. Finally Westley said to me in a whisper: "Goddamn! I'm tired o' sitting here. Let's get up and be saved." So he got up and was saved.

7   Then I was left all alone on the mourners' bench. My aunt came and knelt at my knees and cried, while prayers and songs swirled all around me in the little church. The whole congregation prayed for me alone, in a mighty wail of moans and voices. And I kept waiting serenely for Jesus, waiting, waiting—but he didn't come. I wanted to see him, but nothing happened to me. Nothing! I wanted something to happen to me, but nothing happened.

8   I heard the songs and the minister saying: "Why don't you come? My dear child, why don't you come to Jesus? Jesus is waiting for you. He wants you. Why don't you come? Sister Reed, what is this child's name?"

9   "Langston," my aunt sobbed.

10   "Langston, why don't you come? Why don't you come and be saved? Oh, Lamb of God! Why don't you come?"

knickerbockered: wearing pants that are gathered and banded at the knees

11   Now it was really getting late. I began to be ashamed of myself, holding everything up so long. I began to wonder what God thought about Westley, who certainly hadn't seen Jesus either, but who was now sitting proudly on the platform, swinging his knickerbockered legs and grinning down at me, surrounded by deacons and old women on their knees praying. God had not struck Westley dead for taking his name in vain or for lying in the temple. So I decided that maybe to save further trouble, I'd better lie, too, and say that Jesus had come, and get up and be saved.

12   So I got up.

13   Suddenly the whole room broke into a sea of shouting, as they saw me rise. Waves of rejoicing swept the place. Women leaped into the air. My aunt threw her arms around me. The minister took me by the hand and led me to the platform.

14   When things quieted down, in a hushed silence, punctuated by a few ecstatic "Amens," all the new young lambs were blessed in the name of God. Then joyous singing filled the room.

15   That night, for the last time in my life but one—for I was a big boy twelve years old—I cried. I cried, in bed alone, and couldn't stop. I buried my head under the quilts, but my aunt heard me. She woke up and told my uncle I was crying because the Holy Ghost had come into my life, and because I had seen Jesus. But I was really crying because I couldn't bear to tell her that I had lied, that I had deceived everybody in the church, and I hadn't seen Jesus, and that now I didn't believe there was a Jesus anymore, since he didn't come to help me.

Questions for Critical Thinking

1. *Time* is the most usual way of organizing the narrative essay. Explain why *time* is of particular importance in this essay. Underline all the transitions of time that you can find.

2. From whose point of view is this story told?

3. Why do you believe this piece by Langston Hughes became so immensely popular? What is it about the content that is compelling? What is it about the author's writing that impresses you?

4. Study the use of dialogue or the writer's reporting of what people said. Explain the importance of both of these storytelling techniques in the essay.

Writing in Response

1. Sometimes the events that we look forward to with great anticipation turn out to be bitterly disappointing. Tell the story of just such an event in your own life, or in the life of someone you have known or observed.

2. Religious training for children often involves some very special experiences. If you have grown up in a particular faith, describe a religious experience that left an impression on your life.

3. Write about an experience that convinced you to embrace a teaching of your parents or that convinced you to turn away from a belief held by your parents. Is it possible that as you grow older you may return to these beliefs?

4. What have been the important truths you have learned from older people as you grew up? Do you believe you have more to learn, or do you think most of your belief system is firmly established?

5. Compare two different religious practices that you have observed. What are the values that these religions teach their followers? Are the values the same? If they differ, how wide are the differences?

6. In all religions, there are specific procedures followed by the believers of that faith. For a religion you are familiar with, describe the steps for one of those procedures.

Hot Tub Nirvana for $100

ROY GREEN

The use of the hot tub is an ancient tradition, but it is one that continues to increase in popularity; people enjoy using the hot tub for its ability to soak away the troubles and tensions of modern life. In the following essay, Roy Green goes beyond a description of the benefits of the hot tub experience: he actually shows step by step how you can construct one for your own use.

obtuse: lacking in intelligent design
contortionist: a person able to bend parts of the body into extraordinary positions

1   Unfortunately, the standard Anglo-European household bathtub design is so obtuse that you have to be either a contortionist or a midget to get any benefit. It was obviously designed for a parent to bathe a toddler, and no one else. Even if you can lie in it without your legs protruding, the large water-surface area causes the heat to evaporate within just a few minutes, thereby causing a cold tub, which is almost as effective as a cold shower for diminishing your interest in life in general.

2   Several years ago, however, I found a single-person hot tub invented in the Orient and now I am psychologically dependent upon it. It is small enough to be heated by a standard hot water tank, fits inside a standard bathtub, and is easily portable.

3   The discovery came through a chance visit to an inn in Cork, Ireland, which has made its fortune catering to Japanese tourists. In my bathroom was this amazing little bathtub. At first I thought it had to be a very deep utility sink, but being desperate, I tried it out. It was just barely large enough for me to sit upright with my legs crossed. But with the flotation of the water and the cocoonlike feeling, it was just right.

4   The brochure on the nightstand explained that it is called a *furo*. *Furo* is the Japanese word for a single-person hot tub. The term "low tech" doesn't begin to cover the simplicity and functionality of the design. No bubbles, no jets, no electricity, nothing to break, just deep hot water up to your neck. Asians have known for thousands of years the benefits of sitting alone immersed in hot water. And, as I have since learned, the favorite place for Japanese college students to study is in the *furo*.

5   Basically, it is just a plywood box with a cool Oriental name. At first glance it seems like you may have your knees in your mouth, but this is not the case, due to your natural buoyancy—you feel so good you just don't care. I'm tall for a short person, over 5′10″, and I fit very comfortably.

6   You get the same benefits of a hot tub, but none of the contamination consequences, plus you get to be alone and not feel completely antisocial. Try to remember, did you ever take a tub all alone and not feel self-conscious and wasteful? I did it once and felt as if I were driving a Winnebago to the grocery store.

7   By taking it alone, you don't catch anything you will regret when you get married. By getting the temperature to as hot as you can stand, usually around 104 degrees F, your muscles relax so totally that you feel disconnected from your body. Your lymph system drains. Sweat glands open and all toxins dump like crazy. You will be clean as a whistle when you are done. And when you do get out, you will feel like human Jell-O for about half an hour. And you *will* be sweating. Put on a comfortable bathrobe and sit in an easy chair with a tall glass of water.

8   You can fill the *furo* with your shower, but it is more energy efficient to buy a $20 hand-held shower adapter so you can let the shower nozzle dangle in the bottom of the furo and fill it without letting the hot steam escape. It is best to get in

it while it is filling, because you can stand the heat better if it is a gradual, rather than a sudden, entrance. To empty it, just pull the plug and the water goes into the tub and down the tub's drain.

9   Adding a cup of Epsom salts to the bath can make for an even more pleasurable experience. For a total sinus opening adventure, add eucalyptus oil. To feel like King Tut, add flower petals.

Assembly

10   1. Buy wood and other supplies, and get the wood cut at the lumber yard.

11   2. Take your two 26″ × 28″ sides and screw a 2 × 2 along the 26-inch sides; make sure the 2 × 2 is flush with the top of the panel. Insert the screws every 4 to 5 inches, at about ¾ of an inch in from the edge. Don't worry about an imperfect fit, the waterproof coating will fill the internal gaps later.

12   3. Now take your two 20″ × 26″ side panels and screw them to the 2 × 2s mounted to the 26″ × 28″ side panels. The 20-inch sides should be the top and bottom, thereby making the width 20 inches.

13   Just to double check, when you finish this step you should have a rectangular box that has the 2 × 2s mounted on the outside, with the internal dimensions somewhere near 20″ × 24″. If it doesn't fit, don't worry, be happy, wood is very forgiving, just take it apart and start over. I did.

14   4. Now make the bottom. Take the 20″ × 24″ panel and screw the two 20-inch 2 × 4 pieces to them along the 20-inch side, and then screw the 17-inch pieces along the remaining sides. Then insert the bottom into the box, with the 2 × 4s facing down, and screw through the plywood sides into the 2 × 4s to complete the basic structure.

15   5. Now is the time to get some pretzels or chips to see you to the summit of this project.

16   6. Mark and cut the hole for the drain. You can use a hole saw, jigsaw or ax (depending on your disposition at the moment). The drain assembly should fit perfectly, so tighten it down to about 800 ft/lbs to make sure it's snug.

17   7. Drill screw holes in the ends of the 1 × 2s and then assemble them along the top lip of the *furo* to make it comfortable to enter and exit, and to give it that finely crafted look of a turn of the century shipping crate.

18   8. Now slather up the entire interior with either fiberglass resin, polyurethane, or marine-quality paint. To make it strong enough to withstand hurricane forces, you may wish to line the corners with fiberglass cloth and then slap on a final coat of fiberglass resin. Apply the chemicals outside, in a strong wind, while wearing a respirator to make sure that you do not breathe the fumes, which are very dangerous.

19   This little beauty is designed to fit inside your present mass-produced standard American bathtub. Make sure you get out when your fingers start to look like prunes. You may want to try a variation on the Scandinavian method by taking a cold shower between each hot soak.

Materials

- One 4′ × 8′ sheet of ½″ plywood, (4-ply if possible; you can buy a better grade of plywood if desired) . . .
     . . . cut into 2 pieces that are 20″ × 26″ for the front and back . . .
     . . . and 2 pieces that are 28″ × 26″ for the sides . . .
     . . . and a single 20″ × 24″ bottom piece

- One 8′ 2 x 4 cut into 2 pieces 20″ long and 2 pieces 17″ long, to support the bottom
- One 8′ 2 × 2 cut into 4 pieces that are 24″ long to join the sides together
- One 8′ 1 × 2 cut into 2 pieces 28″ long and 2 pieces 18″ long to trim the top and protect your bottom when you climb into and out of the *furo*
- One tub-drain kit, with plug
- One pound of 1½″ Sheetrock screws
- One quart of fiberglass resin or polyurethane for the waterproof coating inside the *furo*

Tools

Electric drill with Sheetrock screw bit

⅞₄ drill-bit for pilot holes in the 1 × 2s (otherwise they will split)

Jigsaw, or 2½″ hole saw, or ax depending on your attitude

Questions for Critical Thinking

1. Most people today do not grow up learning the crafts that their grandparents or parents acquired as children, watching their own parents. How many students in your class learned a craft from their parents? What crafts are represented?

2. Carpentry is one of the most practical skills to learn. During his travels, Roy Green discovered something that he decided to make for himself. In this process essay, which appeared in a popular magazine, the author provides more than the simple instructions. Divide the essay into parts and then name each section. Do these sections give you hints as to how you might approach a process essay of your own?

3. Achieving humor in writing is very difficult. Find those places in the essay where the author is being humorous. Did you find his humor successful or were you not amused? Why or why not? Do you think the writer is serious about his product, or is the essay all a joke?

Writing in Response

1. Choose a craft that you enjoy. Write a process essay in which you not only tell the reader how to make the craft item, but also provide some commentary such as background information about the craft, or your pleasure in having the finished product in your home, or who taught you how to make it. If you are brave, you may try to add humor to your writing!

2. Many schools no longer teach shop skills, sewing, or cooking. Write an essay in which you argue for or against the belief that these subjects should continue to be taught in the public schools.

3. Write an essay in which you classify the different kinds of hobbies that people have. What types of personalities are attracted to various hobbies? What are the qualities needed for each of them? (For instance, if the hobby is dancing, it helps to be coordinated.)

Ethmix!

BETSY ISRAEL

For most of our country's history, the many ethnic groups that make up our society have tended to remain separate from each other. In recent years, however, more and more people from different backgrounds have been marrying and forming new families. In the following essay, Betsy Israel discusses the kind of person who is the result of this modern trend, the person she calls "an ethmix."

1   Every year at holiday time there was that moment. After shuffling into the high school auditorium and taking our places on the risers below the orchestra, Mr. Callahan, the music teacher, would begin whipping his hands through the air, and we'd burst into *Joy to the World* or *Hark the Herald Angels Sing;* I, standing off to the side, would burst into a cold sweat. For after we'd finish these songs, Mr. C. would turn to me and to the two kids alongside and nod—our cue to start up. "I had a little dreidl, I made it out of clay. . . ." Being asked, at age sixteen, to sing about a clay dreidl was, by itself, fairly humiliating. But it was, for me at least, also confusing.

dreidl: a spinning top, used in Hanukkah games

2   I would be asked to sing the token Hanukkah song because my name was Israel: Clearly I was Jewish. But the truth was that we were only half Jewish, my father having been raised in a traditional Jewish family, my mother, the child of a Cuban immigrant and a Kansas farm boy, on another planet entirely. In our house we had not only menorahs, both electric and manual, but a Christmas tree and stockings and cookies shaped like angels and bells. Being asked, then, to sing *The Dreidl Song*—and told gently that I need not sing any songs referring to Christ (which is to say none of the others)—made me furious. I would walk home later, feeling embarrassed and angry—at my parents in some vague way, at myself for not being cooler, and also at the inevitable dumb girl in too-blue eye shadow and too-tight jeans who would fall in alongside me to ask earnestly, "Is it weird not to have Christmas?"

menorahs: nine-branched candlesticks, used to celebrate Hanukkah

3   That was ten years ago. Back then, attending high school in a town divided strictly along ethnic and religious lines was tough if you didn't have the right answer to the "What are you?" question—and doubly worse if you looked so obviously out of it, nobody bothered to ask. In our town the right answers were always 1. Irish; 2. Italian; and/or 3. Catholic. Needless to say, the few times I was actually asked (I could, some people used to say, pass for Italian), I failed miserably. Today, of course, Jews marrying Gentiles—or Baptists marrying Buddhists, for that matter—is hardly cause for raised eyebrows. It's the odd high school, in fact, that doesn't have its share not only of half Jews and Catholic-Protestants but of black-whites and an ever-increasing number of Asian- or Hispanic-Americans. Coming from a family tossed several times through the ancestral blender is as common now as coming from a family known for its athletic ability or from one in which everyone has freckles.

4   Still, growing up between two worlds, whether the split is religious, ethnic, or cultural, is not quite as easy as growing up in a family that simply shares certain traits or talents. Whether we like it or not, our ethnic and religious backgrounds shape us profoundly. As children, our heritage is a key factor in helping us determine who we are in relation to the outside world—where we fit on the

social spectrum and who else out there is "like" us. Not noticeably belonging to any one group is often upsetting, and these feelings of isolation, of not fitting in, easily carry over into adolescence—a time when everyone, even the fairest-haired among us, must struggle awfully hard just to seem seminormal. Sure, there were days when I felt almost normal, sometimes even lucky (I didn't, after all, have to spend *my* sunny Sundays in church). But there were as many times—usually just after some kid would pass my locker snickering, "Hey, Jew eat yet?"—when I'd feel a little like the cute neighborhood mutt we'd played with as kids: a half-breed, well liked but secretly pitied. At those moments I knew in my bones that growing up hybrid would always be, as we used to say, a truly mixed bag.

5   Feeling weird, it seems, is as common to ethmix kids as feeling bored in church is to others. Patti Rodriquez,* sixteen, of St. Louis grew up in a Cuban-Baptist-Catholic-family and considers herself something of an expert on the subject. "When we were kids, everybody went to Sunday school," she explains. "I felt funny for not having a church to go to. I was scared to tell the other kids I didn't go to church because they would think there was something wrong with me. And I never knew the Bible stories. I didn't know who Jason was or about Rachel. I would get really nervous when the teacher started talking about them. But I was too embarrassed to tell my parents how I felt. I thought it would hurt them."

6   Fifteen-year-old Karen Paulsen of Tallahassee, Florida, is half black, half white and is thus another authority on personal weirdness. "I never noticed color for a long time," she says. "I figured that's just how Mom and Dad are. But once, in fourth grade, my father, who's white, dropped me off at school, and this black kid laughed at me and said, 'Karen, look at your dad, he's *funny*.' And I started getting all inferior, thinking, 'What's wrong with me?'"

7   That was a question I asked a lot as I grew up, and it's a phrase that might well serve as an anthem of sorts for junior ethmixes. There are, after all, many things that you can look forward to outgrowing—having no breasts, for example, or having acne. But what can you do about a funny-sounding last name or eyes that don't look round and American? Not much, and so it's easy, in elementary or junior high school, for an ethmix girl to look at herself and feel doomed.

8   Dr. S. Peter Kim, M.D., an associate professor of psychiatry at New York University Medical Center and the director of NYU's Center for Trans-Cultural Developmental Studies, explains that at "about the time you turn ten the values of the outside world—of friends and teachers—come into play, and it can be hard to form a solid identity if your parents don't seem as American as they should, or as much like everyone else's. Children from bicultural families can have a really rough time adapting, especially since children that age have so little understanding of one another. That's when you get comments like 'You look funny,' which are usually just innocent and inquisitive but still very hurtful."

9   In adolescence, though, "We all suffer," Dr. Kim says. "Our bodies are changing rapidly, which leads to shattering questions about physical appearance: Will I be pretty enough? Will I get boyfriends? If you are the product of a bicultural environment, it can be even harder because you may look different from the kids around you. And the world outside the house becomes so very different from the

---

* All names of teens have been changed.

one inside." Still, he adds, "These kids do adapt and often excel, especially if their parents help them to understand and appreciate their heritage."

10   And it was indeed true that by high school, the pressures, or at least the deep conviction that I was doomed to be forever weird, had faded. Other kids had abandoned their force-fed religions in rebellion. By the ninth grade, it was the strange kid in our school who *wanted* to go to church. (Why go to mass when you could go to the mall or, better, the beach?) There were still moments of isolation—times like Saint Patrick's Day, when the high school would empty and I'd be left to attend an algebra class of three. But I was coming to feel less uncomfortable about it—no longer as angry as the child who'd once demanded to know, "Why can't we just be Catholic?" and instead just annoyed that others *assumed* I must have felt strange. That they felt sort of sorry for me.

11   Karen Paulsen says, "When I got to junior high, I started to wonder about the people who thought my color was weird. We lived in an integrated neighborhood then, and my parents seemed like any other parents; they fought and made dinner just like all the others. I mean, there *were* problems sometimes. I've always considered myself black—I never write 'other' in the space for race—but some blacks didn't, and still don't, accept me. I still get questions like 'What color are you?' I now have a friend who just snaps back, 'She's purple, can't you see?' And my mother supports me, too. Once a girl called me a halfbreed, and when I told my mother about it, she said, 'Forget it. She's a jerk. Blow it off.'" Adds Judy Holtz, a sixteen-year-old from Atlanta who grew up with a different kind of cultural split, a southern mother and a northern dad, "I used to feel weird around my southern relatives, like they were really backward or something. And my dad would be so abrupt with people, not like southerners, who always say 'Y'all come back' and stuff. He was always kind of rude. But I see now that there are two sides to it. Once when I was having a sorority tea, my dad came stomping through the den and didn't even say hello—something a southerner would never do—and kids just turned around to me and said, 'Judy, who's *that?*' I was totally embarrassed. But he is also a real bookworm. We used to get fifty-seven magazines here, and I think my mind was really formed by his being so strict this way, by the northern part of him."

12   Like Judy and Karen, I found the things that bothered or embarrassed me were, by my sophomore year or so, becoming less upsetting and sometimes even sweet and funny—the way, for instance, my Jewish grandmother *still* tried to bribe us to attend Hebrew school (a losing proposition if there ever was one) or the way my mother's mother was turning spooky and spiritual, "seeking the answers" in Christian Science. Patti Rodriquez had always "wanted one of those grandmothers who baked cakes and knitted sweaters," but by high school, she, too, had found that it mattered less. "I had always preferred my mother's American relatives," she says, "because my Spanish relatives were always so emotional, and there was the language barrier. People used to laugh at things my grandmother said because they couldn't understand her. But as I got older, I started to feel a little bad that I hadn't been as close to my father's relatives. Now I feel proud that he came all the way here from Cuba to make a life with my mother and us. I used to think that the Cuban traditions, like 'the gifts from the wise men' at Christmas, were dumb. But now I'm glad we have them."

13   Part of this acceptance comes from looking around and discovering that younger family members have grown up relatively unaffected by the split. Judy Holtz says,

"My little sister, who's seven, is much more southern than I am. I have more of my father in me, while she's more at home with the southern relatives." And Patti adds, "My Cuban grandparents didn't approve of my parents' marriage, and I think my brother and I picked up a lot of my mother's resentment against them. But it's all calm now, and my little sisters don't notice that anything's strange."

14   And accepting a slightly unorthodox cultural setup gets a *lot* easier when you see that it can work to your advantage—especially where boys are concerned. I mean, what was my mother going to say to us? She had, at age twenty, married a Jewish guy ten years her senior. So when one of my sisters began dating a long and increasingly strange string of boys all named Alan (one of them was a tattooed biker), my mother could only say, "Well, we'll see what happens." Patti says that her mother, like mine, "would accept almost anybody." Says Karen, "I go out with boys who tend to share my views—who do not hate others and are accepting of all faiths and races. My mother supports those choices because they support her own view of the world."

15   It is this freedom to choose, born of a tolerance of others, that is perhaps the best part of growing up hybrid. My parents wouldn't flinch if I took up with a Hindu or an American Indian or a black man. And it is because of their basic beliefs that I would consider such choices in the first place. As Patti explains it, "I'm not so closed or one-wayed about things. It's made me a better person, more well rounded."

16   "Bicultural children are more flexible in their world views," says Dr. Kim. "And they are more tolerant in their relationships, more readily accepting. They have a much easier time standing in another person's shoes. And because they're less rigid, they're more mature psychologically, better able to perceive alternative ways of doing things."

17   This tolerance and freedom of choice extends beyond choosing boyfriends. Being exposed to more than one religion makes it easier—and often more meaningful—to choose one for yourself. Patti explains, "My parents gave me a choice— God is God, they said. So in eighth grade I started going to mass with friends, even though my family's only half Catholic. I liked it and wanted to go more, not because I wanted to fit in, but because I wanted to learn more about religion. A lot of people attend church for the wrong reasons. They go for the clothes or the social part. But I think you have to attend because you want to learn something about God."

18   For some of us, having a choice can mean choosing something unexpected, or coming up with a unique way to merge two very different worlds. Felicia Rafalkski, for instance, a fifteen-year-old New Yorker, recently joined a Unitarian church—a church without specific religious affiliation—at the suggestion of a friend. "I was half Roman Catholic and half Episcopalian," she explains, "but I never felt like I had any organized religion. When I would go to a regular Catholic mass, I was really shocked by how strict it was. That's why I joined the Unitarians. You can worship any God you want. It's much more open." A thirteen-year-old boy in her church group adds, "I used to be weakly Jewish and Episcopalian, but I never had formal training. Then I became a Unitarian. Now whenever I go to a Jewish ceremony, it seems really weird—all the emphasis on the Torah. It seems totally strange to worship a book."

19   I don't know whether or not it's strange to worship a book. I still haven't reached any conclusions. But I do know that if I ever feel the need to, I will easily

be able to slip in anywhere, making myself right at home. In the meantime, I can rest assured that my sisters and I *have* grown up to be special people, more tolerant and, I think, more interesting than a lot of the kids we went to high school with. Once upon a time, the endless holidays in our house seemed strange—Hanukkah followed by Christmas; Easter, then a few weeks later, Passover. But I understand now that this was my parents' unique way of showing us how much diversity there was in the world—and how very much to celebrate. As the years have gone by, these holidays—even if noted only by card or by phone call—have become more than just a way of acknowledging our ethnic and religious roots. They have become the way my sisters and my parents and I remain a family, devoted to one another and bound together for life, precisely because there isn't anyone else who does things quite the way we do.

Questions for Critical Thinking

1. Adolescence is a time when many people have difficulty defining themselves and their place in society. When Betsy Israel uses the term "ethmix," she tries to define herself and analyze the issue in all its complexity. What is "ethmix" and how has its reality affected Betsy Israel's life? Give several specific examples from the essay.

2. Review the essay. Mark each paragraph with one of the following labels to classify the writer's examples: *personal experience, observation of those around her, report from outside authorities.*

3. In paragraph three, Betsy Israel remembers that when she was a child, the question "What are you?" was always answered by reference to nationality or religion or both. To what extent has this changed, or is the situation basically the same? In what other ways could people define themselves?

Writing in Response

1. Betsy Israel tells us that a "freedom to choose, born of a tolerance of others . . . is perhaps the best part of growing up hybrid." Write an essay in which you discuss other situations in which a person could be raised that would encourage the person to be tolerant of others. In your essay you might also want to point out situations you believe tend to actively discourage tolerance toward others.

2. Write an essay in which you compare the present social situation that Betsy Israel describes with the situation your parents encountered when they grew up. Based upon what you have heard during family discussions and what your parents have told you, how different is the world you live in, compared with the world your parents knew when they were young?

3. Write an essay in which you describe how you hope to raise your children so that they will be tolerant adults. What will you be able to tell them about your own childhood that will help them understand the need for greater tolerance? How can a parent be frank about the realities that exist in society without discouraging the child?

4. Write a description of the most flexible, unprejudiced person you have ever known. What do you believe was in this person's background that made him or her so free from prejudice?

The Truth about Lying
JUDITH VIORST

Every culture holds up truth as a virtue, while lying is condemned as something that damages people's lives; however, most people accept the fact that at least some kinds of lying are a part of the daily life of our society. In the following analysis of the widespread practice of lying, Judith Viorst classifies the different kinds of lies people regularly tell. As the writer reviews the different types of lies, consider how many of them you yourself encounter on a regular basis.

1 I've been wanting to write on a subject that intrigues and challenges me: the subject of lying. I've found it very difficult to do. Everyone I've talked to has a quite intense and personal but often rather intolerant point of view about what we can—and can never *never*—tell lies about. I've finally reached the conclusion that I can't present any ultimate conclusions, for too many people would promptly disagree. Instead, I'd like to present a series of moral puzzles, all concerned with lying. I'll tell you what I think about them. Do you agree?

Social Lies

2 Most of the people I've talked with say that they find social lying acceptable and necessary. They think it's the civilized way for folks to behave. Without these little white lies, they say, our relationships would be short and brutish and nasty. It's arrogant, they say, to insist on being so incorruptible and so brave that you cause other people unnecessary embarrassment or pain by compulsively assailing them with your honesty. I basically agree. What about you?

compulsively:
uncontrollably

3 Will you say to people, when it simply isn't true, "I like your new hairdo," "You're looking much better," "It's so nice to see you," "I had a wonderful time"?

4 Will you praise hideous presents and homely kids?

5 Will you decline invitations with "We're busy that night—so sorry we can't come," when the truth is you'd rather stay home than dine with the So-and-sos?

6 And even though, as I do, you may prefer the polite evasion of "You really cooked up a storm" instead of "The soup"—which tastes like warmed-over coffee—"is wonderful," will you, if you must, proclaim it wonderful?

7 There's one man I know who absolutely refuses to tell social lies. "I can't play that game," he says; "I'm simply not made that way." And his answer to the argument that saying nice things to someone doesn't cost anything is, "Yes, it does—it destroys your credibility." Now, he won't, unsolicited, offer his views on the painting you just bought, but you don't ask his frank opinion unless you want *frank,* and his silence at those moments when the rest of us liars are muttering, "Isn't it lovely?" is, for the most part, eloquent enough. My friend does not indulge in what he calls "flattery, false praise and mellifluous comments." When others tell fibs he will not go along. He says that social lying is lying, that little white lies are still lies. And he feels that telling lies is morally wrong. What about you?

unsolicited:
without being asked

mellifluous:
smooth and sweet

Peace-Keeping Lies

rationalized: explained, not always correctly, to satisfy oneself

8   Many people tell peace-keeping lies; lies designed to avoid irritation or argument; lies designed to shelter the liar from possible blame or pain; lies (or so it is rationalized) designed to keep trouble at bay without hurting anyone.

9   I tell these lies at times, and yet I always feel they're wrong. I understand why we tell them, but still they feel wrong. And whenever I lie so that someone won't disapprove of me or think less of me or holler at me, I feel I'm a bit of a coward, I feel I'm dodging responsibility, I feel . . . guilty. What about you?

10   Do you, when you're late for a date because you overslept, say that you're late because you got caught in a traffic jam?

11   Do you, when you forget to call a friend, say that you called several times but the line was busy?

12   Do you, when you didn't remember that it was your father's birthday, say that his present must be delayed in the mail?

13   And when you're planning a weekend in New York City and you're not in the mood to visit your mother, who lives there, do you conceal—with a lie, if you must—the fact that you'll be in New York? Or do you have the courage—or is it the cruelty?—to say, "I'll be in New York, but sorry—I don't plan on seeing you"?

14   (Dave and his wife Elaine have two quite different points of view on this very subject. He calls her a coward. She says she's being wise. He says she must assert her right to visit New York sometimes and not see her mother. To which she always patiently replies: "Why should we have useless fights? My mother's too old to change. We get along much better when I lie to her.")

15   Finally, do you keep the peace by telling your husband lies on the subject of money? Do you reduce what you really paid for your shoes? And in general do you find yourself ready, willing and able to lie to him when you make absurd mistakes or lose or break things?

16   "I used to have a romantic idea that part of intimacy was confessing every dumb thing that you did to your husband. But after a couple of years of that," says Laura, "have I changed my mind!"

17   And having changed her mind, she finds herself telling peace-keeping lies. And yes, I tell them too. What about you?

Protective Lies

supersede: replace

18   Protective lies are lies folks tell—often quite serious lies—because they're convinced that the truth would be too damaging. They lie because they feel there are certain human values that supersede the wrong of having lied. They lie, not for personal gain, but because they believe it's for the good of the person they're lying to. They lie to those they love, to those who trust them most of all, on the grounds that breaking this trust is justified.

19   They may lie to their children on money or marital matters.

20   They may lie to the dying about the state of their health.

21   They may lie about adultery, and not—or so they insist—to save their own hide, but to save the heart and the pride of the men they are married to.

22   They may lie to their closest friend because the truth about her talents or son or psyche would be—or so they insist—utterly devastating.

presumptuous: to go beyond what is proper

23   I sometimes tell such lies, but I'm aware that it's quite presumptuous to claim I know what's best for others to know. That's called playing God. That's called manipulation and control. And we never can be sure, once we start to juggle lies, just where they'll land, exactly where they'll roll.

24   And furthermore, we may find ourselves lying in order to back up the lies that are backing up the lie we initially told.

25   And furthermore—let's be honest—if conditions were reversed, we certainly wouldn't want anyone lying to us.

26   Yet, having said all that, I still believe that there are times when protective lies must nonetheless be told. What about you?

27   If your Dad had a very bad heart and you had to tell him some bad family news, which would you choose: to tell him the truth or lie?

28   If your former husband failed to send his monthly child-support check and in other ways behaved like a total rat, would you allow your children—who believed he was simply wonderful—to continue to believe that he was wonderful?

29   If your dearly beloved brother selected a wife whom you deeply disliked, would you reveal your feelings or would you fake it?

30   And if you were asked, after making love, "And how was that for you?" would you reply, if it wasn't too good, "Not too good"?

31   Now, some would call a sex lie unimportant, little more than social lying, a simple act of courtesy that makes all human intercourse run smoothly. And some would say all sex lies are bad news and unacceptably protective. Because, says Ruth, "a man with an ego that fragile doesn't need your lies—he needs a psychiatrist." Still others feel that sex lies are indeed protective lies, more serious than simple social lying, and yet at times they tell them on the grounds that when it comes to matters sexual, everybody's ego is somewhat fragile.

dissemble:
conceal the truth

32   "If most of the time things go well in sex," says Sue, "I think you're allowed to dissemble when they don't. I can't believe it's good to say, 'Last night was four stars, darling, but tonight's performance rates only a half.'"

33   I'm inclined to agree with Sue. What about you?

Trust-Keeping Lies

34   Another group of lies are trust-keeping lies, lies that involve triangulation, with *A* (that's you) telling lies to *B* on behalf of *C* (whose trust you'd promised to keep). Most people concede that once you've agreed not to betray a friend's confidence, you can't betray it, even if you must lie. But I've talked with people who don't want you telling them anything that they might be called on to lie about.

35   "I don't tell lies for myself," says Fran, "and I don't want to have to tell them for other people." Which means, she agrees, that if her best friend is having an affair, she absolutely doesn't want to know about it.

36   "Are you saying," her best friend asks, "that if I went off with a lover and I asked you to tell my husband I'd been with you, that you wouldn't lie for me, that you'd betray me?"

37   Fran is very pained but very adamant. "I wouldn't want to betray you, so . . . don't ask me."

38   Fran's best friend is shocked. What about you?

39   Do you believe you can have close friends if you're not prepared to receive their deepest secrets?

40   Do you believe you must always lie for your friends?

41   Do you believe, if your friend tells a secret that turns out to be quite immoral or illegal, that once you've promised to keep it, you must keep it?

42   And what if your friend were your boss—if you were perhaps one of the President's men—would you betray or lie for him over, say, Watergate?

43   As you can see, these issues get terribly sticky.

44   It's my belief that once we've promised to keep a trust, we must tell lies to keep it. I also believe that we can't tell Watergate lies. And if these two statements strike you as quite contradictory, you're right—they're quite contradictory. But for now they're the best I can do. What about you?

45   Some say that truth will come out and thus you might as well tell the truth. Some say you can't regain the trust that lies lose. Some say that even though the truth may never be revealed, our lies pervert and damage our relationships. Some say . . . well, here's what some of them have to say.

46   "I'm a coward," says Grace, "about telling close people important, difficult truths. I find that I'm unable to carry it off. And so if something is bothering me, it keeps building up inside till I end up just not seeing them any more."

47   "I lie to my husband on sexual things, but I'm furious," says Joyce, "that he's too insensitive to know I'm lying."

48   "I suffer most from the misconception that children can't take the truth," says Emily. "But I'm starting to see that what's harder and more damaging for them is being told lies, is *not* being told the truth."

49   "I'm afraid," says Joan, "that we often wind up feeling a bit of contempt for the people we lie to."

50   And then there are those who have no talent for lying.

51   "Over the years, I tried to lie," a friend of mine explained, "but I always got found out and I always got punished. I guess I gave myself away because I feel guilty about any kind of lying. It looks as if I'm stuck with telling the truth."

52   For those of us, however, who are good at telling lies, for those of us who lie and don't get caught, the question of whether or not to lie can be a hard and serious moral problem. I liked the remark of a friend of mine who said, "I'm willing to lie. But just as a last resort—the truth's always better."

53   "Because," he explained, "though others may completely accept the lie I'm telling, I don't."

54   I tend to feel that way too.

55   What about you?

Questions for Critical Thinking

1. Judith Viorst set out to make some conclusions about lying, but she tells us in her introduction that the task turned out to be very difficult. Instead, she classifies some different types of lies and presents the moral dilemma that is raised by each type. Take a poll in your classroom by asking the following question: Is it always wrong to tell a lie? Did the essay change anyone's opinion?

2. What is the definition Judith Viorst gives for each of the four types of lies? How many examples does she give in each category that further explain her categories?

3. In the course of reading the essay, did you come across any examples that describe lies you have told? Discuss with the class what you believe would have happened if you had told the truth in each case.

4. Whether or not a person gets caught in a lie, Judith Viorst wonders what the effect is on the person who lies. Is a sense of guilt too great a price?

5. Explain the conclusion of the essay. Why does she end with a question?

Writing in Response

1. Write an essay in which you give your own examples to illustrate the types of lies that Judith Viorst classifies. You could also, of course, construct a different classification system of your own.

2. Write a narration that tells of the effects of someone telling a lie. This could be a true story or a story that you imagine.

3. Children very often are caught lying. Some people say these children really don't fully understand the difference between what is real and what is imaginary. Write an essay in which you discuss how parents and teachers should deal with children who are caught lying. Be sure you include some discussion of the age of the child and the seriousness of the lie.

4. Write an essay in which you argue for or against the telling of lies under certain circumstances.

5. Most of us have had a painful experience in which we have been honest with a friend only to find that they are terribly offended by our comments. Relate an experience in which your honesty caused problems. Would you do it again? Was there perhaps another way you could have handled the situation?

Neat People vs. Sloppy People
SUZANNE BRITT JORDAN

Sometimes we learn about our vices and virtues best when we are told about them in a humorous way. This is what Suzanne Britt Jordan does in the following essay, as she invites us to look for ourselves in one of two groups: those who are organized and those who can only hope to be.

1 I've finally figured out the difference between neat people and sloppy people. The distinction is, as always, moral. Neat people are lazier and meaner than sloppy people.

2 Sloppy people, you see, are not really sloppy. Their sloppiness is merely the unfortunate consequence of their extreme moral *rectitude*. Sloppy people carry in their mind's eye a heavenly vision, a precise plan, that is so stupendous, so perfect, it can't be achieved in this world or the next.

rectitude: correctness

3 Sloppy people live in Never-Never Land. Someday is their *métier*. Someday they are planning to alphabetize all their books and set up home catalogues. Someday they will go through their wardrobes and mark certain items for tentative mending and certain items for passing on to relatives of similar shape and size. Someday sloppy people will make family scrapbooks into which they will put newspaper clippings, postcards, locks of hair, and the fried corsage from their senior prom. Someday they will file everything on the surface of their desks, including the cash receipts from coffee purchases at the snack shop. Someday they will sit down and read all the back issues of *The New Yorker*.

métier: French for "a person's specialty"

4 For all these noble reasons and more, sloppy people never get neat. They aim too high and wide. They save everything, planning someday to file, order, and

straighten out the world. But while these ambitious plans take clearer and clearer shape in their heads, the books spill from the shelves onto the floor, the clothes pile up in the hamper and closet, the family mementos accumulate in every drawer, the surface of the desk is buried under mounds of paper and the unread magazines threaten to reach the ceiling.

5   Sloppy people can't bear to part with anything. They give loving attention to every detail. When sloppy people say they're going to tackle the surface of the desk, they really mean it. Not a paper will go unturned; not a rubber band will go unboxed. Four hours or two weeks into the excavation, the desk looks exactly the same, primarily because the sloppy person is meticulously creating new piles of papers with new headings and scrupulously stopping to read all the old book catalogs before he throws them away. A neat person would just bulldoze the desk.

6   Neat people are bums and clods at heart. They have cavalier attitudes toward possessions, including family heirlooms. Everything is just another dust-catcher to them. If anything collects dust, it's got to go and that's that. Neat people will toy with the idea of throwing the children out of the house just to cut down on the clutter.

7   Neat people don't care about process. They like results. What they want to do is get the whole thing over with so they can sit down and watch the rasslin' on TV. Neat people operate on two unvarying principles: Never handle any item twice, and throw everything away.

8   The only thing messy in a neat person's house is the trash can. The minute something comes to a neat person's hand, he will look at it, try to decide if it has immediate use and, finding none, throw it in the trash.

9   Neat people are especially vicious with mail. They never go through their mail unless they are standing directly over a trash can. If the trash can is beside the mailbox, even better. All ads, catalogs, pleas for charitable contributions, church bulletins and money-saving coupons go straight into the trash can without being opened. All letters from home, postcards from Europe, bills and paychecks are opened, immediately responded to, then dropped in the trash can. Neat people keep their receipts only for tax purposes. That's it. No sentimental salvaging of birthday cards or the last letter a dying relative ever wrote. Into the trash it goes.

10   Neat people place neatness above everything, even economics. They are incredibly wasteful. Neat people throw away several toys every time they walk through the den. I knew a neat person once who threw away a perfectly good dish drainer because it had mold on it. The drainer was too much trouble to wash. And neat people sell their furniture when they move. They will sell a La-Z-Boy recliner while you are reclining in it.

11   Neat people are no good to borrow from. Neat people buy everything in expensive little single portions. They get their flour and sugar in two-pound bags. They wouldn't consider clipping a coupon, saving a leftover, reusing plastic non-dairy whipped cream containers or rinsing off tin foil and draping it over the unmoldy dish drainer. You can never borrow a neat person's newspaper to see what's playing at the movies. Neat people have the paper all wadded up and in the trash by 7:05 A.M.

12   Neat people cut a clean swath through the organic as well as the inorganic world. People, animals, and things are all one to them. They are so insensitive.

After they've finished with the pantry, the medicine cabinet, and the attic, they will throw out the red geranium (too many leaves), sell the dog (too many fleas), and send the children off to boarding school (too many scuffmarks on the hardwood floors).

Questions for Critical Thinking

1. When did you first become aware that this essay is written in a humorous vein?

2. What explanation does Suzanne Britt Jordan give for a sloppy person's behavior? Do you agree with her?

3. In paragraph 3, what examples does the writer list as projects the sloppy person plans to do? Do these plans seem admirable?

4. Does the author use the block method or the point-by-point method to contrast sloppy people with neat people?

5. In paragraph 11, the author states that "Neat people are no good to borrow from." Discuss the examples the author gives to support her statement. What makes them humorous? Suzanne Britt Jordan's ability to provide details that the reader recognizes as true about himself or herself is what makes her writing so appreciated.

6. Do you know anyone who has done the things listed in the concluding paragraph? Which type of person do you think the author is?

Writing in Response

1. Write an essay which takes the opposite viewpoint of Suzanne Britt Jordan. Defend the neat person and criticize the sloppy person.

2. Describe two people you know who have very different approaches to being neat and organized. Explain what it is like to be with each of them.

3. How would you describe the household in which you grew up? In what ways were your parents very organized? In what areas were they disorganized? What are the problems of growing up in a household that is extreme one way or the other?

4. Write an essay in which you give advice to a young couple setting up a household. How would you advise them in being neat and organized?

5. Suzanne Britt Jordan claims that sloppy people cannot part with anything. Write an essay in which you analyze your own attitude about possessions. What are the things you have a hard time parting with? What things do you especially like to collect and save?

You're Short, Besides

SUCHENG CHAN

The author of the following autobiographical essay is a teacher and writer who uses her own situation to ask questions about society's attitudes toward people with disabilities. As you read Sucheng Chan's account of her experiences, you may find yourself rethinking some of your own established ideas about people who have special limitations in their lives.

1   When asked to write about being a physically handicapped Asian American woman, I considered it an insult. After all, my accomplishments are many, yet I was not asked to write about any of them. Is being handicapped the most salient feature about me? The fact that it might be in the eyes of others made me decide to write the essay as requested. I realized that the way I think about myself may differ considerably from the way others perceive me. And maybe that's what being physically handicapped is all about.

salient: noticeable

2   I was stricken simultaneously with pneumonia and polio at the age of four. Uncertain whether I had polio of the lungs, seven of the eight doctors who attended me—all practitioners of Western medicine—told my parents they should not feel optimistic about my survival. A Chinese fortune teller my mother consulted also gave a grim prognosis, but for an entirely different reason: I had been stricken because my name was offensive to the gods. My grandmother had named me "grandchild of wisdom," a name that the fortune teller said was too presumptuous for a girl. So he advised my parents to change my name to "chaste virgin." All these pessimistic predictions notwithstanding, I hung onto life, if only by a thread. For three years, my body was periodically pierced with electric shocks as the muscles of my legs atrophied. Before my illness, I had been an active, rambunctious, precocious, and very curious child. Being confined to bed was thus a mental agony as great as my physical pain. Living in war-torn China, I received little medical attention; physical therapy was unheard of. But I was determined to walk. So one day, when I was six or seven, I instructed my mother to set up two rows of chairs to face each other so that I could use them as I would parallel bars. I attempted to walk by holding my body up and moving it forward with my arms while dragging my legs along behind. Each time I fell, my mother gasped, but I badgered her until she let me try again. After four nonambulatory years, I finally walked once more by pressing my hands against my thighs, so my knees wouldn't buckle.

prognosis: prediction of a medical outcome

presumptuous: to go beyond what is proper

atrophied: deteriorated

rambunctious: full of energy

precocious: unusually early development of mental aptitude

nonambulatory: not able to walk

3   My father had been away from home during most of those years because of the war. When he returned, I had to confront the guilt he felt about my condition. In many East Asian cultures, there is a strong folk belief that a person's physical state in this life is a reflection of how morally or sinfully he or she lived in previous lives. Furthermore, because of the tendency to view the family as a single unit, it is believed that the fate of one member can be caused by the behavior of another. Some of my father's relatives told him that my illness had doubtless been caused by the wild carousing he did in his youth. A well-meaning but somewhat simple man, my father believed them.

4   Throughout my childhood, he sometimes apologized to me for having to suffer retribution for his former bad behavior. This upset me; it was bad enough that I had to deal with the anguish of not being able to walk, but to have to

retribution: something justly deserved

assuage: relieve

assuage his guilt as well was a real burden! In other ways, my father was very good to me. He took me out often, carrying me on his shoulders or back, to give me fresh air and sunshine. He did this until I was too large and heavy for him to carry. And ever since I can remember, he has told me that I am pretty.

5   After getting over her anxieties about my constant falls, my mother decided to send me to school. I had already learned to read some words of Chinese at the age of three by asking my parents to teach me the sounds and meaning of various char-

chagrin: discomfort

acters in the daily newspaper. But between the ages of four and eight, I received no education since just staying alive was a full-time job. Much to her chagrin, my mother found no school in Shanghai, where we lived at the time, which would accept me as a student. Finally, as a last resort, she approached the American School which agreed to enroll me only if my family kept an *amah* (a servant who takes care of children) by my side at all times. The tuition at the school was twenty U.S. dollars per month—a huge sum of money during those years of runaway inflation in China—and payable only in U.S. dollars. My family afforded the high cost of tuition and the expense of employing a full-time *amah* for less than a year.

6   We left China as the Communist forces swept across the country in victory. We found an apartment in Hong Kong across the street from a school run by Seventh-Day Adventists. By that time I could walk a little, so the principal was persuaded to accept me. An *amah* now had to take care of me only during recess when my classmates might easily knock me over as they ran about the playground.

7   After a year and a half in Hong Kong, we moved to Malaysia, where my father's family had lived for four generations. There I learned to swim in the lovely warm waters of the tropics and fell in love with the sea. On land I was a cripple; in the ocean I could move with the grace of a fish. I liked the freedom of being in the water so much that many years later, when I was a graduate student in Hawaii, I became greatly enamored with a man just because he called me a "Polynesian water

nymph: a mythical beautiful creature

nymph."

8   As my overall health improved, my mother became less anxious about all aspects of my life. She did everything possible to enable me to lead as normal a life as possible. I remember how once some of her colleagues in the high school where she taught criticized her for letting me wear short skirts. They felt my legs should not be exposed to public view. My mother's response was, "All girls her age wear short skirts, so why shouldn't she?"

9   The years in Malaysia were the happiest of my childhood, even though I was constantly fending off children who ran after me calling, *"Baikah! Baikah!"* ("Cripple! Cripple!" in the Hokkien dialect commonly spoken in Malaysia). The taunts of children mattered little because I was a star pupil. I won one award after another for general scholarship as well as for art and public speaking. Whenever the school had important visitors my teacher always called on me to recite in front of the class.

indelibly: permanently

10   A significant event that marked me indelibly occurred when I was twelve. That year my school held a music recital and I was one of the students chosen to play the piano. I managed to get up the steps to the stage without any problem, but as I walked across the stage, I fell. Out of the audience, a voice said loudly and clearly, "Ayah! A *baikah* shouldn't be allowed to perform in public." I got up before anyone could get on stage to help me and, with tears streaming uncontrollably down my face, I rushed to the piano and began to play. Beethoven's "Für Elise" had never been played so fiendishly fast before or since, but I managed to finish the whole piece. That I managed to do so made me feel really strong. I never again feared ridicule.

11   In later years I was reminded of this experience from time to time. During my fourth year as an assistant professor at the University of California at Berkeley, I won a distinguished teaching award. Some weeks later I ran into a former professor who congratulated me enthusiastically. But I said to him, "You know what? I became a distinguished teacher by *limping* across the stage of Dwinelle 155!" (Dwinelle 155 is a large, cold, classroom that most colleagues of mine hate to teach in.) I was rude not because I lacked graciousness but because this man, who had told me that my dissertation was the finest piece of work he had read in fifteen years, had nevertheless advised me to eschew a teaching career.

eschew: avoid

12   "Why?" I asked.

13   "Your leg . . ." he responded.

14   "What about my leg?" I said, puzzled.

15   "Well, how would you feel standing in front of a large lecture class?"

16   "If it makes any difference, I want you to know I've won a number of speech contests in my life, and I am not the least bit self-conscious about speaking in front of large audiences. . . . Look, why don't you write me a letter or recommendation to tell people how brilliant I am, and let *me* worry about my leg!"

17   This incident is worth recounting only because it illustrates a dilemma that handicapped persons face frequently: those who care about us sometimes get so protective that they unwittingly limit our growth. This former professor of mine had been one of my greatest supporters for two decades. Time after time, he had written glowing letters of recommendation on my behalf. He had spoken as he did because he thought he had my best interests at heart; he thought that if I got a desk job rather than one that required me to be a visible, public person, I would be spared the misery of being stared at.

18   Americans, for the most part, do not believe as Asians do that physically handicapped persons are morally flawed. But they are equally inept at interacting with those of us who are not able-bodied. Cultural differences in the perception and treatment of handicapped people are most clearly expressed by adults. Children, regardless of where they are, tend to be openly curious about people who do not look "normal." Adults in Asia have no hesitation in asking visibly handicapped people what is wrong with them, often expressing their sympathy with looks of pity, whereas adults in the United States try desperately to be polite by pretending not to notice.

19   One interesting response I often elicited from people in Asia but have never encountered in America is the attempt to link my physical condition to the state of my soul. Many a time while living and traveling in Asia people would ask me what religion I belonged to. I would tell them that my mother is a devout Buddhist, that my father was baptized a Catholic but has never practiced Catholicism, and that I am an agnostic. Upon hearing this, people would try strenuously to convert me to their religion so that whichever God they believed in could bless me. If I would only attend this church or that temple regularly, they urged, I would surely get cured. Catholics and Buddhists alike have pressed religious medallions into my palm, telling me if I would wear these, the relevant deity or saint would make me well. Once while visiting the tomb of Muhammad Ali Jinnah in Karachi, Pakistan, an old Muslim, after finishing his evening prayers, spotted me, gestured toward my legs, raised his arms heavenward, and began a new round of prayers, apparently on my behalf.

20   In the United States adults who try to act "civilized" towards handicapped people by pretending they don't notice anything unusual sometimes end up ignoring

furtively: secretly

handicapped people completely. In the first few months I lived in this country, I was struck by the fact that whenever children asked me what was the matter with my leg, their adult companions would hurriedly shush them up, furtively look at me, mumble apologies, and rush their children away. After a few months of such encounters, I decided it was my responsibility to educate these people. So I would say to the flustered adults, "It's okay, let the kid ask." Turning to the child, I would say, "When I was a little girl, no bigger than you are, I became sick with something called polio. The muscles of my leg shrank up and I couldn't walk very well. You're much luckier than I am because now you can get a vaccine to make sure you never get my disease. So don't cry when your mommy takes you to get a polio vaccine, okay?" Some adults and their little companions I talked to this way were glad to be rescued from embarrassment; other thought I was strange.

jovially: good-naturedly
patronizing: condescending
belligerent: hostile

21   Americans have another way of covering up their uneasiness: they become jovially patronizing. Sometimes when people spot my crutch, they ask if I've had a skiing accident. When I answer that unfortunately it is something less glamorous than that, they say, "I bet you *could* ski if you put your mind to it!" Alternately at parties where people dance, men who ask me to dance with them get almost belligerent when I decline their invitation. They say, "Of course you can dance if you *want* to!" Some have given me pep talks about how if I would only develop the right mental attitude, I would have more fun in life.

qualms: uneasy feelings

22   Different cultural attitudes toward handicapped persons came out clearly during my wedding. My father-in-law, as solid a representative of middle America as could be found, had no qualms about objecting to the marriage on racial grounds, but he could bring himself to comment on my handicap only indirectly. He wondered why his son, who had dated numerous high school and college beauty queens, couldn't marry one of them instead of me. My mother-in-law, a devout Christian, did not share her husband's prejudices but she worried aloud about whether I could have children. Some Chinese friends of my parents, on the other hand, said that I was lucky to have found such a noble man, one who would marry me despite my handicap. I, for my part, appeared in church in a white lace wedding dress I had designed and made myself—a miniskirt!

acculturation: assimilation into a larger culture

duality: having two distinct parts
elicit: draw out

23   How Asian Americans treat me with respect to my handicap tells me a great deal about their degree of acculturation. Recent immigrants behave just like Asians in Asia; those who have been here longer or who grew up in the United States behave more like their white counterparts. I have not encountered any distinctly Asian American pattern of response. What makes the experience of Asian American handicapped people unique is the duality of responses we elicit.

24   Regardless of racial or cultural background, most handicapped people have to learn to find a balance between the desire to attain physical independence and the need to take care of ourselves by not overtaxing our bodies. In my case, I've had to learn to accept the fact that leading an active life has its price. Between the ages of eight and eighteen, I walked without using crutches or braces but the effort caused my right leg to become badly misaligned. Soon after I came to the United States, I had a series of operations to straighten out the bones of my right leg; afterwards though my leg looked straighter and presumably better, I could no longer walk on my own. Initially my doctors fitted me with a brace, but I found wearing one cumbersome and soon gave it up. I could move around much more easily—and more important, faster—by using one crutch. One orthopedist after another warned me that using a single crutch was a bad practice. They were right. Over the years

my spine developed a double-S curve and for the last twenty years I have suffered from severe, chronic back pains, which neither conventional physical therapy nor a lighter work load can eliminate.

25 The only thing that helps my backaches is a good massage, but the soothing effect lasts no more than a day or two. Massages are expensive, especially when one needs them three times a week. So I found a job that pays better, but at which I have to work longer hours, consequently increasing the physical strain on my body—a sort of vicious circle. When I was in my thirties, my doctors told me that if I kept leading the strenuous life I did, I would be in a wheelchair by the time I was forty. They were right on target: I bought myself a wheelchair when I was forty-one. But being the incorrigible character that I am, I use it only when I am *not* in a hurry!

incorrigible: incapable of being corrected or reformed

26 It is a good thing, however, that I am too busy to think much about my handicap or my backaches because pain can physically debilitate as well as cause depression. And there are days when my spirits get rather low. What has helped me is realizing that being handicapped is akin to growing old at an accelerated rate. The contradiction I experience is that often my mind races along as though I'm only twenty while my body feels about sixty. But fifteen or twenty years hence, unlike my peers who will have to cope with aging for the first time, I shall be full of cheer because I will have already fought, and I hope won, that battle long ago.

27 Beyond learning how to be physically independent and, for some of us, living with chronic pain or other kinds of discomfort, the most difficult thing a handicapped person has to deal with, especially during puberty and early adulthood, is relating to potential sexual partners. Because American culture places so much emphasis on physical attractiveness, a person with a shriveled limb, or a tilt to the head, or the inability to speak clearly, experiences great uncertainty—indeed trauma—when interacting with someone to whom he or she is attracted. My problem was that I was not only physically handicapped, small, and short, but worse, I also wore glasses and was smarter than all the boys I knew! Alas, an insurmountable combination. Yet somehow I have managed to have intimate relationships, all of them with extraordinary men. Not surprisingly, there have also been countless men who broke my heart—men who enjoyed my company "as a friend," but who never found the courage to date or make love with me, although I am sure my experience in this regard is no different from that of many able-bodied persons.

insurmountable: impossible to overcome

28 The day came when my backaches got in the way of having an active sex life. Surprisingly that development was liberating because I stopped worrying about being attractive to men. No matter how headstrong I had been, I, like most women of my generation, had had the desire to be alluring to men ingrained into me. And that longing had always worked like a brake on my behavior. When what men think of me ceased to be compelling, I gained greater freedom to be myself.

29 I've often wondered if I would have been a different person had I not been physically handicapped. I really don't know, though there is no question that being handicapped has marked me. But at the same time I usually do not *feel* handicapped—and consequently, I do not *act* handicapped. People are therefore less likely to treat me as a handicapped person. There is no doubt, however, that the lives of my parents, sister, husband, other family members, and some close friends have been affected by my physical condition. They have had to learn not to hide me away at home, not to feel embarrassed by how I look or react to people who say silly things to me, and not to resent me for the extra demands my condition makes on them. Perhaps the hardest thing for those who live with handicapped people is to

know when and how to offer help. There are no guidelines applicable to all situations. My advice is, when in doubt, ask, but ask in a way that does not smack of pity or embarrassment. Most important, please don't talk to us as though we are children.

30   So, has being physically handicapped been a handicap? It all depends on one's attitude. Some years ago, I told a friend that I had once said to an affirmative action compliance officer (somewhat sardonically since I do not believe in the head count approach to affirmative action) that the institution which employs me is triply lucky because it can count me as nonwhite, female, and handicapped. He responded, "Why don't you tell them to count you four times? . . . Remember, you're short, besides!"

sardonically:
sarcastically

Questions for Critical Thinking

1. Make a list of the various ways people are classified. What, for instance, are some of the ways you could describe yourself? Give a listing of terms that would describe you.

2. What are the terms Sucheng Chan finds that others use to describe her? How does she herself wish to be thought of?

3. The author gives us several carefully chosen incidents from her life in order to illustrate what she believes are important truths about her situation. Examine each incident she relates and discuss what point she is making about being "handicapped."

4. What do you think the author reveals about herself when she tells us she designed her own wedding gown—a miniskirt?

5. Discuss the writer's explanation of how different cultures see her disability. Do you know of any other cultural attitudes toward illness or physical disabilities?

6. Why do you think the author includes a section on her health problems?

7. At the end, in paragraph 29, the author gives advice to those who live with a disabled person. What is that advice?

8. The author gets the title from her concluding paragraph. What makes the concluding paragraph so good?

Writing in Response

1. Write an essay in which you discuss the basic problem in placing people into categories. Give several examples to illustrate your points.

2. Write an essay in which you describe yourself by using six or seven carefully chosen words that place you into specific groups of people. Within each category, explain how you fit or do not totally fit into this group. Do you feel a positive identification or a negative identification with these groups? Do you think society sees these groups as positive or negative? Do you think this is a fair way for people to view you?

3. Everyone has some disabilities and no one has the ability to do everything well. Think of something about yourself that you might consider a disability. How has it affected your life? What do you do to compensate for it? What can others do to help you deal with the difficulties this disadvantage presents in your life?

4. In paragraph 17, the writer presents a dilemma that handicapped persons face frequently: "those who care about us sometimes get so protective that they unwittingly limit our growth." Can you be too protective of those you love? Write an essay that discusses the problems of parents who are too protective of their children, or husbands who are too protective of their wives. Give specific examples.

Kids in the Mall: Growing Up Controlled
WILLIAM SEVERINI KOWINSKI

The mall has largely replaced the traditional downtown as the main shopping area for cities and towns. It has also provided an important social center for people young and old. William Severini Kowinski examines the growing importance of the mall on our culture, as he discusses its many effects on young people.

1   Butch heaved himself up and loomed over the group. "Like it was different for me," he piped. "My folks used to drop me off at the shopping mall every morning and leave me all day. It was like a big free baby-sitter, you know? One night they never came back for me. Maybe they moved away. Maybe there's some kind of a Bureau of Missing Parents I could check with."

—Richard Peck
Secrets of the Shopping Mall,
a novel for teenagers

2   From his sister at Swarthmore, I'd heard about a kid in Florida whose mother picked him up after school every day, drove him straight to the mall, and left him there until it closed—all at his insistence. I'd heard about a boy in Washington who, when his family moved from one suburb to another, pedaled his bicycle five miles every day to get back to his old mall, where he once belonged.

3   These stories aren't unusual. The mall is a common experience for the majority of American youth; they have probably been going there all their lives. Some ran within their first large open space, saw their first fountain, bought their first toy, and read their first book in a mall. They may have smoked their first cigarette or first joint or turned them down, had their first kiss or lost their virginity in the mall parking lot. Teenagers in America now spend more time in the mall than anywhere else but home and school. Mostly it is their choice, but some of that mall time is put in as the result of two-paycheck and single-parent households, and the lack of other viable alternatives. But are these kids being harmed by the mall?

viable: practical

4   I wondered first of all what difference it makes for adolescents to experience so many important moments in the mall. They are, after all, at play in the fields of its little world and they learn its ways; they adapt to it and make it adapt to them. It's here that these kids get their street sense, only it's mall sense. They are learning the ways of a large-scale artificial environment: its subtleties and flexibilities, its particular pleasures and resonances, and the attitudes it fosters.

resonances: echoes; having a prolonged, subtle effect
fosters: encourages

incursion: invasion

5   The presence of so many teenagers for so much time was not something mall developers planned on. In fact, it came as a big surprise. But kids became a fact of mall life very early, and the International Council of Shopping Centers found it necessary to commission a study, which they published along with a guide to mall managers on how to handle the teenage incursion.

6   The study found that "teenagers in the suburban centers are bored and come to the shopping centers mainly as a place to go. Teenagers in suburban centers spent more time fighting, drinking, littering and walking than did their urban counterparts, but presented fewer overall problems." The report observed that "adolescents congregated in groups of two to four and predominantly at locations selected by them rather than management." This probably had something to do with the decision to install game arcades, which allow management to channel these restless adolescents into naturally contained areas away from major traffic points of adult shoppers.

7   The guide concluded that mall management should tolerate and even encourage the teenage presence because, in the words of the report, "The vast majority support the same set of values as does shopping center management." *The same set of values* means simply that mall kids are already preprogrammed to be consumers and that the mall can put the finishing touches to them as hardcore, lifelong shoppers just like everybody else. That, after all, is what the mall is about. So it shouldn't be surprising that in spending a lot of time there, adolescents find little that challenges the assumption that the goal of life is to make money and buy products, or that just about everything else in life is to be used to serve those ends.

inestimable: impossible to estimate

8   Growing up in a high-consumption society already adds inestimable pressure to kids' lives. Clothes consciousness has invaded the grade schools, and popularity is linked with having the best, newest clothes in the currently acceptable styles. Even what they read has been affected. "Miss [Nancy] Drew wasn't obsessed with her wardrobe," noted *The Wall Street Journal,* "but today the mystery in teen fiction for girls is what outfit the heroine will wear next." Shopping has become a survival skill and there is certainly no better place to learn it than the mall, where its importance is powerfully reinforced and certainly never questioned.

mores: accepted customs of a particular social group
ramifications: consequences
plethora: an excess
belies: contradicts, misrepresents

9   The mall as a university of suburban materialism, where Valley Girls and Boys from coast to coast are educated in consumption, has its other lessons in this era of change in family life and sexual mores and their economic and social ramifications. The plethora of products in the mall, plus the pressure on teens to buy them, may contribute to the phenomenon that psychologist David Elkind calls "the hurried child": kids who are exposed to too much of the adult world too quickly, and must respond with a sophistication that belies their still-tender emotional development. Certainly the adult products marketed for children—form-fitting designer jeans, sexy tops for preteen girls—add to the social pressure to look like an adult, along with the home-grown need to understand adult finances (why mothers must work) and adult emotions (when parents divorce).

unsavory: distasteful, morally offensive
surrogate: substitute

denizens: citizens

crave: desire intensely

10   Kids spend so much time at the mall partly because their parents allow it and even encourage it. The mall is safe, it doesn't seem to harbor any unsavory activities, and there is adult supervision; it is, after all, a controlled environment. So the temptation, especially for working parents, is to let the mall be their babysitter. At least the kids aren't watching TV. But the mall's role as a surrogate mother may be more extensive and more profound.

11   Karen Lansky, a writer living in Los Angeles, has looked into the subject and she told me some of her conclusions about the effects on its teenaged denizens of the mall's controlled and controlling environment. "Structure is the dominant idea, since true 'mall rats' lack just that in their home lives," she said, "and adolescents about to make the big leap into growing up crave more structure than our modern society cares to acknowledge." Karen pointed out some of the elements malls supply that kids used to get from their families, like warmth (Strawberry Shortcake dolls and similar cute and cuddly merchandise), old-fashioned mothering ("We do it all for you," the fast-food slogan), and even home cooking (the "home-made" treats at the food court).

nurture: help develop
rigors: hardships, strictness

12   The problem in all this, as Karen Lansky sees it, is that while families nurture children by encouraging growth through the assumption of responsibility and then by letting them rest in the bosom of the family from the rigors of growing up, the mall as a structural mother encourages passivity and consumption, as long as the kid doesn't make trouble. Therefore all they learn about becoming adults is how to act and how to consume.

infiltrate: gradually gain entrance

13   Kids are in the mall not only in the passive role of shoppers—they also work there, especially as fast-food outlets infiltrate the mall's enclosure. There they learn how to hold a job and take responsibility, but still within the same value context. When *CBS Reports* went to Oak Park Mall in suburban Kansas City, Kansas, to tape part of their hour-long consideration of malls, "After the Dream Comes True," they interviewed a teenaged girl who worked in a fast-food outlet there. In a sequence that didn't make the final program, she described the major goal of her present life, which was to perfect the curl on top of the ice-cream cones that were her store's specialty. If she could do that, she would be moved from the lowly soft-drink dispenser to the more prestigious ice-cream division, the curl on top of the status ladder at her restaurant. There are the achievements that are important at the mall.

14   Other benefits of such jobs may also be overrated, according to Laurence D. Steinberg of the University of California at Irvine's social ecology department, who did a study on teenage employment. Their jobs, he found, are generally simple, mindlessly repetitive and boring. They don't really learn anything, and the jobs don't head anywhere. Teenagers also work primarily with other teenagers; even their supervisors are often just a little older than they are. "Kids need to spend time with adults," Steinberg told me. "Although they get benefits from peer relationships, without parents and other adults it's a one-sided socialization. They hang out with each other, have age-segregated jobs, and watch TV."

impositions: unfair demands

15   Perhaps much of this is not so terrible or even so terribly different. Now that they have so much more to contend with in their lives, adolescents probably need more time to spend with other adolescents without adult impositions, just to sort things out. Though it is more concentrated in the mall (and therefore perhaps a clearer target), the value system there is really the dominant one of the whole society.

empathy: understanding of another's situation, feelings and motives

disinterested: indifferent

forays: initial ventures outside one's usual area

impertinence: irrelevance

inexorably: relentlessly

Attitudes about curiosity, initiative, self-expression, empathy, and disinterested learning aren't necessarily made in the mall; they are mirrored there, perhaps a bit more intensely—as through a glass brightly.

16   Besides, the mall is not without its educational opportunities. There are bookstores, where there is at least a short shelf of classics at great prices, and other books from which it is possible to learn more than how to do sit-ups. There are tools, from hammers to VCRs, and products, from clothes to records, that can help the young find and express themselves. There are older people with stories, and places to be alone or to talk one-on-one with a kindred spirit. And there is always the passing show.

17   The mall itself may very well be an education about the future. I was struck with the realization, as early as my first forays into Greengate, that the mall is only one of a number of enclosed and controlled environments that are part of the lives of today's young. The mall is just an extension, say, of those large suburban schools—only there's Karmelkorn instead of chem lab, the ice rink instead of the gym: It's high school without the impertinence of classes.

18   Growing up, moving from home to school to the mall—from enclosure to enclosure, transported in cars—is a curiously continuous process, without much in the way of contrast or contact with unenclosed reality. Places must tend to blur into one another. But whatever differences and dangers there are in this, the skills these adolescents are learning may turn out to be useful in their later lives. For we seem to be moving inexorably into an age of preplanned and regulated environments, and this is the world they will inherit.

19   Still, it might be better if they had more of a choice. One teenaged girl confessed to *CBS Reports* that she sometimes felt she was missing something by hanging out at the mall so much. "But I'm here," she said, "and this is what I have."

Questions for Critical Thinking

1. How can neighborhoods compete with malls as places for people, young and old, to gather and connect socially?

2. Based on your own experience, how widespread is the clothes consciousness that the writer notes in paragraph 8 "has invaded the grade schools," and other levels of education?

3. In paragraph 10, the writer states that "the mall is safe." Based upon what you have read in the newspapers or perhaps heard on television or radio, is this an accurate statement? What dangers, if any, are there in today's mall?

4. In paragraph 11 the writer quotes Karen Lansky, who has studied malls and their effects on people, and who reports that teenagers want "more structure than our society cares to acknowledge." Is this true, or do teenagers really want more freedom?

5. In paragraph 17, the writer notes the mall is one of a number of "enclosed and controlled environments that are part of the lives of young people." What are some of these other enclosed environments? How similar are they to malls?

6. The author refers more than once to malls as places where people learn (see paragraph 9). What exactly do they learn? Is this knowledge useful or helpful in any way?

Writing in Response

1. Argue for or against the following statement: It is better for kids to _____ (fill in your own idea here) than to go to the mall as a way of having some low-cost entertainment.

2. Write an essay in which you classify the kinds of activities you were involved in as a teenager. Which of these can you recommend to young people and which would you not recommend? Give examples and your reasons.

3. What are the effects of the mall culture on American young people? Use your own examples as well as ideas you have from reading the essay.

4. How much control should a parent have over a teenager's life? Does it partly depend on the personality and behavior of the child? Classify teenagers into types and describe how the parent should handle them in each case. (Or, classify parents into types and describe how each type deals with young people who are trying to establish their own identities.)

Zero-to-60 in 5 Nanoseconds
TIMOTHY TAYLOR

Everyone agrees this is the computer age, but not everyone believes that the arrival of computers has led to only positive results. Timothy Taylor takes us behind the well-publicized glamour of computers and examines how productive they really are. The writer also suggests that, in the end, if we neglect the human factor we are missing the larger point of technology.

heresy: an opinion at variance with established beliefs

skeptics: those who regularly doubt accepted conclusions

nagging: lingering

macroeconomic: concerned with overall national economy

1   It may sound like heresy, but some skeptics doubt that computers add to economic productivity. Evidence for their nagging suspicions comes from all directions—anecdotes, industry-level studies, and macroeconomic statistics.

2   Anyone who has survived the ordeal of installing a new office computer system will understand the dangers here. Workers are required to take time away from their jobs to sit through dry-as-dirt training sessions. Records are carefully filed away in the computer—and then no one knows how to access that information ever again.

3   Once the system is in place, middle managers are often bewitched by their new toys; they begin to produce and require more status reports and updates than ever before. Once upon a time, the paper companies were concerned that computers would usher in the "paperless office." Actually, computers have led to far more paperwork.

counterproductive: hindering productivity

4   Of course, a few horror stories about counterproductive technology don't make a definitive case. Anecdotes illustrate, but they don't prove anything. However, several academic studies have also found that computers don't contribute much to productivity.

marginal: on the edge, slight

5   In a recent "Weekly Letter" of the Federal Reserve Bank of San Francisco, senior economist Ronald Schmidt describes one study that looked at U.S. and European manufacturing firms, and found that investment in information technology had "little, if any, marginal impact on output or labor productivity while all other inputs into production including non-information technologies capital had significant impacts on output and labor productivity."

6   Another study, looking back over several decades, suggested that manufacturing "firms had over-invested in those information technologies, and that the costs of the equipment exceeded their benefits."

7   Other economic studies (not mentioned by Schmidt) have examined computers in service industries like banking, finance, insurance, and wholesale and retail trade, again without finding much connection between computerization and productivity. There seems to be some truth in the popular stereotype that the high-fangled computers in financial industries have mainly served to move money around in faster and trickier ways, often doing as much to destabilize and unsettle the economy than to support it.

8   The macroeconomic evidence signals yet another caution about computers and productivity; the 1980s were a time when business and individuals invested very heavily in computers, but productivity growth for the economy stayed stubbornly low. One wisecrack, generally attributed to Nobel laureate economist Robert Solow of MIT, is that: "We see computers everywhere, except in the productivity statistics."

Nobel laureate: one who has been awarded the Nobel prize for great achievement

9   But this case for the prosecution is far from unanswerable; the computer revolution has its share of defenders who advance two main arguments.

10   One response is to question the data on productivity. One basic measure of productivity is output per hour of labor; for purposes of comparison, "output" is usually measured by the total dollar value of what is produced.

11   Imagine that a new computer-aided design system allows companies to produce, say, higher quality cars—perhaps with better use of interior space, greater safety, and better fuel efficiency—but these improved cars sell for the same price as the old ones. According to the productivity statistics, the same amount of labor is producing the same dollar value of cars, so the computer added nothing. In short, productivity statistics often fail to capture higher quality.

12   This problem is especially severe in the service-oriented industries that have invested so heavily in computerization. Surely, it would seem that with automatic teller machines and access to accounts by telephone, productivity in banking must be higher than a decade ago? Logic says "yes," but the productivity statistics won't show it.

assimilate: incorporate, absorb

literally: really, actually

13   An alternate defense is to accept that computers haven't increased productivity much so far, but to argue that the economy takes decades to assimilate an invention as far-reaching as the computer. Paul David of Stanford University has pointed out an interesting historical parallel. The technology for the dynamo was available in 1900, but it literally took decades for factories to be electrified, so that they could take advantage of this new capability.

14   Similarly, Intel introduced the silicon microprocessor less than 25 years ago, in 1970. Even a decade ago, desktop computers were relatively rare, and those that did exist would today be considered as slow and obsolete as dinosaurs. On this perspective, the "information age" is still in its infancy. Our society is just beginning to redesign its manufacturing and services, its entertainment and finance, its patterns of commuting and living, to take advantage of information technology.

15   In the end, the case against computer-driven productivity is certainly not proven. In the end, it is difficult to believe that this remarkable technology won't raise the world's standard of living.

16   But the academic argument over computers and productivity has a real-world lesson. Too many people buy computers (and other new technologies) the way they buy cars: paying for zero-to-60 in five seconds, and the ability to drive 140 mph, and other features that they will probably never use.

17   In a world where the boundaries of technological possibility are continually expanding, it's worth remembering that sophisticated technology, in and of itself, is worth nothing. The interaction between technology and people is what counts.

Questions for Critical Thinking

1. In the first paragraph, the author gives us the thesis and lists the kinds of examples he plans to present as evidence. In your own words, state his thesis and list the three kinds of evidence he will present.

2. Divide the body of the essay into the three parts listed in the introduction. Does the author do what he says he will do?

3. How many times does the author actually quote from an expert?

4. Which paragraph begins the conclusion? State the author's conclusion in your own words.

5. Find the place in the essay from which the title was taken and explain its meaning.

Writing in Response

1. Anecdotal evidence is evidence which you **believe** is true because of your experience but which you cannot prove by any scientific means. What anecdotal information do you have about people's experience with computers? What stories can you tell about computers and how they saved people time or money? What stories can you tell about how computers caused problems with loss of time or money? You may want to work in groups to gather stories. Then pick three of these anecdotes that you would like to write about. Each story will be a separate paragraph.

2. Machines are always advertised as saving us time. Pick several machines that you use regularly (or would use regularly if you owned them). Describe how each one saves you or would save you time or money. Describe the problems involved by not having these particular machines.

3. Imagine life before the coming of a particular technology (electricity, for instance). Write about the way people lived then. What aspects of this way of life were better than now? Which aspects were worse?

4. The author believes the effects of computer technology are just beginning. Write your futuristic vision of what life will be like 20 years from now with the advances that computer technology will bring.

Why One Peaceful Woman Carries a Pistol

LINDA M. HASSELSTROM

Few topics today raise such a strong emotional response as that of women being the victims of violence. In the following essay, one woman speaks out as she reports her solution to living with the sense of personal threat.

1 I'm a peace-loving woman. I also carry a pistol. For years, I've written about my decision in an effort to help other women make intelligent choices about gun ownership, but editors rejected the articles. Between 1983 and 1986, however, when gun sales to men held steady, gun ownership among women rose fifty-three percent, to more than twelve million. We learned that any female over the age of twelve can expect to be criminally assaulted some time in her life, that women aged thirty have a fifty-fifty chance of being raped, robbed, or attacked, and that many police officials say flatly that they cannot protect citizens from crime. During the same period, the number of women considering gun ownership quadrupled to nearly two million. Manufacturers began showing lightwight weapons with small grips, and purses with built-in holsters. A new magazine is called *Guns and Women,* and more than eight thousand copies of the video *A Woman's Guide to Firearms* were sold by 1988. Experts say female gun buyers are not limited to any particular age group, profession, social class, or area of the country, and most are buying guns to protect themselves. Shooting instructors say women view guns with more caution than do men, and may make better shots.

2 I decided to buy a handgun for several reasons. During one four-year period, I drove more than a hundred thousand miles alone, giving speeches, readings, and workshops. A woman is advised, usually by men, to protect herself by avoiding bars, by approaching her car like an Indian scout, by locking doors and windows. But these precautions aren't always enough. And the logic angers me: *Because* I am female, it is my responsibility to be extra careful.

3 As a responsible environmentalist, I choose to recycle, avoid chemicals on my land, minimize waste. As an informed woman alone, I choose to be as responsible for my own safety as possible: I keep my car running well, use caution in where I go and what I do. And I learned about self-protection—not an easy or quick decision. I developed a strategy of protection that includes handgun possession. The following incidents, chosen from a larger number because I think they could happen to anyone, helped make up my mind.

4 As I drove home one night, a car followed me, lights bright. It passed on a narrow bridge, while a passenger flashed a spotlight in my face, blinding me. I braked sharply. The car stopped, angled across the bridge, and four men jumped out. I realized the locked doors were useless if they broke my car windows. I started forward, hoping to knock their car aside so I could pass. Just then, another car appeared, and the men got back in their car, but continued to follow me, passing and repassing. I dared not go home. I passed no lighted houses. Finally, they pulled to the roadside, and I decided to use their tactic: fear. I roared past them inches away, horn blaring. It worked; they turned off the highway. But it was desperate and foolish, and I was frightened and angry. Even in my vehicle I was too vulnerable.

5   In my car, my pistol is within instant reach. When I enter a deserted rest stop at night, it's in my purse, my hand on the grip. When I walk from a dark parking lot into a motel, it's in my hand, under a coat. When I walk my dog in the deserted lots around most motels, the pistol is in a shoulder holster, and I am always aware of my surroundings. In my motel room, it lies on the bedside table. At home, it's on the headboard.

6   Just carrying a pistol is not protection. Avoidance is still the best approach to trouble; watch for danger signs, and practice avoiding them. Develop your instinct for danger.

7   One day while driving to the highway mailbox, I saw a vehicle parked about halfway to the house. Several men were standing in the ditch, relieving themselves. I have no objection to emergency urination; we always need moisture. But they'd also dumped several dozen beer cans, which blow into pastures and can slash a cow's legs or stomach.

ostentatiously: in a showy, boastful way

8   As I slowly drove closer, the men zipped their trousers ostentatiously while walking toward me. Four men gathered around my small foreign car, making remarks they wouldn't make to their mothers, and one of them demanded what the hell I wanted.

9   "This is private land; I'd like you to pick up the beer cans."

belligerent: aggressive

10   "What beer cans?" said the belligerent one, putting both hands on the car door, and leaning in my window. His face was inches from mine, the beer fumes were strong, and he looked angry. The others laughed. One tried the passenger door, locked; another put his foot on the hood and rocked the car. They circled, lightly thumping the roof, discussing my good fortune in meeting them, and the benefits they were likely to bestow upon me. I felt small and trapped; they knew it.

11   "The ones you just threw out," I said politely.

12   "I don't see no beer cans. Why don't you get out here and show them to me, honey?" said the belligerent one, reaching for the handle inside my door.

13   "Right over there," I said, still being polite, "there and over there." I pointed with the pistol, which had been under my thigh. Within one minute the cans and the men were back in the car, and headed down the road.

14   I believe this small incident illustrates several principles. The men were trespassing and knew it; their judgment may have been impaired by alcohol. Their response to the polite request of a woman alone was to use their size and numbers to inspire fear. The pistol was a response in the same language. Politeness didn't work; I couldn't intimidate them. Out of the car, I'd have been more vulnerable. The pistol just changed the balance of power.

intimidate: to threaten

15   My husband, George, asked one question when I told him. "What would you have done if he'd grabbed for the pistol?"

16   "I had the car in reverse; I'd have hit the accelerator, and backed up; if he'd kept coming, I'd have fired straight at him." He nodded.

17   In fact, the sight of the pistol made the man straighten up; he cracked his head on the door frame. He and the two in front of the car stepped backward, catching the attention of the fourth, who joined them. They were all in front of me then, and as the car was still running and in reverse gear, my options had multiplied. If they'd advanced again, I'd have backed away, turning to keep the open window toward them. Given time, I'd have put the first shot into the ground in front of them, the second into the belligerent leader. It might have been better to wait until they were gone, pick up the beer cans, and avoid confrontation, but I believed it was reasonable and my right to make a polite request to strangers littering my

property. Showing the pistol worked on another occasion when I was driving in a desolate part of Wyoming. A man played cat-and-mouse with me for thirty miles, ultimately trying to run my car off the road. When his car was only two inches from mine, I pointed my pistol at him, and he disappeared.

18   I believe that a handgun is like a car; both are tools for specific purposes; both can be lethal if used improperly. Both require a license, training, and alertness. Both require you to be aware of what is happening before and behind you. Driving becomes almost instinctive; so does handgun use. When I've drawn my gun for protection, I simply found it in my hand. Instinct told me a situation was dangerous before my conscious mind reacted; I've felt the same while driving. Most good drivers react to emergencies by instinct.

19   We can and should educate ourselves in how to travel safely, take self-defense courses, reason, plead, or avoid trouble in other ways. But some men cannot be stopped by those methods; they understand only power. A man who is committing an attack already knows he's breaking laws; he has no concern for someone else's rights. A pistol is a woman's answer to his greater power. It makes her equally frightening. I have thought of revising the old Colt slogan: "God made man, but Sam Colt made them equal" to read "God made men *and women* but Sam Colt made them equal." Recently I have seen an ad for a popular gunmaker with a similar sentiment; perhaps this is an idea whose time has come, though the pacifist inside me will be saddened if the only way women can achieve equality is by carrying a weapon.

20   As a society, we were shocked in early 1989 when a female jogger in New York's Central Park was beaten and raped savagely and left in a coma. I was even more shocked when reporters interviewed children who lived near the victim and quoted a twelve-year-old as saying, "She had nothing to guard herself; she didn't have no man with her; she didn't have no Mace." And another sixth-grader said, "It is like she committed suicide." Surely this is not a majority opinion, but I think it is not so unusual, either, even in this liberated age. Yet there is no city or county in the nation where law officers can relax because all the criminals are in jail. Some authorities say citizens armed with handguns stop almost as many crimes annually as armed criminals succeed in committing, and that people defending themselves kill three times more attackers and robbers than police do. I don't suggest all criminals should be killed, but some can be stopped only by death or permanent incarceration. Law enforcement officials can't prevent crimes; later punishment may be of little comfort to the victim. A society so controlled that no crime existed would probably be too confined for most of us, and is not likely to exist any time soon. Therefore, many of us should be ready and able to protect ourselves, and the intelligent use of firearms is one way.

21   We must treat a firearm's power with caution. "Power tends to corrupt, and absolute power corrupts absolutely," as a man (Lord Acton) once said. A pistol is not the only way to avoid being raped or murdered in today's world, but a firearm, intelligently wielded, can shift the balance and provide a measure of safety.

wielded: handled with skill

Questions for Critical Thinking

1. In her opening paragraph, the writer provides several statistics to show that many more women are either buying or thinking of buying handguns for self-protection. Why do you think the author chooses to begin her essay with these statistics?

2. Discuss the writer's point in paragraph two where she states that she is angered by the fact that, "Because I am female, it is my responsibility to be more careful." Do you agree that this is society's attitude toward women in terms of their safety?

3. In paragraph 4, the writer describes what she did one evening to a group of men that harassed her on the road—she decided to use their tactic and "roared past them inches away, horn blaring." Is the writer correct in saying that this was a "desperate and foolish" thing to do? What do you think she should have done in that situation?

4. In paragraph 18, the writer argues that "a handgun is like a car," and then uses that paragraph to support her position. Do you agree with her point of view?

5. In her next to last paragraph, the writer concludes that we should be ready to protect ourselves by the intelligent use of guns. Are you persuaded by her essay that having more guns is one way to make our society safer?

6. Notice how long the writer waited before she bought a handgun. Do you think she acted in a responsible way?

7. Do you think that because the writer of this essay lives on a ranch in an isolated part of the country that her attitude toward owning a gun should be different than that of an urban dweller?

Writing in Response

1. In your own words, summarize the main points made by this author in favor of gun ownership.

2. Write an essay in which you give advice to single women who either live alone or must travel alone. How should they protect themselves?

3. Construct an argument on a topic of your choosing. In your argument, use details drawn from your personal experience, to support your own position. You might want to consider the following topics:

   Women should not dress provocatively.

   Women should be able to dress as they please.

   People should not be able to have alcoholic beverages at sports events.

   Drinking at sports events should not be restricted.

Targeting Women for Guns
BOB HERBERT

There is a growing concern about the connection between women and guns in our society; more and more women are deciding to purchase firearms and are learning to use them. In the following essay, Bob Herbert examines some of the economic forces behind the current movement to have women buy guns for their own protection.

1   The circumstances that led up to the shooting are not clear. One version of the story, according to the police in Jackson, Miss., is that late Saturday night 3-year-old Jonathan Hicks, who loved to look at the lights on the family's Christmas tree, was mistaken by his stepmother for a burglar.

2   The stepmother, whose identity is being withheld by authorities, reached for a .380 semiautomatic handgun, went into the living room and fired at the first sign of movement. The boy was shot in the head and died.

3   The police are still investigating and have not ruled out other, more sinister versions. What is not in dispute is that the presence of a handgun in the step-mother's home, legally or illegally, and for whatever reasons, heightened the chances that something terrible would happen.

4   Tremendous sums of money have been made from the manufacture and sale of guns in the United States. But with so many men already armed, new markets must be found. The following quotation is taken from an "Editor's Note" in "S.H.O.T. Business," a trade journal for the firearms industry:

5   "An important mission of this magazine is to show our readers how they can expand their customer base, especially to women and children."

6   Most of us see homicide as a huge problem, but the blood is not flowing fast enough to suit the firearms industry. It is going after women big time.

7   Last week the Violence Policy Center, a research foundation in Washington, released a report titled "Female Persuasion—a Study of How the Firearms Industry Markets to Women and the Reality of Women and Guns." The report explained how the leading trade association of the firearms industry, the National Shooting Sports Foundation, created a series of shooting competitions called the Ladies Charity Classic Events as a way of introducing women to guns.

8   The competitions are now run by an offshoot of the national foundation called the Women's Shooting Sports Foundation. The report said, "By utilizing mainstream charities as beneficiaries, the WSSF entices non-gun-owning women to participate in the Ladies Charity Classic Events. . . . Charities range in size and scope from the 1988 Classic, which benefited a Houston shelter for abused women and children, to 1994's benefit for the Houston chapter of the Susan G. Komen Foundation for breast cancer research and treatment.

9   "As the National Shooting Sports Foundation noted in 1992, 'Each [WSSF] regional event will include a shooting clinic prior to the tournament and an association with a charitable cause; both recognized as key factors in motivating women who are not shooters to participate.'"

insidiousness: the spreading of harm in an underhanded way

10   It is just about impossible to overstate the insidiousness of seeking out women concerned with issues like domestic violence and breast cancer for the sole purpose of putting guns into their hands. But nothing is beneath the gun merchants, who have yet to find a sewer too slimy to swim in.

altercations:
fights or arguments
lethal: deadly

11   What firearms marketers never point out—to men or to women—is the extent to which the ready access of guns leads not to self-protection but to the destruction of gun owners and their loved ones. An analysis of gun deaths in the home that was published in The New England Journal of Medicine in 1986 found that more than 80 percent of the homicides occurred during arguments or altercations. In those kinds of situations, individuals often reach "for the most lethal weapon readily available."

12   Guns are particularly dangerous—and particularly dangerous to women—in households that are prone to domestic violence. That's another taboo topic for firearms marketers. So is suicide. Most gun deaths in America are the result of suicide, not homicide.

13   Men and women are being sold a fraudulent myth by the gun merchants. The route to personal safety is not more and more firepower in the hands of more and more Americans. The Violence Policy Center noted that "research over several decades has consistently shown that a gun in the home is far more likely to be used in suicide, murder or fatal accident than to kill a criminal."

14   That fact holds no interest for gun merchants, who, like cigarette manufacturers, make a wonderful living from the sweet smell of death.

Questions for Critical Thinking

1. In the first paragraph of her essay, "Why One Peaceful Woman Carries a Pistol," Linda M. Hasselstrom provides numbers and statistics to underscore how popular it has become for women to carry guns; in paragraphs 11 and 12 of his essay, Bob Herbert cites statistics of his own that argue against women possessing guns. Which set of numbers and statistics do you find more convincing?

2. In this essay, the writer does not use any personal experience to make his points, but Linda M. Hasselstrom's essay is filled with personal experiences. Is one essay more convincing because of its use of personal experience? Is the other piece more persuasive because it is filled with objective reporting?

3. In paragraph 13 of his essay, the writer tells us that the way to personal safety "is not more and more fire power in the hands of more and more Americans." However, the author does not say what would be the way to more personal safety. How important is it to the effectiveness of his argument that he does not present an alternative solution?

4. In what paragraphs does the writer anticipate the position of the other side to his argument and then answers his critics? How effective is this technique?

5. Bob Herbert's conclusion is very effective. Study the last two paragraphs of his essay and discuss how he achieves his dramatic impact.

Writing in Response

1. Write an essay in which you agree or disagree that the presence of guns in a home increases the chances of violence in that home.

2. Write an essay in which you discuss what you believe would be the best approach to increase the personal safety of all of our citizens.

Photo Credits

Page 14 Tony Stone/Scott Robinson

Page 45 Courtesy of Swanson Dinners

Page 45 Courtesy of News America

Page 57 Tony Stone/Chip Henderson

Page 91 AP/Wide World Photos

Page 107 Tony Stone/Lori Adamski Peek

Page 117 Tony Stone/Andy Sacks

Page 341 New York Times

Literary Credits

Excerpt from ANNIE JOHN by Jamaica Kincaid. Copyright (c) 1983, 1984, 1985 by Jamaica Kincaid. Reprinted by permission of Farrar, Straus & Giroux, Inc.

GAYELORD HAUSER'S TREASURY OF SECRETS by Gayelord Hauser. Copyright (c) 1963 by Gayelord Hauser and copyright renewed (c) 1991 by Anthony A. Palermo. Reprinted by permission of Farrar, Straus & Giroux, Inc.

"It's Time We Helped Patients Die" by Howard Caplan. Copyright (c) 1978 by Medical Economics Publishing Company. Reprinted by permission from MEDICAL ECONOMICS magazine.

"The Difference Between a Brain and a Computer" from PLEASE EXPLAIN. Copyright (c) 1973 by Isaac Asimov. Reprinted by permission of Houghton Mifflin Co. All rights reserved.

Excerpt from AIDS What Does It Mean to You. Copyright (c) 1974 by Margaret O. Hyde and Elizabeth A. Forsyth. Reprinted by permission of Walker and Company, 435 Hudson Street, New York, New York 10014, 1-800-289-2553. All rights reserved.

"Goodbye, Mom's Apple Pie" by Colleen Brosnan. Reprinted by permission of Colleen Brosnan.

"Where Have All the Fathers Gone?" editorial page, 6/18/95. (c) Copyrighted Chicago Tribune Company. All rights reserved. Used with permission.

"Life in Front of the Tube" is reprinted from the Jan/Feb 1996 issue of AMERICAN HISTORY ILLUSTRATED with the permission of Cowles History Group, Inc. Copyright AMERICAN HISTORY ILLUSTRATED magazine.

"Clinton's No Carter" by David Broder. (c) 1992, Washington Post Writers Group. Reprinted by permission.

"A Valentine Lost at 3, Kept in Mind for 51 Years" by John Lang, 2/14/96. Copyright (c) 1995 by the New York Times Company. Reprinted by permission.

"Sea Island Daughter" by Tina McElroy Ansa. ESSENCE magazine, July 1995, p. 49. Reprinted by permission.

"There Goes the Neighborhood" by Jim Shahin. AMERICAN WAY magazine, February 15, 1996, p. 30.

"Woes of a Part-Time Father" by Nick Chiles. This essay was reprinted with permission of Nick Chiles.

"Salvation" from THE BIG SEA by Langston Hughes. 1940 Hill & Wang. (Division of Farrar, Straus & Giroux.) Copyright renewed in 1968.

"Ethmix" from SEVENTEEN magazine, November 1986 by Betsy Israel. Reprinted by permission.

"Hot Tub Nirvana for $100.00" by Roy Green from MOTHER EARTH NEWS, Dec./Jan. 1996, p. 48. Reprinted by permission of MOTHER EARTH NEWS, copyright (c) 1996 (Sussex Publishers, Inc.).

"The Truth about Lying" by Judith Viorst. Copyright (c) 1981 by Judith Viorst. Originally appeared in REDBOOK.

"Neat People vs. Sloppy People" by Suzanne Britt. Reprinted by permission of the author.

"Your Short Besides" from MAKING WAVES by Sucheng Chan, copyright (c) 1989. Reprinted with the permission of the author.

"Kids in the Mall: Growing Up Controlled" from THE MALLING OF AMERICA by William Severini Kowinski. Copyright (c) 1985 by William Severini Kowinski. Reprinted by permission of William Morrow & Co., Inc.

"Zero-to-60 in 5 Nanoseconds" by Timothy Taylor from the San Jose Mercury News, May 28, 1993. Reprinted by permission of the author.

"Why One Peaceful Woman Carries a Pistol" from LAND CIRCLE: WRITINGS COLLECTED FROM THE LAND by Linda M. Hasselstrom (c) 1991. Fulcrum Publishing, Inc., 350 Indiana St. #350, Golden, CO 80401 (303) 222-1623.

"Targeting Women for Guns" by Bob Herbert, 12/7/94. Copyright (c) 1994 by the New York Times Company. Reprinted with permission.

INDEX